Liberating WORD

Also Available by Rev. Piazza

Prophetic Renewal
Hope for the Liberal Church

The Real antiChrist
How America Sold Its Soul

Gay By God
How to Be Lesbian or Gay and Christian

Queeries
Questions Lesbians and Gays Have for God

A Daily Reflection for Liberals,

Volume One, The First Testament

By Rev. Michael S. Piazza

LIBERATING WORD

A Daily Reflection for Liberals, Volume One, The First Testament

Published by Sources of Hope Publishing
5910 Cedar Springs Road
Dallas, Texas 75235-6806
800-501-HOPE (4673)

ISBN: 978-1-887129-14-5

Printed in the United States

Table of Contents

ACKNOWLEDGEMENTS

While the thoughts and understandings of the scripture that follow cannot be blamed on anyone other than the author, the fact that they have arrived in your hands is the result of the efforts of many.

Dr. Tim Seelig, Director of *Art for Peace & Justice*, was the person who was most persistent in encouraging and harassing me to write. He is also the one who believed so much in this project that he turned it into a book by the sheer force of his will … a substantial will, I must add.

Two people who have given their efforts to spreading the message of liberation are David McCollough and Kevin DeCloux. In addition to being incredible advocates and encouragers, they are the gifted members of the *Hope for Peace & Justice* staff who enabled these thoughts to arrive on the screens of tens of thousands of computers. They were assisted in their efforts by DeSorrow Golden who is a member of the *Hope for Peace & Justice* board of directors and a faithful volunteer.

Coy James is the artist, marketer, and sometimes, den mother of this team. He has been a tireless supporter of my ministry for more than two decades. Such friends and partners are all too rare I have found.

When the idea for this project arose, I am not sure any of us anticipated the strain of producing something every single work day that would be read around the world. Hopefully, there were times when the writings were inspired. Clearly, there were also times when the blessing was that they were written at all. My thoughts, no doubt, were less than coherent at times. If you do not notice this, it is because they first passed through the hands of my editor, David Plunkett. I learned years ago that my writing benefited by being proofed, corrected and rewritten by David. More than anyone, he invested himself in these devotions, and I consider him a genuine partner on many levels. Also, I want to thank our new friend, Anissa Sanborn, for her work on the final edit and layout of the book.

Finally, I must thank the thousands of people who took the time to reply to these devotions when they were in email form. Often, it was to challenge or disagree with some thoughts. I am genuinely grateful to all who made the effort to engage them so seriously. As I said when we introduced this project, if I don't challenge and even anger you, then I have failed. We have no need of another commentary to simply restate what we already have heard or believe.

There also were thousands of you who took the time to give me encouraging feedback. This work was written at a time when I had two fulltime jobs: Dean of the Cathedral of Hope United Church of Christ, and President of *Hope for Peace & Justice.* It was also a time when I had two teenage children … enough said. Your kind words kept me reading, studying, praying and writing. I can never thank you enough.

Creating this work has greatly strengthened my faith, and I think that is a gift that cannot be measured. My prayer is that this team can share a bit of that with you.

These thoughts are dedicated to the many courageous preachers, teachers and writers who dared to think differently about the scripture and gave me the courage to follow their example.

AND

This book is dedicated to the Board and Staff of Hope for Peace & Justice.
There are many who dream of a better world,
but these are among the few who give their lives to making it so.
They are midwives of the world of peace and justice for which we all long.

INTRODUCTION

Changing the world is a daily struggle. In part, it is a struggle to keep the world and the dominant culture from changing us. While they do not reflect the faith of the majority of Americans, fundamentalists have succeeded in commandeering the public discourse. The result is that they have become the ones to define orthodoxy and, to a large extent, faith itself.

Liberating Word is designed to be daily nourishment to strengthen progressive people of faith. For the world to be transformed into a place of peace and justice, WE must enter the fray. It is tempting to duck our heads and just let things pass. It is easy to become so overwhelmed by life itself that we simply don't have the energy to challenge what is said and done. However, if we do not, then who will?

Fundamentalists—both Christian and Muslim—are programmed by daily doses of authoritarian, fear-based, religious rhetoric. They can quote scripture and recite the mantras of oppression more quickly than a liberal can formulate the question. In a sound bite/bumper sticker world of communication, that gives fundamentalists a distinct advantage. Often we disagree with their interpretation of faith, theology and scripture, but since we haven't been programmed, it is more difficult to respond with conviction. *Liberating Word* is deliberately designed to invite you to ponder issues and grapple with questions, so when these subjects arise, you will be able to thoughtfully respond with as much conviction as any fundamentalist.

These are not devotions, but are designed to evoke our devotion to the principles of justice and peace rooted in the Hebrew and Christian scriptures. If you don't find at least one a week with which you disagree, then this project has failed. Its purpose is not to answer your questions but to strengthen your questioning. My hope is not that you will agree, but that you will consider your faith in a whole new way.

GENESIS

In the beginning God ...

Genesis 1:1

The Hebrew and Christian scripture begins with the story of Creation. At the dawn of another new year, perhaps that should be our starting point as well. There are many lessons to be drawn from this ancient story written first as a song or poem.

The insistence of fundamentalists that these words be taken literally would be humorous if fundamentalists of any brand had the slightest sense of irony. Perhaps the difference between us and them is that we don't take ourselves or anything so seriously that we can't honestly and courageously engage it. Nothing is so sacred that it cannot be questioned, challenged or earnestly examined. That includes the one we may call God and the words we may call scripture.

Beginning with the creation song in Genesis, we ask questions that we will ask all our lives. *In the beginning God* ... There is no introduction, no preparation, no explanation to this one referred to in the English version of the story as "God." Without apology or apologetics, you either begin there or you don't. Believe or not.

Accepting the **possibility** that there is something, or someone, which precedes existence itself is the first tenet of all religions. That is something we accept and trust by faith because it cannot be proven. If it could be proven as a scientific fact, then faith would not be required, which is another irony fundamentalists seem to miss. By demanding that creationism be taught in public schools, they are trying to give away to secular society the foundation tenet of their faith. Faith doesn't concern itself so much with the *how* of creation but with the w*ho and* perhaps, the *why*. Those are questions that science cannot address.

In this new year, let us liberate our faith from the mundane questions like "how?" Ask more profound questions that might lead us to discover our life's meaning and purpose. Only fundamentalists miss the fact that, while answers change, these questions are what endure because these questions are eternal. **Let this be the year we have the courage to ask *any* question.**

GENESIS

In the beginning God created the heavens and the earth ...
Genesis 1:1

God created ... The Divine is revealed first as the artist of all creation. While Jews, Christians and Muslims agree on this fact, the importance is forgotten. It is a foundational tenet of our common faith that the physical creation is a sacred product of God's own will.

Fundamentalists seem to get tied up in the "how" of creation, insisting that public schools teach the Bible's description as a scientific fact rather than as a spiritual teaching. Although many of us thought that battle was long over, Christian fundamentalists have worked to take over local and state school boards, determining which science textbooks are utilized. Teaching "creationism" as a scientific explanation does harm to both science and faith.

The point of Genesis was not to describe how God was the originator of creation, but to remind us of the fact that the common source of all creation was God. While trying to force the Bible to make the other argument, fundamentalists fail to connect with the more important truth. People of faith ought to be fanatical environmentalists because the very first point our common scriptures make is that God is the source of creation. It is divine in origin and deserving of our tender concern.

I am increasingly convinced that the true religion of Americans is Capitalism. Therefore, the fundamentalists have enthusiastically sacrificed the Divine's creation on the altar of Capitalism. The prophets of profit have decided our environmental policy is based on economic principles, not Biblical ones. The idolatry of Capitalism serves only one purpose, and that is profit. As revealed in Genesis 1:1, we who serve the God of Creation must become as passionate about protecting creation for our God's sake as others are about exploiting it.

We are the ones to challenge people of good hearts to think differently. It may be simply a matter of asking our family and friends who attend conservative churches to take the first verses of the Bible seriously and to remember that the first commandment is to serve no other gods. Surely these are two verses on which we all agree. In that case, they should be our allies in preserving God's good creation rather than destroying it in the name of the gods of Capitalism. What are you doing to save the environment?

GENESIS

And God saw everything that had been made and beheld it was very good.
Genesis 1:31

The goodness of creation is an amazing statement of faith to have been asserted so many thousands of years ago. This is especially true when you consider that the authors of the Bible had never seen the blue water of the Caribbean, or even the Mediterranean for that matter. They had never watched the sun set behind snowcapped Rockies. They never beheld the amber waves of grain that stretched as far as the eye can see. The authors lived in a relatively harsh environment where they struggled simply to subsist and feed their families. Still, they looked around them and noticed that the world into which they had been born was an amazing place. It was very good.

In today's world, this is a reality that can seldom be experienced driving down the road at 60 miles per hour. Our busy, cluttered lives deprive us of one of the first and most basic of spiritual experiences. God "beheld" everything and pronounced it good. Our spiritual ancestors didn't have our advantage of viewing the whole earth from space or any part of it from our computers or television. The advantage they did seem to have, though, was that they had the capacity to "behold."

Perhaps this difference offers an antidote to the epidemic of cynicism that seems to grip us all these days. Politics, business and even personal relationships can leave us feeling that the world is anything but good. The cycle of deception and disappointment can color the lens through which we look at life. While we might otherwise resist becoming bitter or cynical, "resistance is futile" when we are exhausted or overwhelmed.

The word "behold" is very different from the word "notice." It is more deliberate and powerful. You might "notice" something casually or accidentally. To behold something, you must deliberately and intensely focus your attention on it. Stop and be still for at least a moment, undistracted and centered. Pause to "behold" a flower, a baby's smile or even the grace of a building's design and it may change the rhythm of your day. It may break the cycle of cynicism and let you choose to live in a different space.

God is the source of creation. The world in which we live is good—it is not perfect or we couldn't be here—but it is still very good. You are a part of the goodness of this world. Don't let the circumstances around you cause you to forget it. Consider who makes the world "good" for you!

GENESIS

Let us make humans in our image; male and female God created them.
Genesis 1:27

The traditional understanding of this verse is simply that God created boys and girls. This is the first of two descriptions of God's creation of two genders. (There is a later version that involves Adam's ribs.) Scholars believe that the two versions were by different authors and written at different times. I believe the first editor of Genesis decided to include both of them because they make different spiritual points. While that makes perfect sense to me, I'm always curious how fundamentalist defenders of Biblical inerrancy explain the two versions that use different names for God.

This version of human creation is intriguing for two reasons. First the pronoun "us" that is used implies that God was speaking to someone. While we could speculate about whom that might have been, it would be pure speculation on our part. What is more productive, though, is to recognize that the author of the story seems to sense that human creation, unlike that of the sun and moon and stars, was a communal effort. So integral to human nature is community and connection that the writer intuited that it was a core principle of creation.

The other interesting factor is that, despite the sexism, some would say misogyny, of the age, the author is very clear that women and men are created equally by God in God's image. That is an amazingly progressive statement made to a culture in which women were consistently inferiorized. One might say that this is proof of true divine inspiration of the writing.

It always has seemed important to me that lesbian and gay people read this verse even more carefully. You see, if being male and female is a reflection of the image and likeness of God, then we who are aware of our dual nature have an advantage. God is **BOTH** masculine and feminine, and so are we. Embracing the "bothness" of our nature is a spiritual act that should move us closer to God and allow us to more fully reflect the likeness of God.

Far from being a cause for shame or embarrassment, women who accept and embrace their masculine sides and men who are in touch with their feminine sides are actually honoring the very nature of God in which they were created. Increasingly, psychology is demonstrating that those women and men who embrace their dual nature are much more mentally healthy than those who do not. Perhaps this is something the Bible revealed thousands of years ago.

Maybe nelly men and butch women are just more God-like … or maybe the more fully we accept our true nature the more God's image is expressed and God's likeness can be seen.

GENESIS

"... but of the fruit of the tree of the knowledge of good and evil you shall not eat."
Genesis 2:17

The story of Adam and Eve and the apple is one of the best known parables in the world. It has a prominent place in pop culture and has often been depicted in art. Frequently through the ages, it has been used to justify Western society's sexism. Few people, however, have tried to understand its most significant point. Nowhere does an apple appear in the story, but what does appear is one of the most important and difficult of human concepts.

Ultimately, the writer was trying to find a way of expressing the reality that, from the very beginning, humans were created with **free will**. Although we surrender it often, and frequently try to blame God for the consequences of our choices, this parable's point is that the world in which we live was set up in such a way that, although God has the power to control us, God chose not to do so.

Taking the story of the tree, the fruit and the serpent literally makes the story a silly fable. However, if we engage the story as a significant parable, we discover that the idea of human volition is something philosophers and theologians have struggled with since the beginning of time.

We believe in an omnipotent God. We believe that God is good. How, then, do we explain the bad things that happen in a universe where God is both all powerful and good? If God is "in control," as so much pious music claims, then God is to blame for every child who is molested and abused. So much piety, if taken seriously, makes a terrible monster of God. The author of Genesis is telling this parable to explain that humans can't get off the hook nearly that easily. Even in a perfect and idyllic garden setting, we somehow found a way to mess things up **AND** God allowed it.

In the ancient parable, Adam (mankind) and Eve (womankind) decided to disobey the will of God. When they made the choice and acted on it, God was not present to interfere. What an amazing story to illustrate that, right from the start, God created us and gave us space to shape our lives as we choose. Despite our pious wishes, God is **NOT** in control of us, and everything does **NOT** happen for a reason, and **NOTHING** is "meant to be."

Still, this is one more example of where too many people of faith claim to take the Bible literally, but fail to take it seriously. We always have choices. From the start, God wanted the best for us, but did not make us puppets to be controlled or manipulated. The "fruit" represents the freedom and choices we are given, and the rest of the story represents the fact that the consequences also belong to us.

GENESIS

God banished man from the Garden of Eden,
to work the ground from which he was taken.
Genesis 3:23

Original sin is the doctrine that the sin of Adam and Eve in the Garden of Eden (called "the fall") changed human nature, so that all human beings since then are innately predisposed to sin and are powerless to overcome this predisposition without divine intervention. This doctrine is shared in one form or another by most Christian churches. Traditionalists insist that because of this "fall," humans must be externally "saved" from eternal damnation. Many of us who grew up in conservative churches got "saved" when we were young, but am I the only one who woke up the next morning still feeling shame, out of place, and not very God-like?

Writer and Catholic laywoman, Nancy Meirs, discussed the fact that the words "safe" and "saved," share common roots. Every human has a deep longing to feel safe. It seems to be another thing we lost when we chose to live apart from God. It could be argued that we feel more safe—or more saved—if we are able to identify and point to those who are not saved, but Nancy Meirs wrote:

> *Every human stands in desperate need of salvation from sin, death, the guilt, and the shame which torments us. Isn't it ironic then that Christianity has reduced salvation to a commodity, creating "haves" and "have-nots" as though God, the All-Embracing Parent, would gather some children into safety and shut the rest out in the cold?*

She also notes that St. Paul seems to make salvation contingent on some formula in several of his writings, but she is clear that:

> *The difference between the believer and the nonbeliever lies not in God's treatment of them but in the way they experience themselves in the world.*

The ancient writer of Genesis was clear that we are all children of the God who created us and whose very breath gives us life. He was also clear that our messed up lives are not how God intended them to be. Nowhere is it even hinted at that God has a plan to give paradise back to some while keeping others out. Rather, the message is that, in this world, we have tribulation and that much of it is our own doing because we choose to live apart from God.

The amazing thing, though, is if we can make that choice to live apart from God, we are also free to choose the opposite. Jesus was a living example of one who made a different choice. It didn't eliminate the trials and tribulations from his life that were common to all humanity, but through his trials, he discovered his sense of place in the family of God. I also believe he recovered, to a remarkable extent, the image and likeness of God in which we were all created. Then he said, "If I can do it, so can you … ALL of you!"

Maybe what we need is a faith that focuses more on God's original love and less on our "original sin." That sure seemed to work wonders for Jesus.

GENESIS

Am I my brother's keeper?

Genesis 4:9

The first story the Bible tells after humans lose paradise is the story of Cain and Abel. As a kid, I was curious to know that if Adam and Eve had two sons named Cain and Abel, how were there any grandkids? Where did Cain and Abel find wives? No one ever adequately answered my questions because the truth is a child's innocence can disprove nonsensical theology.

It is a sad statement that one of the first stories of the Bible talks about "horizontal violence." The point of Genesis 1 and 2 is that we are ALL sisters and brothers, yet we keep killing our sisters and brothers.

These boys didn't have to have lots of company on earth to find an enemy willing to destroy them out of jealousy and rage. Thousands of years have passed, and we are no longer primitive like our ancestors. Rather than beating our brother or sister into the ground with a club, we can now drop bombs on them from thousands of feet in the air. We no longer have to look them in the eye when they die. We do not have to dig the hole for their bodies with our own hands. We no longer have to feel the guilt and shame or rationalize our deeds by asking God if we are our brother/sister's keeper.

Recently while reading a newspaper, I read of a man who hired someone to kill his relative. At the trial, he received the same punishment as the person who committed the actual murder. On that very same page of the paper was a description of how American bombs had struck a school, killing a dozen or so innocent children. As I read those side-by-side stories, I was deeply disturbed that MY tax dollars paid for the bombs and the training of the pilots who killed those precious children, slaughtered as they learned their ABCs.

I didn't drop the bombs … "Am I my brother's keeper?" the original murderer asked.

GENESIS

God saw that the evil of humanity was immense in the earth and that every inclination of the thoughts of their hearts was only evil all day long.
Genesis 6:5

This verse is offered as an explanation for the great flood that provides the setting for the story of Noah. Actually, there are three legends of floods in the traditions of the ancient Near East. The stories are similar, but the reasons offered for the flood vary greatly. In the Sumerian version, the gods sent the flood because humans were too loud at night and they were keeping the gods awake. In a later Babylonian story, the gods decide to destroy humanity because they are becoming too self-sufficient, or "too big for their britches," as my mother would say.

In the Hebrew story, though, the rationale offered for God sending the flood was God's justice in the face of human injustice. The flood was a strategy for interrupting human inhumanity, violence and abuse.

I've always found it odd that the story of Noah is a children's favorite since it is about the wholesale destruction of so much life. You never see the children drowning in the flood; rather you see two giraffe heads poking through the port hole of the ark. It seems unfortunate to me that we have missed the point of this ancient parable.

In a pre-scientific world, natural disasters like floods were explained as "acts of God." While we know today that weather is not the result of a divine temper tantrum, the author's spiritual insight that the Creator of the universe is unhappy with human violence and injustice is important.

The Judeo-Christian faith is rooted in a primal belief that injustice is an evil that is reprehensible to God. Our struggle to transform the world into a more just and peaceful place is not just some nice liberal notion; it is one more way in which we are created in the image and likeness of God. Our passion for justice synchronizes our heartbeat with the pulse of the divine.

GENESIS

Then God said (to Noah), "As for me, I am establishing a covenant with you and your descendants after you and with every living creature ..."

Genesis 9:8

The idea of "covenant" is woven throughout the scriptures. This statement by God to Noah is one of the first occurrences. In this passage, God is establishing a covenant with all of creation. Every human—regardless of their race, or gender, or sexual orientation, or religion—is named and claimed by God in this covenant. It is utterly and completely inclusive. No conditions, no restrictions, no limits.

One would think that people who claim God to be the source of **all** creation would understand that this reality makes every human our sister or brother. Apparently, the ancients missed the point, so the Bible tells us this story of starting over. A remnant of humanity is saved, and from this single family, all humanity is descended.

Clearly this is a parable, not a description of a historical event. The point of the parable that religious people seem to continue to miss is that we are all family related by a common covenant made with us by God. Not only that, but God makes that covenant with every living creature. So every time another species becomes extinct a divine covenant is severed. How differently we would treat one another if we could remember that not only are we all related, but that the "other" person is someone with whom God has a covenant.

What would the lifestyle be of a person who lives in covenant with God? Perhaps remembering that God has made covenant with us could heal our insecurities and fears. That alone would change the world in which we live, and change how we live in the world. We share a covenant relationship with God, with every other person, and every other living creature. Mutuality and devotion is the only appropriate way to live with that understanding of life.

GENESIS

God said, "This is the sign of the covenant that I make between me and you and every living creature ... I have set a bow in the clouds and shall be a sign of the covenant between me and the earth."

Genesis 9:12-13

Kermit the Frog (of Jim Hensen's Muppets™) sings about the rainbow connection between us all. The rainbow has become a powerful symbol of the lesbian and gay community. Originally, though, it symbolized the covenant God made with humanity in the time of Noah. The story of Noah is an attempt by ancient people to explain a cataclysmic flood. In the wake of that awful disaster, they managed to find signs of hope and promise.

Until then, ancient people believed rainbows were actually the bow from which God shot arrows of lightning. These mysterious and frightening bolts from the blue became connected with a God whom they feared. The rainbow was transformed from a source of fear to a sign of promise. The story of Noah was the beginning of the revelation that God was not the force of life we needed to fear.

The different colors that come together to form a covenant sign from God seem to be most appropriate for people who value diversity. I just wish it did a better job of reminding us that we value diversity. Nothing is more disappointing to me than to discover huge reservoirs of racism or sexism in the lesbian, gay, bisexual and transgender community. How can that be? How can people who were once excluded and punished by society for being different not treasure others who are different from the majority?

Rainbow flags, stickers and t-shirts become symbols of the rankest hypocrisy **unless** they symbolize our celebration of authentic diversity. The rainbow was chosen as a symbol first by God—the God who created every single star, snowflake and person to be utterly unique and then pronounced it all good, very good.

When our differences become a source of our strength rather than fear and division then we will understand what the rainbow means.

GENESIS

Now the whole earth had one language and the same words ...
Genesis 11:1

Following the story of Noah is a rather strange story about the Tower of Babel. This is another parable that also is found in other religions in different ways. It was the storyteller's attempt to explain why people speak different languages. Frankly, it as good an explanation as any I suppose.

The tribal people for whom the author originally wrote had very limited knowledge of the world beyond their own small region. When they began encountering people who spoke different languages they sought an explanation of how that could be. The legend of Babel was the explanation upon which they settled.

According to the story in Genesis 11, back in the day when all people spoke the same language, humankind decided that it could build a tower tall enough to reach to heaven. That work became the common task of the human race, and as a result, all other work was neglected. The ancient parable explains that, to stop this foolishness, God caused people to speak different languages, so their cooperative effort ceased. Thus humans speak a wide variety of languages to this day.

Many cultures totally removed from the Hebrews have stories in their folklore that are, at least, similar in purpose to this story. An ancient Sumerian legend holds that, at one time, all humanity spoke the same language, the language of the gods, or the language of heaven if you will.

There are some fragments of another legend that tell of a time when communication was done with the mind and simple symbols. Language was seen as a result of distrust. This legend is actually quite accurate. The dominant, masculine-oriented, right-brained thinking that most of us use regards language as the means of communication. In reality, we are beginning to learn that a significant portion of communication is actually non-verbal, subliminal and even subconscious. Language, in fact, often serves as a hindrance to genuine effective communication.

So, the parable of the Tower of Babel, as strange as it is, has a lesson to teach us even today. If we are finding communication a challenge, perhaps we ought to try using something other than words: a touch, a smile, a gift, a prayer. Love doesn't always require words; otherwise none of us would have pets. Imagine a world where we treat one another with the same deliberate tenderness with which we treat our non-verbal furry and feathered friends.

GENESIS

God said to Abraham, "Go from your country and your kindred and your father's house to a land that I will show you."

Genesis 12:1

The story of the Tower of Babel marks the end of the Biblical stories about *humanity in general*. From this point on, the Bible is a record of a *specific people*. All of that begins with the story of a person. Initially, he is called Abram and, ultimately, he becomes known as Abraham.

"Strangers in a strange land" pretty well describes the history of the Jews. It is how they got their start and how they have spent most of their history. Muslims and Christians also trace their roots as a people back to Sarah and Abraham. Perhaps the lesson for us all is that we were, and are, called to leave behind what we know and are comfortable with, and travel through this life as sojourners.

Fundamentalism's great appeal for Christians, Jews and Muslims has been that it offers absolute answers and promises a permanent place. There seems to be something in every one of us that finds that appealing. Yet, if our common story has any meaning at all, it is that faith is about living without those things.

It isn't easy, but I suspect that every one of us has done that in various areas of our lives. You have left your "father's house" when it comes to your attitudes about homosexuality, or about race, or about women. The challenge is to spend a lifetime examining our values and the things we once were taught to be "true," and discovering whether or not they are true for us. This kind of relentless quest requires as much courage as Abraham and Sarah's journey required of them.

Leaving behind what we have always "known" without knowing where the journey will lead is a frightening prospect for most of us. I believe it was Socrates who said, "The unexamined life is not worth living." I would suggest that "the unexamined belief is not worth holding."

So, do you have the courage to question what you believe about the Bible, or heaven, or Jesus, or war, or patriotism, or capitalism, or capital punishment? This is the hardest truth I have ever had to deal with: ***The fiercer my resistance to reconsidering my opinion, the more likely it is not truly mine.***

Are you ready to leave your security and follow the Spirit to a new place?

GENESIS

Now the LORD said to Abram, "Go from your country and your kindred and your father's house to the land that I will show you. I will make of you a great nation, and I will bless you, and make your name great, so that you will be a blessing."

Genesis 12:1-2

In this verse you have the essence of the Jewish faith and, perhaps, the core of what should be our faith as well: ***You are chosen by God to be blessed AND to be a blessing.***

All too often when people are blessed they forget that the last part of that phrase is the other side of the coin. Without BOTH sides the coin is counterfeit and worthless. If we ever sing or say "God Bless America" without remembering why God would, or should, bless America, we are uttering our prayer to some idol other than the God of the Bible.

The land that our European ancestors killed the indigenous people in order to take is an incredibly rich and abundant land. The unique blend of people who formed this country worked very hard to exploit its resources and create great wealth. We have been far from perfect, but this country has done a great deal of good with its wealth. However, if we allow our success, strength and abundance to convince us that we are somehow superior then I believe we are in serious spiritual trouble. Arrogance rooted in abundance is a grave sin for an individual or a nation.

This is a lesson that our leadership—both Republican and Democratic—seems to have forgotten **completely**, and, in so doing, they have endangered the very soul of our nation.

I believe that to say "God bless America" is a sin unless we intend to use those blessings to bless others who have less. To seek strength for any purpose other than peacemaking is coercive, abusive and manipulative. To seek abundance for any purpose other than compassion is self-indulgent. If we ask for God's blessings for any other reason than to bless others we are guilty of idolatry because we are not praying to the God of Abraham, Sarah and Jesus Christ.

GENESIS

God brought Abraham outside and said, "Look toward heaven and count the stars ... so numerous shall your descendents be."

Genesis 15:5

It is important for us to understand the story of Abraham if we are to understand what is going on among Christians, Jews and Muslims, but, as these passages illustrate, the story of Abraham has a great deal to teach us spiritually as well.

Most of us know how Abraham and Sarah were childless well into their old age and how Sarah suggested that Abraham have a child with her handmaid, a slave named Hagar. The child born to Hagar and Abraham was named Ishmael.

Now, according to the Prophet Mohammed, the Arab people are the descendants of Ishmael, who was the first born of Abraham, and the heir of the promises of God. Even the Hebrew Bible is clear that God also makes covenant with Ishmael. There is not a word of judgment or condemnation for Abraham fathering a child with Hagar. It was a very common practice in those days.

Of course, Sarah eventually also becomes pregnant, and Isaac is born. Because only fatherhood mattered in ancient inheritance laws, Sarah became very insecure that her slave girl's son would be the heir rather than her own son. The story of how Ishmael and Hagar were abused by Sarah and ultimately sent away by Abraham is often cited by the Arab people as proof that the Jews will never allow the Palestinians to live with them in peace.

Thus the history we must live with begins …

Now, this 4,000-year-old story is not the cause of the conflict between modern Israel and the Palestinians. However, it is an important symbol of how one conflict can lead to long-term dire consequences. For this reason, *Hope for Peace & Justice* seeks to equip people of faith to resolve conflicts in their own families, communities and households of faith. Imagine if you had been there that day and had the skill to help resolve the conflict between Sarah and Hagar. The world might be a different place.

Learning to make peace is our responsibility as descendents of Abraham, Sarah and Hagar.

GENESIS

So Sarah laughed to herself ...

Genesis 18:12

We got a bit ahead of the story yesterday when we talked about the conflict between Sarah and Hagar over who would be Abraham's rightful heir. We need to back up a bit to the day when the aging Sarah heard that she was going to have a child. (Genesis 18:1-15) A messenger comes from God and tells Abraham the good news, and Sarah, who is standing outside the tent, overhears. Her response is to laugh out loud. Now, when the messenger confronts her about this later, she denies it. In fact, when her son is born to her when she is 90 years old, he is named Isaac, which, in Hebrew, means "laughter."

We don't often associate our faith with laughter, which is a shame. There are more New Testament references to joy than there are to weeping, mourning, anger, sadness and distress put together. Biblical scholar Arthur Dewey of Xavier University, in exploring Jesus' oddball, off-the-wall humor, says that, "There is more of David Letterman in the historical Jesus than Pat Robertson."

Jesus' humor didn't send people rolling in the grass, to be sure. He wasn't a stand-up comic, or some first-century Jerry Seinfeld, but those who heard him would have laughed occasionally, and smiled knowingly. The more scholars know about the life and times of Jesus, the more they appreciate his style of world-mocking wit, outrageous proverbs, and teasing irony. Jesus often used humor to puncture the pompous piety of people who made great show of their religion and sat in judgment of others.

I do wonder about all the things we believe so fervently that make God laugh. We act so certain about things we really know nothing about. I also wonder if our religion might not be closer to true faith if we were able to laugh at ourselves a bit more. The next time someone is arguing with you about your faith, pause for a moment and stand there silently with your eyes closed. When they ask you what you are doing, tell them that you are just listening for the laughter of God.

GENESIS

In the Bible's sojourn with Abraham and Sarah, Genesis 19 is a most disturbing detour. There we find the story of the destruction of Sodom. It is interesting to me that nine out of 10 fundamentalists who would tell you that Sodom was destroyed because of homosexuality could not find the story in the Bible. I suspect that nine out of 10 of them also have never read the story.

It is one of those passages of scripture that is talked about often but seldom actually read. The legend of Sodom was the storyteller's attempt to explain the destruction of an ancient city. The story has frequently been used to justify prejudice against lesbian and gay people. The word "sodomy" is, of course, derived from this story, and the rank depravity of Sodom's inhabitants ensures that the word will forever have a negative connotation.

However, a simple naïve reading of the story is all that is required to reveal that the evil of Sodom had nothing to do with homosexuality, but everything to do with the inhospitality toward, and the abuse of, strangers.

Today, take the time to open your Bible and read Genesis 19:1-29. This will serve several beneficial purposes. First, the story will be revealed to you. Secondly, it will give you the knowledge to defend this passage the next time Sodom is mentioned in conversation. You'll know where it is in the Bible, you'll know the story and you can ask if they have read the story themselves. You see, in arguments with fundamentalists, it doesn't take much to become the resident expert.

GENESIS

Now that you've read the story of Sodom, you know that two strangers visited the city. They are called "angels," but that word simply means "messengers from God." These strangers didn't have wings and were probably dressed pretty much like everyone else. Something about them clued Lot into the fact that they were strangers, though. Maybe Sodom was so small a city that he knew all the men by sight.

As they walked into town, Lot spotted them and offered them the hospitality of his home. While that sounds excessive to us in modern times, it was actually quite common then. In fact, even to this day, the desert Bedouins of the Near East follow a very strict hospitality code that requires them to provide for travelers. In that region, it is a matter of survival, so it is one of their highest values.

Lot knew that he had a moral obligation to welcome strangers and provide them with shelter, food and drink because, someday, he too, might be a stranger and his survival would depend on someone providing for him. Understanding many of the stories of the Bible requires us to understand this principle. It is the root of many values of our faith traditions. Hospitality to strangers is not a peripheral Biblical value, but a central one. When Jesus sent his disciples out, he commended those who received them and cared for them and warned that those who did not would suffer the same fate as Sodom. (Matthew 10:15) He saw *inhospitality* as the sin of Sodom, *not* homosexuality.

The prophet Ezekiel seemed to take a similar view:

> *As I live, says the Lord God, your sister Sodom and her daughters have not done as you and your daughters have done. This was the guilt of your sister Sodom: she and her daughters had pride, excess of food, and prosperous ease, but did not aid the poor and needy. They were haughty, and did abominable things before me; therefore I removed them when I saw it.*
>
> Ezekiel 16:48-50

Now, given this reality, ponder for a moment how the United States is treating immigrants, the strangers among us. Given what Ezekiel said, consider the opulence on one side of the Rio Grande and the poverty on the other, and ask yourself what the REAL sin of Sodom is today.

Because of his hospitality, and because he protected these strangers who were sent from God, Lot and his family were spared from the destruction that rained down on Sodom. Lot, who is Abraham's nephew, was considered a "righteous man." I'm not so sure about that, though.

I mean, did you read the story? He takes these strangers into his house, and, soon, ALL the men of Sodom are gathered outside his door demanding that he send them out so that they might "know them." Now, some scholars suggest this is a sexual term, which is possible. If that is true, though, what is being demanded is not gay sex, but male rape. The men of Sodom wanted to *rape* these strangers as a way of humiliating them. Those who suggest that the sin of Sodom is gay sex simply don't understand that rape is not an act of sex; it is an act of violence. ANY rape counselor could explain this if fundamentalists were willing to listen.

It matters little if the rape being proposed was homosexual or heterosexual. This story in the 19th chapter of Genesis suggests that Sodom was destroyed because its residents were so depraved that their hospitality consisted of rape.

Now, I must admit that, as disgusting as that is, I think Lot was just as depraved, because he offers his virgin daughters as a substitute. (Genesis 19:8) What kind of man suggests that they should rape his daughters rather than these strangers??? Even MORE disgusting than Lot or the men of Sodom are all the preachers who have used this story to stir hatred toward lesbian, gay, bisexual and transgender people without EVER decrying the sexism that made Lot's offer seem perfectly reasonable. This story is about RAPE—men's violence primarily against women. Where are the sermons about that sin? The violent abuse of women continues to be a worldwide epidemic.

In a world where fundamentalist males misuse their spiritual power, offering young girls for rape is the act of a "righteous man," while seeking to rape another man is a sin worthy of the destruction of a city. Who is the pervert here???

As a gay man, I'm pretty comfortable saying that the story of Sodom has NOTHING to do with my lifestyle.

So Lot escapes just as sulfur and fire rain down upon the city of Sodom. In a footnote to the story, Lot's wife disobeys the order of the angels and looks back at the city and is promptly turned into a pillar of salt. Also, Lot's sons-in-law thought he was kidding when he tried to get them to leave, and, apparently, they stayed behind.

Then the story takes one last perverted twist. After their escape, Lot and his daughters hide in a cave. That night, his daughters decided to get him drunk and seduce him. Both women get pregnant and give birth to sons. One boy is cited as the ancestor of the Moabites, the other as the forefather of the Ammonites. (Genesis 19:34-38)

Genesis 19 has a lot of stories about sex. Funny, isn't it, how this chapter has been used. I don't think I've ever heard a single sermon on Lot offering his daughters to be raped or the fact that he fathered children with both of them. It seems Sodom became synonymous for how God hates homosexuals.

We have spent a good bit of time on this chapter because it is important for us to learn to read the Bible for ourselves and to challenge what we have always been told. Simply discarding it will not lead our cause forward. However, if we decide not to be ignorant about what the Bible REALLY says, we can push back against those who would believe what fundamentalist preachers TOLD them the Bible says. Clearly, in this chapter, the moral issues center mostly on heterosexual behavior. In fact, the Bible has just a passage or two about same-gender behavior but hundreds of passages about heterosexual misbehavior.

As the African proverb goes, "So long as the hunter tells the story the lion will continue to be defeated." We must learn to tell the WHOLE story.

GENESIS

We end this week of strange stories with just one more. This one is much more familiar. You may remember it from Sunday school.

In Genesis 22, Abraham THINKS he hears God tell him that he is supposed to take his son Isaac up on the mountain and slay him as sacrifice. This text traditionally has been used to prove Abraham's great faith and his willingness to obey God, no matter what.

I'm not so sure Isaac would agree. If he lived today, he would spend the rest of his life in therapy because his father tied him up and was about to slit his throat with a knife. Fortunately, before Abraham could succeed, Isaac was saved when his father spotted a ram whose horns were caught in bushes.

It doesn't take a psychologist to tell you that this event probably did great emotional damage to the teenaged Isaac. As any person who was abused as a child can tell you, being betrayed by one of the people you trusted your life to does damage that may never be healed. Still, preachers have made a hero out of Abraham because he was willing to sacrifice his child.

The trouble is if this makes a hero out of Abraham, what does it make out of God?

What kind of monster tests a parent's devotion by asking them to butcher their own child? Is God so insecure that this kind of proof was needed? Did God not already know Abraham's heart?

Frankly, I understand the story this way: Abraham was feeling great grief over how he had allowed his first born son to be cast out because his mother was a slave-girl. This sacrifice of Isaac was never God's idea. If God played any role at all it might have been to nudge that ram into the brambles in order to save the boy's life. I have no doubt Abraham *thought* God called him to sacrifice Isaac. But he was wrong, because God is not a monster.

Any time a parent disowns a child because of their religion, they make a monster out of God. A religion that would come between a parent and a child is not from God. Now consider for a moment the implications of what we sometimes believe about Jesus' death. What kind of God would require an innocent person to die so that she or he could love everyone else? Hmm?

GENESIS

In the marriage of Isaac and Rebekah we have the story of the merging of two really dysfunctional families. We know how Isaac's parents cast his step-brother Ishmael and his mother Hagar out like yesterday's trash, and how Abraham thought God had called him to slaughter Isaac as a test of faith. Who can blame Isaac for being a bit dysfunctional? Rebekah's family isn't much better as we will see in days to come.

Did you hear about the man who had his genealogy done? He had a complete family tree done for him. A friend said, "Oh that's interesting. I've been thinking about doing that. Do you mind me asking how much it cost?" "It cost me $5,000 total," the guy answered "Five thousand dollars!" she said. "That sounds expensive to me." "Well", he explained, "It cost me $1,000 for them to look it up, and $4,000 for them to hush it up."

That may be how many of us feel about our family trees. We're afraid to look at it closely. The problem is that, like cancer, pretending a tumor doesn't exist won't keep it from making you sick or even killing you.

Having some bent branches on your family tree is nothing of which to be ashamed. The stories of the descendents of Abraham and Sarah are sometimes painfully honest. The behavior of some of the most revered people in the Bible can make our own families look amazingly healthy by comparison. Almost every branch of Abraham and Sarah's family tree is twisted, but that didn't keep God from loving them. It didn't keep God from blessing them, and it didn't keep them from serving God.

So no more excuses. Let's get to work. If God can use Isaac and Rebekah, God can surely use you, but the first step is being honest about our family. You know, the same thing applies to a nation. Given our recent history of torture, preemptive war, convicting and executing innocent people, exploiting the environment in which our children must live, we've been a pretty dysfunctional family. It doesn't mean God doesn't love us, but it does mean we could use a healthy dose of confession and repentance to start the healing.

GENESIS

The trouble with dysfunctional heterosexual families is that they often have children who can keep the dysfunction alive from one generation to the next. This is the case with Isaac and Rebekah. They had twin sons, Esau and Jacob.

These boys are fraternal twins. The time for the birth came. According to the tradition of that time (a tradition which still exists in many cultures today), even though the boys were twins, all the rights and privileges went to the first-born son. This couldn't have been truer if the boys had been born a decade apart rather than just seconds. The technical term for this is "primogeniture." It means that the first born son is the heir. In this case, that would imply that the promises God made to Abraham and Sarah would pass to Esau and his heirs, but since that isn't how it happened, the author has to offer some explanation.

What follows is a strange way of legitimizing your ancestors. Rather than tell some heroic tale of how Jacob became the chosen one over Esau, what we get is a seedy story of family dysfunction and intrigue. Perhaps the storytellers recognized that dysfunction and competition were far more common in families than heroics.

It is easy enough to live out our dysfunction. We just have to keep doing "what comes naturally." However, heroics require courage and choices. Most people have more courage than they think. The challenge is choosing justice over dysfunction. That choice requires us to put the needs of others above or at least on par with our own. It seems that the Bible acknowledges our dysfunction, but longs for us to become heroes who resist the patterns we inherit and choose a more noble way.

Do you know someone who has done that?

GENESIS

The Bible describes Esau, the first born twin, as red and hairy. It is unclear if the color is intended to describe his skin tone or his hair color or both. Red hair was apparently far less rare in the Middle East than it is today. The other boy is born grasping the heel of Esau, so they called the second son Jacob. The name is connected to the Hebrew word for "heel." Jacob is regarded as a heel in many ways, and his name comes to mean "deceiver" or "usurper" or "supplanter." The narrative then moves very quickly:

> *The boys grew up. Esau was a skillful hunter, a man of the field, while Jacob was a quiet man, living in tents. Isaac loved Esau because he was fond of game, but Rebekah loved Jacob.*
>
> Genesis 25:27-28

Again we have a classic picture of a dysfunctional family. Imagine growing up in a home where one of your parents obviously loves your sibling but not you. The word "quiet" is an odd one to use here. Basically what the author is trying to say was that one was butch and one was not. Isaac loved the butch boy and Rebekah loved the nelly boy.

Isn't it odd that a 4,000-year-old story depicts what happens so often today? Fathers often are closer to their "tomboy" daughters than to the more feminine ones. Mothers are often closer to their sensitive sons than to the more classically masculine ones. Of course, just the opposite can also be true. Many parents also despise or abuse the child that is less stereotypic.

Decades ago, the Kinsey Institute at the University of Indiana did a through study of factors that were predictive of a child growing up to be lesbian or gay. They eliminated all the circumstances like birth order, or parental age, or being an only child, and identified only one predictive factor. Apparently when they were children, lesbian and gay people were significantly more likely to play with toys thought to be typical of the opposite sex.

Many parents of course reacted by trying to force their sons to play with guns rather than dolls, but that behavior didn't change their sexual orientation, it simply added to those poor children a burden of shame and isolation. The lesson we should have learned is that sexual orientation is just one more factor with which we are born. When will we learn to celebrate the diversity of God's human creation?

Jacob and Esau would have been happier and healthier people if both their parents had been healthy enough to love both sons just as they were. Do we have the capacity to expand our love to those we don't understand or fully appreciate?

GENESIS

In Genesis 25:27-34, there is a brief story about how Esau sold his birthright to Jacob for a bowl of red bean stew. That was the heroic deed which Jacob did to earn the right to inherit God's promises to Abraham and Sarah – he exploited his own brother's hunger. You have to admire the Bible's honesty…

Esau came in from hunting and was famished and exhausted. When he entered the house the smell of Jacob's cooking hit him like a physical blow. He suddenly felt the full impact of his body's needs. He asked his brother for a bowl of the stew, but Jacob holds out asking Esau to sell him his birthright. Esau exclaims that his birthright will do him no good if he dies of starvation and so he agrees.

Every time I read this story I have an internal debate. Which of these two should be named the Patron Saint of American Citizens? I can make a case for both:

> Esau: What people have been more epitomized by our obsession with instant gratification? Americans sit down to meals and eat more of than is needed to be considered healthy. It is as if people, who have never known actual hunger, are afraid this meal is their last. We spend rather than save or give our money and then we act as if we are poor. We are addicted to our cars, our plastic and our electric appliances because we want what we want NOW, regardless of the consequences for the environment or future generations. Spiritual disciplines are utterly disregarded and then we wonder why our lives are so spiritually impoverished. We have sold our birthright as children of God. We were created to be spiritual beings but we have become only physical, which is why we desperately fear death.
>
> Jacob: On the other hand, Jacob has a strong argument as well. After all, we have shipped our low paying jobs and pollution south of the border. The people working for American corporations still can't provide for their children, so they risk their lives to become "illegal immigrants." We love the lifestyle allowed by cheap products provided by slave wages. Rather than sharing our bread with our sisters and brothers, we exploit their need then depreciate them for being desperate for what we have. Yes, Jacob could be our patron saint for this and other issues.

Perhaps it is time Americans choose a new patron saint…maybe Jesus, he who said, "What YOU do to the least, YOU do to me."

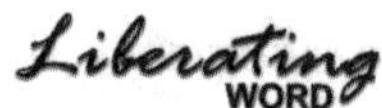

GENESIS

Jacob was not finished abusing his brother. In Genesis 27 we are told how, with his mother's assistance, he uses animal skins to make himself seem like his hairier brother Esau, and thereby tricks his old blind father into giving him the blessing that rightfully belonged to Esau.

When Esau comes into the house and learns what has happened, he falls on his knees in front of old and dying Isaac and plaintively begs, "Have you only one blessing, my father? Bless me also my father!" (Genesis 27:28) But although Isaac was sad and grief stricken, the only thing he offered to his son was the promise of a tough life.

Perhaps Isaac should be the patron saint of modern Americans. We live as if there is a strict limit to the number of people who can live blessed lives. We fight to keep immigrants out rather than helping them to find the blessed life in their home countries. A study revealed that the test grades/failures of third-graders are a perfect predictor of how many prison cells would be needed eighteen years in the future. So rather than spend our tax dollars on education, we spend them on more prisons.

It is almost as though we have a vested interest in creating a permanent under-class. We live as if we believe that if their lives were blessed, ours would be less blessed. This heresy is even more tragic in the church where we live as if God only has enough love for those who believe "the right thing" or behave "the right way." It is almost as if we are afraid that if God loved everyone equally then there would be less love for us. We make our lists of those who are "in" and those who are "out" as if we fear that if one more person gets into heaven we will lose our place.

Isaac thought he could only bless one of his children and the other would just have to fend for himself. I'm grateful that God didn't go to the Isaac school of economy. I hope you didn't either. There is more than enough to go around for us all! If we keep using our blessings to build bombers, we shouldn't be surprised when one of the "unblessed" straps a bomb to her body and stands next to us.

GENESIS

For the past several days we have looked at the dysfunctional family of Isaac and Rebekah and their twin sons, Esau and Jacob. As you may recall, Jacob wrangles Esau into swapping his birthright for a bowl of stew. Then, his mother pushes Jacob to trick his blind and elderly father into giving him the blessing that legally belonged to his older brother. When he learned of this deceit, Esau was so angry that Jacob was forced to flee. His mother sent him off to her brother Laban's to hide. In the end, Rebekah loses her favorite son, and Jacob loses his family, because they have acted dishonestly and selfishly.

Despite that, Jacob may have been relieved to escape his dysfunctional family. What he forgot, however, is that, "Wherever you go, there you are." That is to say, Jacob's family dysfunction traveled with him, in part, at least, because it traveled *within* him. Tomorrow, we will look at how his Uncle Laban swindled him in much the same way that Jacob swindled Esau … and so it went from one generation to the next.

Conservatives insist that raising children is a private matter, which is fine if every family in which a child is reared is healthy. However, as the epidemic of modern public massacres has demonstrated, when a child grows up in a severely dysfunctional or abusive home, the resulting pain is not just private. Hillary Clinton has been ridiculed by the Right for her book about children entitled *It Takes a Village,* but she is reflecting ancient wisdom that deserves modern attention.

The pain of Jacob and Esau is a perfect symbol of what happens when two parents live out their own dysfunction in a nuclear family with two children. Their family was an anomaly of that day because there was no apparent extended family. The result is ancient and Biblical proof that children thrive much better when surrounded by the love of more than two people. Considering massacres in high schools, malls and college campuses, we liberals need to stop letting fundamentalists define "family values," because that is just one example of how we all pay when the family fails.

GENESIS

Jacob fled his brother Esau's wrath and went to his Uncle Laban's house. Laban had two daughters, Leah and Rachel. Before he had even arrived, Jacob met Rachel and fell in love. He offered to work for his uncle for seven years in return for the approval to marry Rachel. Despite the fact that Rachel and Jacob are first cousins, theirs is held up as a great Biblical love story.

Of course, Laban was the brother of Jacob's mother Rebekah. Like his sister and his nephew, he was more than a little dysfunctional. Since Rachel was the younger sister, Laban wanted to make sure he got Leah married off first. So Laban got Jacob drunk on his wedding night, and, the next morning, Jacob awakened to discover that he married Leah rather than Rachel. Not to worry though; in exchange for another seven years of labor, Laban allows him to marry his other daughter too.

Ultimately, Jacob has 12 sons, some with his cousin Leah, a couple with his cousin Rachel, and a few more with Leah and Rachel's handmaids Bilhah and Zilpah. These sons became the patriarchs of the 12 tribes of Israel. Thus we have an ancient and highly esteemed example of **BIBLICAL family values**!

For years, I have fought against lesbian, gay, bisexual and transgender people simply adopting the heterosexual version of the family as our own. While a husband and wife, 2.4 kids, and a house in the suburbs might work for a FEW people, by and large, it has resulted in 50 percent of all heterosexual marriages ending in divorce, children who spend years in therapy, an incredibly high rate of alcoholism and drug addiction, and a general diminishing of the quality of American life. Heterosexuals bought a lie and modeled their families after an illusion.

Extended families, clans, tribes and villages are the more pervasive and certainly more Biblical. Those are the models to which we should pay attention.

Eventually, Jacob has enough of the treachery and deceit of his Uncle Laban, and, maybe, he has enough of his own. He decides to go home, perhaps hoping Esau has forgiven and forgotten the past. Along the way, though, he learns that Esau is headed toward him with a sizable army of 400 men.

Jacob sends peace offerings, but he is deeply distressed. That night, he camped at a brook called Jabbok, and there, late in the night, Jacob has his famous wrestling match. When I was a kid, I learned that he wrestled with an angel. The word "angel" simply means "messenger of God," so that is possible. The text simply says, "And a man wrestled with him until daybreak." (Genesis 32:24) It seems that they wrestled to a draw, though Jacob's hip apparently was displaced. As morning came, the mysterious wrestler tried to leave, but Jacob wouldn't let him go. Jacob insisted that the mysterious angel could not go until he blessed him. The wrestler blessed Jacob by giving him a new name of "Israel."

To this day, the Jewish nation calls itself by that name. This story is important and amazing in many ways. Sigmund Freud, who was Jewish, could have spent his career unpacking this dream. Let me give you my short-hand interpretation:

Jacob had seen what he looked like in the life of his Uncle Laban, and he didn't like it. Faced with a brother who, all these years later, was still furious and determined to kill him, Jacob might have fled as he had done years earlier. He might have devised a scheme or deception. What he did instead was wrestle honestly with who he was and what that looked like to him. This time, Jacob refused to let it go until he found the blessing in it, and with a new name, he found being in the world.

Like me, you may have grown up in a home, school, community and culture that shaped you in ways you'd like to leave behind. For example, I grew up in rural South Georgia. For many years, I denounced the racism of that culture and prided myself of being free of it. What foolish arrogance. Although it took a long time, I eventually was able to acknowledge that I was a product of my family and culture, and simply pretending to be more sophisticated and liberated didn't make it so. Like an addict, I had to accept that true liberation was to accept that I would wrestle all my life against values I no longer wanted to be mine.

I don't think we are ever really redeemed/saved/transformed. The truth is we, at best, are **being** redeemed/saved/transformed by authentically wrestling with the angels/messengers from God who often come in the most annoying forms.

Consider who in your life might be struggling today.

GENESIS

Yesterday we talked about Jacob's wrestling match. He wouldn't let go until he got the blessing out of it. That may be one of the most important liberating lessons in this story. In a disposable society, we often give up too soon. We discard clothes when there is still a lot of wear left in them. We also discard relationships when they become worn, tired or difficult. Unfortunately, we also discard the relationship before we get the blessing from them.

A friend was complaining recently to me that after the death of her mother everyone kept trying to "help her get over it," "cheer up", and "move on." She said, "What they don't know is that my dad and I had lots of unresolved issues, and I'm afraid that, if I simply move on, those issues will remain unresolved for the rest of my life." What a wise woman. Our culture does seem to try to put away its grief way too early. A pet dies, and we go out and replace it. A relationship ends, and we do the same thing. The trouble is if we don't wrestle with the ending, we take the same issues into the next relationship.

When Jacob refused to let go until he got a blessing from his struggle, the Wrestler said to him, "You shall no longer be Jacob (the deceiver) but Israel, because you have struggled with God and with humans and prevailed." Wow!

Figuring out a formula to get God's blessing is popular in modern Christian circles by tithing, obeying the rules, praying the right prayer, etc. According to this story, spiritual blessing comes from wrestling/struggling/grappling with the Divine. Light, easy, superficial relationships with God don't seem to result in transformation or genuine blessings. Far from being a bad thing, when we are struggling with our faith, we may well be on the right path to becoming the person God created us to be.

Politically, we've seen the results of leaders who are not reflective—people who don't struggle, but have absolute confidence that they know the mind of God. Maybe we need to embrace leaders who are willing to acknowledge that they don't know and are not sure. Maybe we need to embrace the struggle in our own lives. Apparently, that is where the blessing can be found.

Jacob, who is now named Israel, arises from a night of wrestling, and rather than running away, he sets out to meet the brother he long ago had deceived. Esau comes toward him with an army of 400 men. What is amazing is that Esau doesn't attack him, but he embraces him. Why was that?

Had Esau long ago forgiven his brother? Was he a man of grace? Perhaps, but why employ the army? Maybe when he saw his brother, Esau recognized that he was a changed person. He was no longer Jacob the deceiver, but Israel the struggler. Maybe it was the fact that Israel's struggles had left him with a limp for the rest of his life.

Modern-American-Success-Christianity seems to suggest that life should be smooth, easy, prosperous, confident and wrinkle-free. Israel's wrestling with God left him with a lifelong limp. St. Paul wasn't delivered from his "thorn in the flesh," and when the risen Christ met the doubting Thomas, his body bore the scars of crucifixion. So where did we get the idea that God was a god of the perfect, the strong, the confident, the flawless?

What a difference it might have made in our world if, after the events of 9/11, America had limped a bit in our response. At that moment, almost the whole world responded with support. We didn't limp, though; in our arrogance, we launched not one, but two wars to prove that we were the great military might. Our desire for revenge guided us, and the result was that we are now weaker, poorer, less safe and without the support we were offered at that moment.

Arrogance rarely makes a brother or sister out of an enemy. Esau embraced his brother when he saw him limp toward him. Despite superior military power, he decided not to use it against his brother. Arrogance sees enemies, where humility might have seen a brother.

GENESIS

In our study thus far, we have discovered the origins of the 12 patriarchs of the 12 tribes of Israel. They were the great-grandsons of Abraham and Sarah, and the grandsons of Isaac and Rebekah, and the sons of Jacob/Israel and his two wives, Leah and Rachel, and two of their handmaids. Thus far, it has been a pretty dysfunctional family picture.

There is probably one more episode of dysfunction that we should examine before we let the subject drop. If you recall, Jacob was his mother's favorite while his father favored his brother, Esau. Unfortunately, Jacob didn't seem to learn from the pain that favoritism caused. Instead, he perpetuated it by playing favorites with his own sons. His favorite was Joseph, one of his younger sons who was born to Rachel, the woman with whom he first fell in love.

Tomorrow, we will look at the unfortunate results of this favoritism in Joseph's life. Today, please ponder how parental favoritism can be unhealthy and painful. Why, then, do we insist on projecting such dysfunction onto God?

Do we really believe that God loves some better than others? Do we really believe that any healthy parent would love some of their children for eternity, and torment others because they didn't believe a certain way? And what does this say about our prayer life?

If you have a moment, I encourage you to listen to the song "Held" performed by Natalie Grant. It can be found on www.youtube.com.

GENESIS

Thanks to composer Andrew Lloyd Webber, many of us know the story of "Joseph and his Amazing Technicolor Dreamcoat." At least, many of us are familiar with *his* version. The coat, which Jacob gave to his son Joseph, was seen by Joseph's brothers as a sign of their father's favoritism. To compound matters, Joseph had these dreams in which his brothers were subservient to him, and he was immature enough to report the dreams to his brothers. This only magnified their dislike, and eventual hatred, of him.

Joseph's dreams foretold a future none of them could anticipate and which turned out to be quite different from what they understood the dreams to mean. Still, the critical lesson is that we all must learn to be winners without making other people out to be losers. We must create a society in which our dreams can come true without the dreams of our sisters and brothers being ground into the dirt.

We live in a world capable of meeting the needs—though not the greeds—of us all. Everyone can have adequate housing, but not if a minority of us insists that we should have lavish housing just because we can afford it. Everyone can have a job, but not if executives insist on making more than their 500 lowest paid workers combined. Everyone can have an education, but not if the affluent are willing to pay for private education for their own children but not willing to pay a little more in taxes so that poor children can have adequate education.

That list can go on and on, but, in this story, there are two lessons to be learned.
First, we must cease to see life in terms of win/lose. We can all win if those with power don't insist on running up the score.

The other thing we must remember is what Joseph seemed to forget: They are our brothers and sisters, not strangers, enemies or aliens. They are as worthy of love and dreams and fullness of life as we are. We must live more simply so that our sisters and brothers may simply live.

How different would our immigration policies be if our starting point was that we are all sisters and brothers, and our goal would be to help their dreams come true?

GENESIS

Joseph's preferential treatment, his special robe, and his dreams all resulted in his brothers hating him so much that they sold him into slavery and told their father that he had been killed. That is an awful lot of hatred. Maybe it was also fear. Maybe they were afraid that Jacob would discard them and turn their inheritance over to Joseph. Or maybe they were just afraid that there wasn't enough love to go around.

In a world where fundamentalists are willing to blow themselves up to hurt others who don't agree with them, we need to ask ourselves, "What are they so afraid of that they would hate us so?" Also, along with Joseph, we must take some responsibility. How Joseph acted and how he treated his brothers certainly didn't justify what they did to him. Still, if he had been emotionally healthy and mature, he would have known that, while he could not do anything about how his brothers felt and what they did, he could take responsibility for his role in the dynamic that was created.

I have yet to hear an American political leader suggest that now, with a little distance from September 11, 2001, it would be an emotionally healthy and mature attitude to consider what we did to create such hatred in so much of the Muslim world. We are not responsible for the actions of the terrorists, and we can't fix them. What we are responsible for is our role in the dynamic that created that event.

This attitude is not disloyal to our country or to the memory of those who died. Rather it is the spiritual practice of self-examination, confession and repentance. I'm not optimistic that we have the leadership to advocate a spiritually mature road for our country. I am more hopeful that you and I can do this when we encounter people who are angry and hateful to us.

So, in Genesis 37:25-36, we read the story of Joseph's brothers selling him to a group of traders from Midian on their way to Egypt. There, he is bought by Potiphar, Pharaoh's right-hand man. Before, Joseph had been spared having to tend the flocks to stay at home where he kept the books for his father. In Potiphar's house, despite being a slave, those skills and that experience served him well. He soon advanced in rank and became overseer of the entire household.

There is a parable in that somewhere. Many of us graduated from high school or college with dreams of how we were going to conquer the world. Maybe, like Joseph, our dreams were about how we were going to succeed and prove to our brothers and sisters how wrong they were about us. We even may have dreamed of how we would leave this world a better place.

So, how are those dreams going for you? Yeah, that's what I thought. Somehow life never quite turns out like we thought it would. We aren't in charge of the universe; heck, we aren't really in charge of our own lives. Circumstances pick us up and take us to places we never wanted to be: divorce, disabled, unemployed, depressed …

What do we do when we find ourselves living lives that are not of our own making? Maybe Joseph is a role model for when we find ourselves enslaved. Perhaps it is the advice of Solomon that we need: "Whatever your hand finds to do, do with all your might." (Ecclesiastes 9:10) Or maybe St. Paul, who said, "Whatever your task, put your whole self into it, as if you are doing it for the Lord, not your masters." (Colossians 3:23)

There are times in our lives when the only liberation we can know is the freedom to decide who we will be and how we will live in any given circumstance. Perhaps if we refuse, like Joseph, to become enslaved within, we may find freedom, happiness and blessings, despite our circumstances.

GENESIS

According to Clare Boothe Luce, "No good deed goes unpunished." I'm not sure what prompted that devout Catholic woman to make that observation, but Joseph sure could have spoken those words. Sold into slavery by his jealous brothers, Joseph ended up as a house slave of Potiphar, a ranking official of ancient Egypt. Joseph worked so hard that Potiphar eventually made him the head of his household.

Genesis 39:6 says, "Now Joseph was handsome and good-looking." As I read that, I wondered what the distinction between handsome and good-looking was. Actually, as a gay man, I know what I mean by that, but I couldn't help but wonder what the writer of Genesis had in mind. Since presumably he was not a gay man, it is a clue that something is about to happen that is caused by Joseph's good looks.

Sure enough, Potiphar's wife, who is not named in the story, tries to seduce Joseph into having sex with her. Joseph has more integrity than to betray his employer who has trusted him with his household, so he refuses. After one rejection, Joseph literally has to flee from her grasp, leaving behind his outer garment. With the garment as incriminating evidence, she falsely accuses Joseph of rape. Thus Joseph's integrity landed him in prison.

One would think that this would put the lie to simplistic theology that life rewards those who behave and punishes those who do badly. Unfortunately, that kind of dualism seems to endure in many forms. Even those of us who know that life is not fair and that bad things do happen to good people are still programmed by this theodicy enough to wonder when bad things happen to us what we might have done wrong. Perhaps spiritual maturity is being able to face one of life's injustices and, rather than asking "Why me?" ask, "Why not me?" We may not deserve the pain, suffering or struggle life brings us, but then who does?

GENESIS

After two years in prison for the crime he did not commit, Joseph is summoned to interpret the dreams of Pharaoh. Joseph says that Pharaoh's dreams predict seven years of good crops, followed by seven years of famine. The good thing is that, because of his education and training, Joseph is able to suggest a tangible plan for how to handle the crisis. In the end, Pharaoh puts Joseph in charge of the plan. In fact, Pharaoh was so impressed that he made Joseph the prime minister over all of Egypt.

The cliché, "Everyone's a critic," has never been more true than today. What made Joseph so special was not his ability as a prognosticator who could predict the bad things that were to come. Instead, he was special because he offered a solution and then took responsibility for making a bad situation better.

It seems that Christians tend to forget that Jesus called us to be "the salt of the earth" and the "light of the world," **NOT** "the critics of the earth" or "the hecklers of the world." Like Joseph, we are called to be a people who should offer solutions **AND** take responsibility for positive change. People of faith are not folks who use prayer to ask God to make situations different; rather we must be people who ask God to use us to make things better.

So, what situation have you been fussing about lately? What can you do to help make it better? Nothing? What about praying? Are there any circumstances that cannot be improved if we are willing to care, help find a solution, and take responsibility?

GENESIS

Joseph was 30 years old when he became prime minister of Egypt. During the seven years of abundance, he carefully carried out a plan that would allow the nation to survive seven years of famine that he saw in the dreams. In fact, not only did Egypt survive, but, because of Joseph's management, when famine spread across the region, Egypt prospered. In fact, their neighbors had to come and buy grain from Joseph.

This reality leads to a family reunion for Joseph and his brothers. In Genesis 42, we are told that Jacob heard that Egypt still had grain, so he sent his sons to make a purchase. Little did the brothers know that the person from whom they would have to buy grain was the brother they had callously sold into slavery and later told their father that he had died.

It is a small world … too small when it comes to how easily our bad deeds come back to haunt us. It usually doesn't happen quite as directly or as globally as it did to Jacob's boys, but if there is one Biblical law that seems to be fundamentally true, it is "What you sow, you shall also reap" or, in more modern terms, "What goes around comes around."

Sooner or later, in one form or another, we must face the consequences of our choices. Those consequences may seem completely disconnected, but at the very least, our bad choices diminish us as humans. That is no small price to pay. We whittle away at the stature of our souls, and ultimately, living with the person we have become is worse than any sentence a moral court might pass upon us.

Jacob's boys were about to confront the brother they had so badly mistreated. In some ways, though, they were the lucky ones.

GENESIS

As the famine progressed, Joseph's days were spent dealing with supplicants who he alone had the power to feed. No one was more surprised than he, when one day, he recognized the faces of the ten men who stood before him. They did not recognize him, however.

That is usually how it is. In order to abuse another person, we have to somehow dehumanize them. We couldn't treat them as we do if we recognized them as our brother or sister, so we divide the world up into "them" and "us." Dehumanizing allowed the Nazis to treat Jews as if they were objects to abuse. It is the key to stereotyping, scapegoating and racism, and it is what allows humans to commit genocide.

Joseph's brothers didn't see Joseph as one of them, so when they needed something from him, they didn't recognize him. Prejudice would never allow them to see someone they disregarded and discarded as a person of position and power. They could no more recognize Joseph than educated people can hear the profound wisdom of someone whose subjects and verbs don't agree, or affluent people can understand the joy of someone who has chosen to live more simply.

Progressive people usually make an extraordinary effort to eradicate overt prejudice from our lives. Unfortunately, that sometimes leaves us incapable of recognizing the more subtle ways we dehumanize others by patronizing, discounting or making assumptions about them.

Today's exercise is to think of a time when you made an assumption about someone only to discover that you were wrong. Confess that recalled experience to others. Becoming more honest invites more honesty and frees us to see our sisters' or brothers' faces in unexpected places.

GENESIS

So Joseph's brothers come wanting to buy food. Joseph recognizes them immediately, but he doesn't tip his hand. What follows is difficult to understand if we idealize Joseph as the heroic victim of his nefarious brothers. He speaks to them sternly, makes them wait for an answer, accuses them of being spies, and then holds one of them hostage while sending the rest to fetch his youngest brother.

He did not come out to them, but, to the brothers' credit, as they experienced this time of testing, they began to talk among themselves about how their difficulties were the result of how they had treated the brother they sold into slavery. They had no idea that Joseph could understand their language since he had always spoken to them through a translator.

Some scholars suggest that this was the change of heart that Joseph had been awaiting. Perhaps, or maybe the guilt they expressed over what they had done caused Joseph to have a change of heart. Maybe in that moment he decided that, even if they hadn't treated him like a brother, he had to treat them like his brother.

Viktor Frankl, an Austrian neurologist and psychiatrist who survived a concentration camp and lost so much to the Nazis' persecution, once wrote, "Everything can be taken from a person but … the last of the human freedoms—to choose one's attitude in any given set of circumstances, to choose one's own way." In that moment, Joseph decided that he would not allow his brothers' actions and abuse to determine who he was as a person.

Forgiveness is just a nice theory, **until** we have something major to forgive.

Joseph eventually identified himself to his brothers. This seemed to cause them to be more afraid than when they thought Joseph was simply an Egyptian official who suspected them of being spies. Joseph's reaction to them, and his theology of life, is summarized in a startling statement found in Genesis 50:20. Joseph says to his guilt-ridden brothers about their actions in selling him into slavery: "You intended it for evil, but God intended it for good."

Joseph refused to see himself as a victim. Whatever circumstances of life he found himself in, Joseph found a way to do his best, make a contribution and rise to the top of the situation. His ability to do that may have well been rooted in his trust that, whatever happened, his life belonged to God.

Romans 8:28 says that, "God causes all things to work together for the good of those who love God." On the face of it, you might understand that to mean that God will only let good things happen to those who love God. The trouble is that isn't true. Lots of bad things happen to good people. Lots of bad things happened to Joseph.

A more accurate understanding of this passage in Romans, and Joseph's statement might be:

> ***Living as someone who believes she/he is loved by God allows good things to come out of even painful circumstances.***

God is the source of life, and when we cooperatively trust life's source, somehow things work out for the best. It doesn't mean bad things don't happen, but it does mean that we don't make it worse by becoming bitter, vindictive or cynical.

Cooperating with life in every circumstance is always a better choice. Even if others may intend to harm us, we must live as people who trust that God's only intent/desire for us is good. Trusting God is faith, and Jesus said faith could move mountains.

So, we come to the end of the story of the life of Joseph, as well as to the end of the book of Genesis.

Joseph's brothers and father all move to Egypt to escape the famine that has spread across the region. Joseph's interpretation of Pharaoh's dream, and his management of Egypt, had prepared that nation. Despite their abuse of him, Joseph welcomed his brothers and their families to settle in Egypt.

Most Christians are aware that the people of Israel were slaves in Egypt and know the story of how Moses led them out. What you may not know is how the Israelites ended up in Egypt in the first place. Now you know. The Israelites ended up in Egypt because when they were faced with hunger in Canaan, Israel/Jacob's son Joseph invited them there.

Isn't that how we all end up "in Egypt?" Medication that helps us deal with pain or sleep at night soon leaves us dependent or addicted. People who make us feel good about ourselves soon have the greatest power to shatter our self-esteem, or at least ruin our day. Salary increases soon enslave us to a job we hate …

I've never known someone to deliberately marry someone abusive, or to set out to become an addict, or to graduate from college hoping for a meaningless career. We become enslaved by promises to solve our problems, ease our pain or relieve our stress. We also become enslaved by our desire to take the shortest route, or to avoid all pain or discomfort, and by the artificial lure of the easy road to the "good life." Sacrifice is a concept that is hardly known at all outside the gym. Not only are we unwilling to make sacrifices for others, we don't want to strain too much for our own happiness. Hence, like Israel/Jacob and family, we end up as slaves because we follow the easy road to stop our stomachs from growling.

GENESIS

The Bible says that Joseph died at the age of 110. He lived to see his great-great-grandchildren, nieces and nephews. While he lived, his family prospered as guests and welcomed immigrants in the land of Egypt. Joseph wanted his final resting place to be with his ancestors. He knew that the day would come when his family would return and he asked that they take his bones with them when they made the trek home to Canaan.

My mother always says that she doesn't care what we do with her after she is gone. I've known other people who felt that way. There was a time during the worst of the AIDS crisis when several pastors on staff had someone's ashes in their offices.

On the one hand, it is easier when people die with confidence that death is not final and their future is not determined by where their remains end up. On the other hand, I can't help but wonder, what if the last thing I can do with myself is return to the earth to renew it for future life?

Of course, that isn't what happens when a person is embalmed and placed in a casket that is then sealed inside a vault. The final disposal of our body is not really the point of this. While it would be nice if all of us were organ donors, the question is are we life-givers?

Joseph wanted his bones to be returned to the land of his ancestors. Although we are getting ahead of our story, the book of Exodus says that, despite centuries having passed, when the Israelites went home, they took Joseph's bones with them. I wonder what it would take to live in such a way that years later people would take me with them wherever they go.

While I don't want my remains left behind to collect dust in some office, the real desire of my heart is that when I'm gone I will leave behind a positive mark in the lives of those who remain. If the positive deposit we make in another person's life is strong enough, it just might live on forever.

EXODUS

Named after the event it records, the second book of the Bible is called Exodus and is the core event in the identity of the Jewish people. Exodus is probably the most exciting book in the Bible and is an epic adventure story. Although it is the story of thousands of people, it is also the story of one person and his own personal exodus.

In the King James Version of the Bible, this book is called "The Second Book of Moses." This is an indication of the former belief that Moses wrote the first five books in the Bible. The books themselves do not identify the author; it is just tradition that Moses wrote them. However, the tradition is unlikely since he dies in one of the books.

It is accurate however to call Exodus "a book of Moses." He is the star of the exodus and the chief character of this book. Most of the lessons about our journey of faith that we learn from the exodus we learn from Moses' life. He teaches us many negative lessons; that is he teaches us some things we shouldn't do. By and large, he is an incredible person and leader. The Bible is honest about him.

The blunt honesty of the Bible about its heroes' faults is remarkable considering how reluctant those who claim the Bible as scripture are to acknowledge their own faults or make allowances for the failings of others. A leader today is terrified by the threat that others will learn of their deficiencies, and their fears are well grounded. While we blithely say we are "only human," God forbid someone else shows a bit too much of their humanity. We put leaders on a pedestal and then delight in knocking them off. In the end, of course, that says more about us than it does about them.

Religious people need to remember is that it says NOTHING about God who seems to delight in putting treasure in cracked pots.

EXODUS

The Book of Exodus begins with a brief description of how the descendents of Jacob multiplied in their adopted land. At first, they were welcomed as guests and friends. They lived among their Egyptian neighbors as friends and co-workers. Although they spoke a different language and worshipped a different God, the two groups of people worked together to make Egypt the most powerful nation on earth.

Then something happened. I wonder if the grain Joseph had stored began to run out. Perhaps it was simply the fear that it might. Somehow, most of our prejudice ends up being rooted in the fear that there is not enough. Have you ever thought if "they" get theirs, I might not get mine? That fear, which seems to shape our attitude toward immigration and immigrants, is an ancient one. Neighbors and partners in prosperity suddenly become threats.

Over a recent Christmas holiday, I drove through South Georgia. Because of migrant farming in the area, there is now a significant population of Hispanic immigrants. As I drove along the back roads to my parents' house, I noted how sparsely populated that area was. While Georgia is the largest state east of the Mississippi, almost half of its population lives in metropolitan Atlanta. There is little danger of overcrowding in the rural areas. The back-breaking farm work is done by migrants who are paid below minimum wage because no one else will do the work. They aren't taking anyone's job, but their slave wages contribute to the prosperity of others.

Fear is seldom rational. One day the Egyptians looked around and were afraid that, if the Hebrews prospered, they might take something that rightfully belonged to the Egyptians. So they labeled them illegal immigrants and forgot they were neighbors and friends. Labels seem to help humans do that.

EXODUS

The book of Exodus offers only one sentence to explain how the descendents of Jacob went from being inhabitants in the land of Egypt to being slaves:

> *Now a new king arose in Egypt who did not know Joseph.*
>
> Exodus 1:8

This kind of amnesia seems to be epidemic. Leadership arose who forgot that it was a Hebrew who led the nation during lean years. It was a Hebrew who saved the Egyptians from starvation. They forgot their history, so the new king turned the Egyptians against the Hebrews. He made them afraid: "Look the Israelites are more numerous and powerful than we …" (Exodus 1:9)

That could hardly be true, but leaders who use fear to divide and manipulate people have a very low regard for truth.

I was talking to my father about the immigration issue that America faces. Unfortunately, my parents most often watch Fox News, so their information is, well, slanted at best. I'm not sure his opinion could be swayed even if he would have listened to the generally more progressive CNN network. My father was concerned about all the "illegals" who were settling in their small South Georgia town.

In the course of our conversation, I tried to help him see that crime was no worse in that town than it was when I was growing up, and that, if he read through the list of arrests that had been made over the weekend, he wouldn't find many with Latin surnames. Again, facts have little strength in the face of fear. I also tried to talk to him about how industries like poultry packing were dependent on immigrant workers because no one else was willing to do the work. He agreed but seemed stuck on the fact that they were here illegally.

Finally, I reminded him that both of his parents had come to this country from Italy. They had been brought here as children by parents who couldn't make a living and who desperately wanted more for them and him. "Yes," he said, "but they came here legally."

"They did," I answered, "because they could. That is really the only difference. Who decided that they could, but the current immigrants can't? Did God? I don't think so."

Like Pharaoh, we forget that, unless we are Native Americans, we, too, are descended from people who came here and stole land by force from indigenous people. Amnesia is epidemic.

EXODUS

When I was in high school, I worked at the local Piggly Wiggly as a stock clerk. During those years, I came to love an "old" African-American man and his wife. They both were probably 50 at the time, but to a teenager, that seemed ancient. It was the first time my carefree soul confronted racism in its rank and brutal form.

This good man and his wife both worked fulltime at the store, and they both held down other part-time jobs. They were the hardest-working people I had ever known. One day, Tom's paycheck and mine were accidentally placed in the wrong envelopes. That was when I discovered that, though I was only 17 and working part-time, I actually earned a dime more an hour than this grandfather of three.

Perhaps I should have just kept my mouth shut and pretended not to notice, but I expressed my outrage to my friend about this injustice. He had worked fulltime for this store for almost a decade. Tom simply said to me, "You know how you learned in school that slavery ended in 1863? Well, they lied. It never really ended."

In Exodus 1:11, we read about how the Egyptians enslaved their neighbors. The captors didn't suddenly put shackles on their ankles and wrists; they simply made life a greater and greater burden for them. Maybe it was a scenario like they neglected the schools the Hebrew children attended so they soon did not qualify for better positions. Perhaps colleges wouldn't accept Hebrew children because they couldn't pass the tests the Egyptians devised. Hebrew parents had to work two jobs because of their low wages. The Hebrew children were neglected and often got into trouble, so the Egyptians felt justified in locking them up like animals.

One day the manager at the Piggly Wiggly called my friend "Unc." When I asked him what that meant he said, "You know, like Uncle Tom." That was the day I realized that slavery still existed in this country.

EXODUS

The Egyptians gave the Hebrews all the tasks no one else wanted to do. Today I guess they would collect our garbage, harvest summer crops, work in poultry- and meat-packing plants, or in the kitchens of restaurants in which they could never afford to eat. Still, that didn't seem to satisfy the Egyptians:

> *The Egyptians became ruthless in imposing tasks on the Israelites, and made their lives bitter with hard service in mortar and brick and in every kind of field labor. They were ruthless in all the tasks that they imposed on them.*
>
> Exodus 1:13-14

Fascinating, isn't it, that thousands of years later the people in power still enjoy a quality of life afforded them by immigrants whom they resent, even hate. Many advocate spending millions of dollars to round up all the undocumented immigrants in this country and return them forcibly to their country of origin. Of course, the cost of living would escalate substantially since every restaurant, factory, construction site and farm would need to pay much higher wages and provide much greater benefits to fill the vacant jobs. Those who complain about the immigrants don't really want to do the low-wage manual labor, and they show little interest in reducing their standard of living because of how prices would soar.

The Egyptians abused the immigrant Hebrews who lived among them. Although they enjoyed the palaces and pyramids the Hebrews built, the Egyptians despised and were even prepared to kill them by ordering the Hebrew midwives to murder all the boy babies who were born. (Exodus 15-17)

Funny, isn't it? Who are the Egyptians and who are the Hebrew children-of-God in our day? Next time immigration is debated, remember this story and whose side God was/is on.

EXODUS

Exodus 1 tells us the names of two amazing women. Although you probably do not know their names, Shiphrah and Puah are true heroes. Though we do not know their husbands' or fathers' names these are among the first women in history whose names are recalled. It is quite possible that they were not married, or perhaps what we have here is the first lesbian couple. That may be reading a bit too much into the story, but I want you to understand how unheard of it was in that day for a woman to be so noted for her own virtue and value that her name was recorded.

Shiphrah and Puah were very courageous, deliberately defying the orders of the Pharaoh, the most powerful person on earth at the time. These women were midwives who were ordered to kill any male babies born to the Hebrews. Girl children were allowed to live.

Apparently, while the Egyptians didn't want to lose their cheap labor; they wanted to ensure that they could control and dominate the slaves. These two heroic women thwarted that plan by doing what they thought was right and refusing to kill any babies born under their care.

Of course, when their defiance was discovered, Pharaoh ordered the Egyptians to throw every boy child in the Rio Grande … uh, I mean the Nile. The analogy is not accurate, of course, but it is important that we understand that issues such as dealing with immigrants is nothing new. The debate about whether we will provide education and healthcare to undocumented residents living among us is often very close to simply throwing children away because of the choices their parents make in order to keep them from starving.

EXODUS

While few people know the names of Shiphrah and Puah, the midwives whose courage saved the lives of Hebrew baby boys, Christians know the name of one of those boys. Moses' mother hid him for three months, but once that became impossible she placed him in a waterproof basket and floated him down the Nile. She then assigned his older sister Miriam to keep watch over him to ensure his safety.

What amazing courage this mother had. Like her, sometimes we must be willing to let go of the thing we love the most in order to save it, and us. Clearly, Pharaoh trying to kill babies was not God's will, but the writer of the book of Exodus saw the hand of God. Pharaoh's daughter found baby Moses, and at his sister Miriam's suggestion, arrangements were made for Moses' biological mother to be his wet nurse.

Jochabed, Moses' mother, exercised extraordinary courage in her willingness to give up her child to save his life. That courage was rewarded, but let's not make the leap that anytime we do what is right we get rewarded. I'm not sure quite where that theology came from, given the fact that none of the other mothers who lost their babies, or those children who lost their lives, did anything wrong. Besides, where does that theology fit in a faith where the founder was tortured on a cross and all of his disciples were executed or imprisoned?

If we make courageous decisions in hopes of ending up as a prince or a princess in Pharaoh's house, we are certainly not following the example of Jochabed, or, for that matter, Jesus.

EXODUS

So Moses grows up as a grandchild of Pharaoh. Perhaps because his birthmother was in his life, he strongly identified with the oppressed Hebrews. One day, as an adult, Moses witnessed an Egyptian slave-master beating one of the Hebrews. Moses became so enraged that he killed the Egyptian. As a result, he fled the country and became a fugitive.

Both Mahatma Gandhi and Martin Luther King, Jr. were fond of saying, "An eye for an eye will leave the whole world blind." Such wisdom seems almost too noble for the human soul. Somehow, like Moses, we are more prone to use violence to end violence; war to bring peace; torture to end terrorism.

Before Gandhi or King, it was Jesus who called us to try another way: forgiving enemies, turning the other cheek, going the second mile. It was Gandhi who so poignantly observed about Christianity, "I like your Christ; I do not like your Christians. Your Christians are so unlike your Christ."

It is easy to rage against a "Christian nation" [sic] that practices preemptive war, gives tax cuts to the wealthy, and reduces help to the poor. Yet the truth is there are probably plenty of ways that we allow our anger to cause our Christianity to utterly disappear. No, we don't murder anyone, but if looks could kill we would probably leave several dead drivers in our path …

EXODUS

The Israelites groaned under their slavery, and cried out. Out of the slavery their cry for help rose up to God. God heard their groaning, and God remembered the covenant with Abraham, Isaac and Jacob. God looked upon the Israelites, and God took notice of them.

Exodus 2:23-25

Memory loss is said to be a sign of aging. If that is true then we are in real trouble. According to this verse, God was already getting forgetful 4,000 years ago. Imagine how much worse it must be now …

That is silly, of course, but so is the idea that scripture puts forth that God had forgotten all about the covenant with Abraham, Isaac and Jacob. Do people who claim to take the Bible literally honestly believe God had a memory loss and, only upon hearing the Israelites moaning, remembered them?

That does seem to be what the author is saying, but maybe the truth that is hidden here is that, in times of suffering, it sure feels an awful lot like we have been forgotten, even by God. Perhaps what the author is trying to say is that, even when our struggles seem to go on and on, God has not abandoned us.

Although our oppression seems as if it will never end, the core message of the Bible is that God never really forgets God's own, even though it does feel that way sometimes. Exodus is not just the name of this book in the Bible; it is the promise of God to those living in oppression … and it is a warning to oppressors then and now.

EXODUS

Chapter three of Exodus begins with one of the most famous stories in the entire Bible: the burning bush. Tomorrow's devotion will focus on that story, but today I want to call our attention to one thing.

Notice what God did when God heard the cry of the oppressed people in Egypt. No magic words were spoken. No lightning came down from on high. God responded to cries of the Hebrew immigrants by calling a single individual to do something about it.

Moses was tending the sheep of his father, Jethro, when he saw a bush on fire. Since the bush didn't seem to be consumed, it caught Moses' attention, and he turned aside. The turning aside from his every day routine and work allowed him to hear the voice of God. I suspect there were many days when Moses wished he had just kept on walking and minded his own business.

Whoops! By taking time out of your busy day, **you** have turned aside. What is God calling you to do? There are plenty of God's children out there who are still oppressed by the empire's forces of racism, sexism, classism and homophobia. Today, as then, God is trying to set them free. The trouble is no matter how many bushes burn are we too busy to heed God's call to do something?

I pray that today, in conversations or the news or something you witness, you will see the signs of oppression and **know** that God is calling you to turn aside and get involved.

Liberation never happens by magic. It happens when ordinary people like shepherds care enough to do something.

EXODUS

The burning bush is treated as if it is a miracle of the Bible. Maybe it is, or perhaps it was a natural occurrence. Apparently, there are bushes in the desert that excrete combustible oil that coats the leaves to protect its scarce moisture. It is possible for that oil to burn without the bush burning.

So, what Moses turned aside to see was really a natural phenomenon that was rare enough to be appreciated. It was from this phenomenon that God spoke to Moses' heart. I believe God still works that way today, but we are too busy to turn aside.

For a short time in Texas, the blooming of the wildflowers is amazing. The view is beautiful! The wildflowers don't last long, and by the time they are gone, the dry heat will set in and things will turn brown. Still, when the wildflowers are in bloom, Texas is a wonderful place to be.

It is a source of frustration to me when driving along in the car that people don't notice the wildflowers. I often have lectured my daughters—and some of the adults riding in my car—because they were too busy reading or talking to turn aside and behold the beauty of God's creation. Those amazing moments **ought** to make our spirits attentive to the God of creation.

Whether it is at the beach or the mountains or the side of the road, those moments of blazing beauty are the Spirit's call to us to turn aside. If we simply whiz by life at 65 mph, it is likely we will never hear God's voice. Maybe that is the real reason we fill our lives with so many things that ultimately don't really matter. That way we ensure there is no time left in our life for God to call us to do justice.

EXODUS

> *Then Moses said, "I must turn aside and look at this great sight, and see why the bush is not burned up." When the Lord saw that he had turned aside to see, God called to him out of the bush, "Moses, Moses!" And he said, "Here I am."*
>
> Exodus 3:3-4

The dialogue between God and Moses at the burning bush is interesting. Now, we've talked about how the bush may have been a rare natural phenomenon, so we need *not* to think that Moses heard God's voice with his ears. That isn't how God speaks. Most of the time with me it is with gentle, inner nudges that I'm never completely sure are from God. There are times when there is a nagging feeling or a thought that just won't go away, but God never speaks in an audible voice. A few times in my life the inner voice was loud enough to seem audible, and the nudge was more like a shove, but those times have been very rare.

Maybe this was one of those rare times for Moses when he was so focused on the bush but was not consumed that the suddenness of God's voice seemed to ring off the canyon walls. Notice that the first word God speaks is Moses' name.

God didn't call out to just any and every shepherd in the desert, but spoke to Moses specifically by name. Who knows, but, just on the other side of the mountain, God might have been calling Anna to go and do some other small work of justice. In our story, though, the name spoken was "Moses." I suspect that the truth is most of us are more like Anna, whose name and deeds are forgotten. Maybe we are like Anna in another way.

Notice that the passage says, "When God saw that Moses turned aside, God called to him." I suppose God learned a long time ago to save His/Her voice unless we are willing to turn aside. Anna may have been too busy to turn aside or too noisy to hear.

EXODUS

> *God called to him out of the bush, "Moses, Moses!" And he said, "Here I am." Then God said, "Come no closer! Remove the sandals from your feet, for the place on which you are standing is holy ground."*
>
> Exodus 3:56

Having fair skin, I am the original tenderfoot. I rarely ever go barefooted, even at home. So, what does this scripture mean?

Actually, there are many layers of meaning, but, for us on our progressive journey of faith, let me suggest just one. When you walk around barefooted, you have to be much more careful. Things you might do and places you might go with shoes can extract a painful price if you go with bare feet. Considering and ordering our steps become critical on bare feet.

Remember that God was about to call Moses to become the leader of the Hebrews, and to confront the most powerful ruler in Moses' world. This story seems an apt reminder that any leadership is best done barefooted. Walking through life on bare feet is a humbling experience, reminding you of the significance of the smallest stone. It is also a good reminder that those who follow us have tender feet as well and may require great patience and compassion.

Perhaps, if we lived more in bare feet and less in designer shoes, we would discover that all people are God's people and that God is always with us, ever speaking and therefore, all the ground of life is holy.

<u>EXODUS</u>

Last week we began looking at the story in Exodus chapter three when Moses turned aside to see a bush that was on fire, but was not consumed. That image stays in my mind. I wonder what it meant as a spiritual parable. ***How do we sustain our spiritual passion and energy to avoid burn-out?***

I am not sure I have an answer for that, but I have discovered in my own life, that burnout has little or nothing to do with how hard I work or how much time off I take. Burnout seems more rooted in how I feel about the work I am doing rather in the number of hours I am working.

In the life of the church, we have volunteers who work a fulltime job and then give countless hours to their ministries. Through the years, I have, at times, tried to protect these volunteers from burning out and have been rebuked for my efforts. One woman told me that her ministry was what allowed her to get up and go to work everyday. When I looked puzzled, she explained, "Listen, the work that I do from 9 to 5 is because I need to make money. The work I do here at church is because I need to make a difference. I'm not sure I could do the *money thing* unless I got to do the *meaning thing*."

The people who seem to get burned out are those who lose sight of the meaning of what they are doing. I wonder if Moses had finally gotten to the point in his life where he was tired of following sheep around all day and was ready to make a change. Perhaps he'd reached the age or station in life where he was ready to go from being a successful shepherd to a significant servant of God.

The bush burned but wasn't consumed, and God was about to assign Moses the toughest task of his life. Moses would need to be completely and totally on fire with the task of leading the Hebrews out of slavery. It would be tough … almost as tough as being a liberal person of faith today.

EXODUS

Then the Lord said, I have come down to deliver them from the Egyptians, and to bring them up out of that land to a good and broad land, a land flowing with milk and honey.

Exodus 3:7-8

From slavery and oppression to a "good and broad land, a land of milk and honey." That is the intent of God. That is the reason God says, "I have come down to deliver them …"

Now, if Moses had been smart he would have stood up right then and said, "That's great. Let me know how that goes," and run in the opposite direction.

You know, you ought to have done the same thing, because … tag, you're it. God is still coming to deliver people from oppression and leading them to a land of milk and honey. And God is still doing it the same way: tapping people on the shoulder and saying, "Let's go. You do the work and I'll be with you." Did you feel that tap when you started reading this Liberating Word? No? Well, take my word for it; God is tapping you to help with this liberating work.

I love the image of a land flowing with milk and honey. God is promising to lead God's people from a place of oppression where their efforts only benefit others, to a place of abundance, sweetness and life. We don't need to feel guilty because we have a good life. It is God's will for all God's children, and God is pleased that you are not feeling hungry or oppressed. But it is God's will for ALL God's people.

It is not God's will that those who live north of the Rio Grande have to rent storage units while those who live just on the other side have no hope of a better life for their children. It is not God's will that those who live on one side of town are safe and secure while those on the wrong side of the tracks live in mortal danger. It is not God's will that some people can get face lifts while others can't afford lifesaving surgery.

If you haven't felt God coming down and tapping your shoulder then maybe the shoulders of your designer jacket are too padded. All of us who enjoy the milk and honey of enough are called by God to work to make sure God's other children taste life's sweetness too.

EXODUS

"So come, I will send you to Pharaoh to bring my people, the Israelites, out of Egypt." But Moses said to God, "Who am I that I should go to Pharaoh?"

Exodus 3:10-11

So God has come down to liberate the Hebrews from slavery, and Moses is going to be the instrument of that liberation. Moses wasn't exactly overjoyed by this prospect. In fact, this passage begins a long discourse of excuses from Moses about why he shouldn't be the one.

I wonder if God would have chosen Moses in the first place if Moses had been so arrogant to believe he was capable of handling the job. A limited ability never seemed to disqualify someone from God's service. Moses complains that he is not a good speaker. God doesn't care. Our past doesn't get us off the hook either. Remember that Moses killed the Egyptian who was beating the Hebrew slave. Moses is a murderer, but that doesn't get him off the hook either.

In fact, about the only thing that seems to disqualify you from serving God is hubris—thinking you are qualified to be used by God.

Throughout the Bible, you find that the people God calls always think that they are not qualified … and they are always right. It isn't ever a false sense of modesty. God really does seem to like to hang out with the riff-raff of life. However, that alone doesn't seem to be a qualification. There are lots scoundrels who do not hear the call of God. Apparently the qualifier isn't being unqualified; it is knowing you are not qualified to be God's partner.

God didn't call Moses to be a partner in liberation because Moses wasn't qualified; God called Moses because he was a person free of hubris. Moses knew he wasn't qualified and couldn't do it on his own, which made him the perfect partner for the God who seeks to do the work of liberation through us and to us. The best liberators are people who know we still need a bit of liberating.

EXODUS

But Moses said to God, "If I come to the Israelites and say to them, 'The God of your ancestors has sent me to you,' and they ask me, 'What is his name?' what shall I say to them?"

Exodus 3:13

Before the bush died down, Moses wanted to know the name of this God who was sending him back to Egypt. Of all the things he could have asked, that question would have been low on my own list.

What I find most interesting about this passage is that Moses is concerned about what he will tell the Israelites rather than the Egyptians. I mean, wouldn't you think he'd be more worried about what he was going to tell the Egyptians when they asked by what authority he came demanding that they simply let their slaves go?

Perhaps Moses knew that oppressors know that they are on the wrong side of moral authority. Oppressors ratchet up the volume and animosity to cover the reality that they know they are on the wrong side of what Dr. Martin Luther King, Jr. called "the arc of the moral universe."

Or perhaps Moses wanted a name to give to the Israelites because he knew that oppressed people take some persuading to throw off the shackles they have internalized. If they were no longer slaves, who would they be? How would they live? What would they moan and complain about?

Obviously, there are many types of slavery. I have found that people who have been sold into the slavery of capitalism are the hardest souls to deliver. We work our lives away, not really filling our needs, but mostly filling our greeds. Almost all of us could live more simply and be more free to make different choices with our lives. Instead we work because we HAVE to … we are slaves.

Moses seemed to know that we are the ones who are hardest to convince that God's deepest longing is our genuine freedom.

EXODUS

God said to Moses, "I AM WHO I AM." He said further, "Thus you shall say to the Israelites, 'I AM has sent me to you.'" God also said to Moses, "Thus you shall say to the Israelites, 'The Lord, the God of your ancestors, the God of Abraham, the God of Isaac, and the God of Jacob, has sent me to you': This is my name forever, and this my title for all generations."

Exodus 3:14-15

This is one of the most sacred and inscrutable texts in the Bible. There are as many understandings of its meaning as there are Biblical scholars who are paid to explain it. The truth is no one really knows what it means, so I won't claim that I do.

Although I do not understand it, I do like it. The truth is I am always frustrated by those who are on a first name basis with God. I love the theologian who said, "Anything you say about God is wrong." What he meant was that language itself is too limited and limiting to contain the Living God.

"I am who I am" has been translated in a variety of ways, but none really explain the meaning. Taken at face value, it seems that Moses understood God simply to be God and that there wasn't adequate language to say any more.

One of my daughters once flippantly referred to God as "The Big Guy." I said, "What makes you think he is big? Does he need to go on a diet? And where did you get the idea that God is a guy? You didn't get it from me or our church." After this rapid fire litany, she asked, "Well, if I can't say 'big' or 'guy,' can I say 'the'?" The truth is that is about all Moses got from the conversation.

When fundamentalists start talking about God in excruciating detail and with conclusive certainty, you had better run. Their one certitude about God will not include us bearing much family resemblance.

EXODUS

Moses kept saying, "Why me?" God wouldn't quit until finally Moses said, "Why **not** me?"

In Exodus 4:18 we find Moses returning from the backside of the desert to his father-in-law Jethro in order to ask for his leave. I can't help but wonder if Moses didn't secretly hope that Jethro wouldn't let him go. But he does, and, in Exodus 4:21, we find a verse that has always given modern Christians trouble. Since this statement occurs in one form or another 18 times throughout the next few chapters, we probably ought to take a moment to look at it:

> *When you go back to Egypt, see that you perform before Pharaoh all the wonders I have put in your power; but I will harden his heart so he will not let my people go.*
>
> Exodus 4:21

The idea of hardening Pharaoh's heart occurs in many different ways. First, God hardens Pharaoh's heart. Secondly, Pharaoh's heart was hardened. Finally, Pharaoh hardens Pharaoh's heart.

What does it mean to have a heart hardened? In this case, it refers to Pharaoh's stubborn refusal to listen to Moses, as well as to be persuaded by God or Moses' persuasion. Pharaoh's soul was callused and unresponsive. He was obstinate and inflexible.

As far as the Hebrews were concerned, God was in charge and in control. If something happened, it was God who did it or caused it to happen. The Hebrews did not make the distinction between God's permissive will and God's intentional will. To them it was the same if God allowed someone to contract a disease and die or if God personally infected them with the virus. The scientific era would not come for many centuries. Without any other explanation, the Hebrews did what primitive people still do today by attributing anything that was beyond their control to God.

How primitive is your faith? Do you instinctively look to heaven and ask, "Why me?" Or are you able to consider the bigger picture and ask, "Why **not** me?"

EXODUS

Exodus chapter 5 begins the long process of persuading Pharaoh to let his Hebrew slaves go free. I'm sure that no one expected Moses' effort to succeed on his first try, but it doesn't appear that people anticipated just how strongly Pharaoh would react either.

In Exodus 5:6, we are told that, in response to Moses' request, Pharaoh simply made things harder for the Hebrews. One of the main jobs of the slaves was to make bricks for the many structures being built. Since these bricks were sun-dried, they used straw to hold them together until they hardened. Structures made of these bricks still stand today.

One of the burdens added to their load was that they were no longer provided with straw. They had to gather their own straw while still fulfilling the same quota of bricks. In verse 21, the Hebrews confront Moses and Aaron saying, "You have made us abhorrent in the sight of Pharaoh and in the sight of his servants, to put a sword in their hand to kill us."

Moses tried to do what he thought was right, but, in the end, the very people he was trying to help were hurt. He was trying to help the Hebrews, but when things didn't go the way they thought they should, they turned on him.

It is a fantasy for us to believe that "doing the right thing" is always rewarded. Moses did what he was told by God to do, but it only made matters worse. We don't confront oppression or oppressors because we will be rewarded, or even be loved by those whose liberation we seek. We do what is right because it is right.

Often, as Moses (or Jesus) knew, doing the right thing only makes our own lives more difficult and painful. That is why doing justice requires courage. If it was rewarded, everyone would be doing it.

EXODUS

Yesterday you read that when Moses first asked Pharaoh to let the Hebrews go free the only thing accomplished was that Pharaoh made the people's lives harder. For Moses' effort, he only managed to make his own people mad at him.

When Rosa Parks and Martin Luther King, Jr. launched the Montgomery bus boycott, many African-Americans in that city were forced to walk. Some of them lost their jobs because they couldn't report to work on time. At the time, many people resented what Parks and King tried to do. Like Moses, they discovered the truth in the saying, "No good deed goes unpunished."

Actually when you think about it, it is not surprising that the Hebrews resented Moses. These are people who had been slaves for a long time. The circumstances of their lives had forced their gaze downward for years. Every time they tried to look up and see the horizon, there was someone there to remind them who and what they were while shattering any dreams.

It wasn't long before the dirt into which they were constantly forced to gaze upon soon got into their souls. Their self-esteem was completely destroyed. They were not only enslaved, but they had become slaves. Their oppression had robbed them of their hopes and dreams, and that is the cruelest enslavement of all.

In the lesbian, gay, bisexual and transgender community it is called internalized homophobia, and the results are an increased addiction problem, higher rates of smoking and other self-destructive behavior, and conflicts that make long-term relationships more difficult.

True liberation will never come until we are able to quit enslaving ourselves. Unfortunately, like the Hebrews, we resist paying the price for true freedom and often turn on those who try to lead, confront or challenge us.

EXODUS

Like any liberation movement, the cost of getting the Hebrews out of Egypt was high. The plastic façade we call freedom is far removed from the cost that is freedom's reality.

Moses was trying to do the right thing, but for a time, he only succeeded in making matters worse for the very people he sought to help. To be rebuffed by Pharaoh was one thing, but it is quiet another to have your own people turn on you.

What Moses does next is a pattern for how he will handle these kinds of situations in the future.

> *Then Moses turned again to the Lord and said, "O Lord, why have you mistreated this people? Why did you ever send me? Since I first came to Pharaoh to speak in your name, he has mistreated this people and you have done nothing at all to deliver your people."*
>
> *Then the Lord said to Moses, "Now you shall see what I will do to Pharaoh: Indeed by a mighty hand he will let them go; by a mighty hand he will drive them out of his land.*
>
> Exodus 5:22-6:1

God goes on to remind Moses of the context of the covenant between God and the Hebrews. In Exodus 6:9 Moses goes to the Hebrews to tell them the good news and remind them of God's faithfulness, but they "would not listen because of their broken spirit and their cruel slavery."

We who seek to listen to God's ***Liberating Word*** have a tough challenge when it comes to telling good news to oppressed people. They are expecting bad news. They know how to deal with bad news. Like the Hebrews, we have elevated whining, complaining and criticizing to an art form. They are what make many people thrive.

I think it is amazingly insightful that the writer of Exodus recognized that the Hebrew's broken spirit caused them to be unable to hear the tender words of love and acceptance that God tried to speak to them. Maybe the writer was insightful because he realized how poorly he had heard God's liberating word.

EXODUS

Physician Dr. Boris Kornfeld was a Russian Jew during the early days of communism. Although he was young and brilliant, he made a very foolish remark about Stalin. It was reported and he was immediately sent to Siberia.

While he was there, he had the good fortune to become friends with a gentle, generous man who was imprisoned because he was a Christian. Eventually, Dr. Kornfeld became the prison doctor, and he converted to become a Christian.

Dr. Kornfeld was determined to be a good Christian, so he began to stand up for the prisoners and report abuses by the guards. As a result, he was repeatedly beaten, and, one time, the whole camp was punished because he refused to perform a cruel experiment on a young girl.

One evening, the doctor sat down beside the bed of a young man on whom he had performed surgery for cancer of the intestines. As the boy moved in and out of consciousness, the doctor prayed for him and shared his faith in Christ.

Later that night, the young lad was awakened by a great commotion in the adjoining room. He learned later that Dr. Kornfeld had been clubbed to death by guards.

One could say that Boris Kornfeld's faith made matters worse for him. Perhaps he simply should have remained silent and minded his own business.

Well, one person who would argue against that opinion was the young man on whom he had operated; the young man whose life he saved and whose faith he gave. You see, if Boris Kornfeld had not been willing to live out his faith obediently, even though it might cause trouble, the world might never have known the Nobel Prize efforts of Aleksandr Solzhenitzyn whose life he saved that night.

Doing what God calls us to do may not always bring the results we expect or desire. If it does, it may be on God's timetable, not ours. If Pharaoh simply had let the Hebrews go, they forever would have attributed their freedom to his kind nature. Or perhaps they would have thought Moses was an amazing orator.

As it was, things got worse for them for a time, but when at last they were free, they knew that liberation was God's will and God's doing. Then they knew that all the things Moses had said about God's faithful love for them was true. They might have gotten freedom quicker, but would God's liberating love ever have gotten such a firm hold on them if they had?

So, what about the challenges that plague you? They probably aren't sent to you from God, but could God use them to liberate you?

EXODUS

Every child who attended Sunday school remembers the stories of the plagues. Plagues were exciting stuff and Sunday school often needed some excitement.

Although modern scholars have tried to explain the plagues away, it is remarkable how deeply we have come to believe in the "God of the plagues." The Jews saw the calamities as a result of Pharaoh's stubbornness. Again and again, he refused to respond to what God asked him to do. In their eyes, Pharaoh brought the plagues on himself. The ancient prophets were not above using the plagues as illustrations for what could happen to God's own people if they didn't re-evaluate their behavior.

The other perspective from which the Hebrews have always viewed the plagues is that they demonstrate just how deeply God loved them. The fact that God brought this series of devastating afflictions on the most powerful person/nation on earth was, for them, a sign of how serious God was about the covenant between God and their grandparents.

In their perspective, the plagues were signs of God's love for the Jews, God's unwillingness to relinquish what belonged to God, God's faithfulness to promises, and God's ultimate justice.

While we might not agree with their primitive understanding of God, spiritual maturity for us might well be defined as a faith system that is able to sense the love and presence of God even when our lives are feeling plagued.

EXODUS

The first plague involves the water of the Nile River turning into blood.

Those seeking a natural explanation for how these events occurred have suggested a volcanic eruption near the headwaters of the Nile was the catalyst for each of them. As a result, the river became polluted with reddish clay that made the waters appear to be blood.

Whether the water became blood, or just became *blood-like*, the point was to get the Egyptians' attention. The life of the people of Egypt then and now depended almost completely on the Nile River. So profoundly important was the river that it was regarded as a deity. The attack on the Nile was a frontal attack on all that they believed and depended. It was an assault on their very source of life.

Obviously, God didn't destroy the Nile or dry it up, but turning the Nile to blood, or even just making it look like blood, certainly struck the Egyptians where they lived. **It was a call to re-evaluation!**

How about your own life? I'm not suggesting that God has brought disasters upon you, but I am confident that, from the pain that each of us experiences, God is calling us. God uses life's "plagues" to shake our assumptions and make us re-evaluate some of our priorities.

Have you heard the old preacher's story about the farmer who bragged that her mule was always cooperative and obedient? When her neighbor borrowed the mule and couldn't get it to cooperate at all, the farmer had to come over and show him how. She took a two-by-four plank and hit the animal over the head. She explained, "First, you've got to get the mule's attention."

Do you know someone who has had a cancer scare? Some people allow an experience like that to change them forever. Others go right back to the way they have always lived. God didn't destroy the Nile, but turning it blood-red should have been a whack up side the head to get the Egyptians' attention. Maybe it would be better to attend to what is important and try to skip the two-by-four step altogether.

EXODUS

Exodus 8:1-15 recounts my favorite plague. The Nile turns blood-red, and all of the frogs crawl out and take to the land. This plague is not particularly dangerous. Have you seen a frog up close? If you have, you realize frogs can't hurt you but they can make you hurt yourself.

Whenever I read this passage about the plagues in Egypt, I can't help but wonder why on earth, when Moses asked Pharaoh when he wanted the frogs removed, he answered, **"Tomorrow!"**

Tomorrow?! Why not today? Why not tonight? Why not right now?

Can you imagine? Well if you can't, you probably have never lived with frogs like Pharaoh and I have lived with frogs.

I think there are a number of things in our lives that can qualify as frogs. There are many things with which we continue to live. We all have habits or ways of behaving that have proven self-destructive or harmful, but somehow we continue them. We all have attitudes that drag us down, and almost all of us know better than we do. Like Pharaoh, we put off getting rid of those frogs until tomorrow.

After all, we've waited this long. Maybe tomorrow it will be discovered that cigarettes don't really cause cancer. Or maybe they'll discover that jogging does. Maybe tomorrow my mate will listen to me and discover that I was right all along. Maybe tomorrow I'll confront those negative folks in my office and quit being one of them. Maybe tomorrow …

If I just hold out, a miracle may happen. The frogs just may disappear by themselves, and I won't have to change, or I won't have to make any sacrifices. Maybe I won't have to admit that I'm wrong. Somehow tomorrow seems to never get here for some of us.

I want to lay some profound South Georgia wisdom on you. I think I may have told you this before, but it bears repeating: "If you've got a frog to swallow, don't look at it too long." Wait, that's not all: "If you've got more than one to swallow, swallow the biggest one first."

That is great wisdom! Waiting until tomorrow often allows whatever it is we need to change to continue to damage our lives. Tomorrow may be too late. Ask God to help you get rid of those frogs **now!**

There were seven other plagues, including lice and flies. In chapter nine, the livestock began to die.

You see, the suffering that Pharaoh's stubbornness caused moved beyond aggravation and harassment to the destruction of property. The sixth plague, boils, came with actual physical pain. With this plague, even Pharaoh's own advisors were convinced that Moses' God was powerful and dangerous.

The seventh plague was hail, and all the crops are damaged.

Locusts, the eighth plague, devoured the crops. Historical records outside the Bible document a massive swarm of locusts that covered 2,000 square miles.

The ninth plague was darkness.

> *Then the Lord said to Moses, "Stretch out your hand toward heaven, that there may be darkness over the land of Egypt, darkness which may even be felt."*
>
> Exodus 10:21

That is the progression of a life led in willful disobedience to the God of life and light. The darkness that ultimately envelops us is so powerful that it can be felt. It is the darkness of un-creation.

In Genesis, we read of how God began all life with creating light. Light was created four days before the sun and moon and stars were created. There is a light that is beyond what our eyes perceive. This light is the essence of life. It is the kind of light about which it was said of Jesus:

> *In him was life, and the life was the light of humanity.*

Pharaoh's disobedience moved himself and his people in an act of "un-creation." Each step of rejecting God's signs took him further into evil until the final result was darkness and death. There can be no stronger warning to us than that. Whatever the source of life's problems, struggles, challenges, or if you will, plagues, we dare not close our hearts to what God is seeking to tell us.

EXODUS

Before we leave the week spent with the plagues of Egypt, let's do a theology check.

Yes, the ancient Hebrews understood the story of how God visited plagues upon the Egyptians as literally true. The ancients saw God as the cause/source of all things good and bad. Today we understand that bacteria, viruses and germs cause disease. To the ancient Hebrews, the invisible cause must have been God.

Many people still hold God responsible for the bad things of life. However, people of progressive faith understand that God has given us free will and that true freedom means that we live in a world in which God's intervention has been greatly limited. Our freedom is dependent on the self-limitation of God; otherwise we are mere puppets of a "Cosmic Master."

Personally, I don't believe God sends plagues. However, Romans 8:28 says that, "All things work together for good for those who love God." Notice that it does NOT say that all things **are** good, but it does teach that all things work together for good for those who love God. The lesson is that, when we synchronize our hearts with the heartbeat of God, life begins working out in a way that is ultimately good.

God doesn't send plagues, but if our lives are in sync with Life, then God can use even plagues for our good.

EXODUS

In Exodus chapter 10, after the seventh plague, even Pharaoh's advisors try to get him to give up the self-destructive course:

> *Pharaoh's officials said to him, "How long shall this fellow be a snare to us? Let the people go, so they may worship the Lord their God; do you not yet understand that Egypt is ruined?"*

So Pharaoh takes their advice. He calls Moses and Aaron to tell them that they can go and worship their God, but they must leave their children behind. Obviously, this was not something that was acceptable to the Jews, so the eighth plague comes, just as Moses warned it would. Locusts swarmed, eating all the plant life in the land.

Again, Pharaoh confesses his mistake (Exodus 10:16), and tells them they can go. However, he again changes his mind and won't let them go. Giving up something that is financially lucrative, even though it is wrong, seemed to be as tough back then as it is today.

We complain about air pollution, but support "Big Oil" when we insist on driving our big comfortable cars. We deplore how China treats its citizens and the trade deficit, but buy Chinese products at places like Wal-Mart because they are so cheap. We don't want to provide citizenship for undocumented immigrants, but neither do we want to pay higher prices that would allow them to make a living wage in their own country.

Finally, after the ninth plague, Pharaoh came to the place to which everyone arrives who plays such games. He strikes out in anger. He doesn't pretend to want to change anymore, but threatens to kill Moses if he ever sees him again.

Apparently, then as now, getting angry with someone else was easier than reflecting honestly on our own guilt and paying the price for changing our ways.

EXODUS

The final plague is death, and the result is an event known as the Passover. What the crucifixion and resurrection of Jesus is to Christians, the Passover is to the Jews.

The plague of death hit the Egyptians very hard. The angel of death passed over the homes of the Jews if they had placed the blood of a lamb on their door posts.

In the Jewish tradition, this event has been a constant reminder that they are a "protected people." By telling and retelling the story of how they were spared in the night of terror, the Jews have survived the last 3,000 years as a people. The Jews, as we all know, have been persecuted severely throughout history for their faith. At times, they have been exiled from their homelands, they have been imprisoned and murdered in the places where they sought refuge—in fact, in Colonial America, Jews that were not killed were exiled to the colony of Rhode Island because it was the only place that would accept them—and millions were killed in Nazi concentration camps just over 60 years ago.

Theirs is a faith, however, that sustains them because they have been passed over. Telling and retelling the stories of their faith has kept them alive for generations.

While we might understand God differently from our Jewish sisters and brothers, we honor their faith and their faithfulness. We should learn from their example of remembering their story and the dangers of forgetting ours. Young women don't want to hear the stories of old feminists. Young lesbian and gay people think Stonewall is irrelevant. Young African-Americans have moved on from the oppression of the last century. The grave danger is that those who forget their stories are often doomed to repeat them … or, at the very least, never to complete them.

EXODUS

So, while the Egyptians buried their dead, the Hebrew slaves packed fast to get out of town. The unleavened bread of the Passover is eaten as a reminder that, as people of faith, we must be ready to act when the opportunity presents itself.

Perhaps that is supposed to be one difference between people of faith and those who do not believe in the goodness of God. I often use this quote attributed to Charles Lindbergh: "Take lots of chances, but leave nothing to chance." It seems to me that people who trust in the love of God are able to take more chances, believing that things ultimately will work out all right.

That is very different from saying that people of faith get more breaks from life than others. That "prosperity gospel" seems to forget that we are disciples of one who was falsely accused, arrested and, ultimately, executed as a criminal by the state. Jesus didn't get special treatment. Still, he gambled his life on the human capacity to change and to love.

The Gospel of Jesus' death and resurrection is to liberate Christians in much the same way that the death of that first Passover night liberated the Hebrews. The point of the unleavened bread was that, when freedom comes to us, we cannot be distracted by things like waiting for bread to rise. The circumstances might not be perfect, but we can acquire a taste for flatbread if that is the price of freedom.

Waiting for everything to be ideal may mean we wait too long. While Pharaoh let the Hebrews go in the wake of the plague of death, he quickly changed his mind and pursued them. Just imagine having to spend the rest of your life enslaved because you wouldn't "settle" for unleavened bread.

EXODUS

One of the most famous scenes in cinematic history is Charlton Heston, as Moses, parting the Red Sea in Cecil B. DeMille's *The Ten Commandments.*

I actually prefer the animated version of the Exodus in Disney's *The Prince of Egypt*:

Either of them is an impressive display of God's power to rescue God's people when their enemies are in hot pursuit. Passing through the sea became a symbol of the faithfulness of the God of the Jews. It is a symbol of the kind of God we all want to believe in: God of the cavalry riding to the rescue.

There is an ancient rabbinic story that I love about this passage. A student asked his teacher if God always enjoyed all that God did. In response, the rabbi told this story:

> *And it came to pass that the Almighty sent some angels to ensure that the Hebrews made it safely out of Egypt. Later that morning, God came upon these same angels who were dancing and cheering. When God asked them what the fuss was about, they said, "Look, look. We got 'em; we got 'em." And the Almighty saw the Egyptian soldier and chariots and horses swept away by the sea and said to the angels, "You are dismissed from my service." "Why?" they asked. "Because, how can you celebrate when some of my children are drowning?"*

While we must trust in the providence of God, we must not let our trust become presumption.

EXODUS

> *When the horses of Pharaoh with his chariots and his chariot drivers went into the sea, the Lord brought back the waters of the sea upon them; but the Israelites walked through the sea on dry ground. Then the prophet Miriam, Aaron's sister, took a tambourine in her hand; and all the women went out after her with tambourines and with dancing. And Miriam sang to them: "Sing to the Lord, for God has triumphed gloriously; horse and riders have been thrown into the sea."*
>
> Exodus 15:19

What is most fascinating in this passage is that the Bible identifies Miriam as a prophet. While it would take centuries before the Jews allowed women to be rabbis—and much of the church still is mired in sexism—clearly, from the start, God picked leadership based on gifts, not gender.

Another thing that Moses apparently had learned about leadership is that it is best done with a team. Remember, when Moses offered his excuses to the burning bush about why he shouldn't be the one to go, God answered him by assigning Aaron to go with him.

While Moses is honored as the principle leader of the Exodus, Miriam and Aaron both are acknowledged as co-leaders. Our culture still seems to struggle with the idea of authentic leadership teams. Instead, we insist that a single charismatic person have all the wisdom, strength and gifts to be an omnipotent leader/CEO/president/pastor.

Sane and healthy people, like Moses, recognize their weaknesses and are comfortable asking for help and partnering with others. One of the fallacies of the fundamentalists' need for messianic leadership is that healthy people who are genuine enough to know their weaknesses often don't step forward to lead because they fear that they have to do it all alone.

Fortunately for the Hebrews, Moses wasn't so insecure or sexist that he thought he had to go it alone. Maybe he knew there was but one Messiah, and he was not the One … neither are we.

EXODUS

Exodus chapter 15 begins with singing and dancing. God has liberated the people from their oppression. Now, on the far side of the Red Sea, they have great cause for celebration. This season of joy doesn't last very long, though.

It is amazing that the human heart can vibrate with gratitude one moment, and then clench with anger the next. For 21 verses, the people follow Moses and Miriam in song and celebration of their miraculous deliverance. Then verse 22 says:

> *Then Moses ordered Israel to set out from the Red Sea, and they went into the wilderness of Shur. They went for three days in the wilderness and found no water. When they came to Marah, they could not drink the water of Marah because it was bitter. And the people complained against Moses, saying, "What shall we drink?"*

Okay, so tell me you have never had a time when you went to church and sensed the overwhelming presence of God during worship, only to find yourself fighting with your spouse or your children before you got out of the parking lot. Or do you remember a time you were deeply moved by the beauty of creation, only to find yourself whining about some petty mishap moments later? Sometimes I wonder how God puts up with us.

The juxtaposition of the attitude of the people of God in chapter 15 is pretty amazing. Granted, needing water in that region is no small thing, but turning against their liberating leader after only three days of hardship seems a little shallow to me. It wasn't Moses' fault that there was no water, but leaders soon discover that the gratitude of those they lead has a very short shelf-life.

It always has amazed me that people will follow a leader for years, and then, with one disagreement or one disappointment, the entire relationship shifts and a supporter becomes a critic. A friendship of years suddenly can be defined by a single conflict and all the good experiences are completely forgotten.

Has anything like that happened to you? Have you fallen out of favor with someone in your life? It is important that, if we want to be judged by the sum of our lives rather than a single moment, we offer that same grace to others. Somewhere I have read, "What you sow, you shall also reap."

EXODUS

The Israelites were three days from the Red Sea, and they were thirsty. They found water at Marah, but the water was bitter. It wasn't poisoned, but it tasted awful. There seems to be a spiritual parable here. You see, the water of Marah was bitter. Although it was clear and cool, it was laced with calcium and magnesium. The high mineral content is what made the water bitter. All around the edge of the pool was a white powdery residue.

The Bedouins have a saying about the pool at Marah: "One swallow and you go for a week." What they mean is that you can't even wet your fingers and put them in your mouth because the waters of Marah serve as a powerful laxative.

The Hebrews discovered that the water was bitter and they began to grumble. So God showed Moses the branch of a particular tree, the sap of which changed the chemical balance of the water and made it sweet and good to drink.

There is a parable in that, too. Beside every bitter pool, there is a tree that can make the bitter water sweet. It is what Paul meant in Romans 8:28 when he wrote, "All things work together for good for those who love God." Notice he doesn't say all things ARE good, but that all things work together for good. Perhaps he could have said that for people of faith, God is able to bring resurrection out of every Good Friday.

The events of your life may be bitter, but God's grace can transform the bitterness. That is not to say that tough times don't come to people of faith; rather, if we trust God, there is some good that can come out of the toughest time rather than only bitterness.

Faith is no insurance or insulation from life's tragedies. Even Jesus wasn't able to avoid Good Friday. What our faith offers us is an antidote to bitterness. We who trust in the ultimate goodness of God may not find the silver lining in every cloud, but we just might find that the rain will help us grow.

Like Jesus, we all must drink from life's bitter cup from time to time. If we can avoid letting it make us bitter, though, we just might take away some good. That doesn't make the pain any less, but the choice is not to have pain or not. To live is to know pain. The choice is to find some good even through the pain, or be left with only the bitter dregs.

EXODUS

Okay, I warn you in advance that today's "Liberating Word" may be the strangest that you have ever read yet. Yesterday, we talked about how the waters of Marah were bitter because of the high chemical content. Magnesium is a powerful laxative, so it is little wonder that the Israelites didn't want to drink the water. I wonder, though, if that bitter water wasn't just what the doctor ordered.

In Egypt the water of the Nile River, then and now, is filled with *amoebic dysentery.* The people of Egypt have one of the shortest life expectancies on Earth. You may remember that when Joseph's father Jacob arrived in Egypt, the Pharaoh was very surprised with how old he was. The Hebrews lived in Egypt for 400 years, and the many life-shortening diseases that afflicted the Egyptians had begun to afflict them.

The stagnant water used for irrigation for farming was full of the parasite that causes *bilharzia*, a debilitating disease carried by snails in the fields. Even today, amoebic dysentery and bilharzia infect 80 percent of the peasant population of modern Egypt.

This story of the Hebrews at Marah ends with this strange verse:

> *There the Lord made for them a statute and an ordinance and there God put them to the test saying, "If you listen carefully to the voice of your God, and give heed to God's commandments, I will not bring upon you any of the diseases that I brought upon the Egyptians; for I am the Lord who heals you."*
>
> Exodus 15:25-26

What was it that God wanted them to obey? Well, eventually God would give them dietary restrictions that, to primitive people, must have seemed bizarre. But I think God had something more immediate in mind for the Hebrews that day. Perhaps God wanted them to drink the bitter waters of Marah rather than grumbling.

If they drank the water, they would experience extreme cramping and awful diarrhea, but they also would have purged their systems of the diseases and parasites that they carried inside of them. I don't want to push this analogy too far, but you see, God got the Hebrews out of Egypt and now wanted to get Egypt out of the Hebrews.

Let's forget about physical amoebas and parasites for just a minute and think about some of the mental and emotional parasites we have internalized over the years. What are some of the things God would like us to purge from our systems so that we might be free from the dis-ease that plagues the world in which we live? Are there bitter waters from which God is asking you to drink? Is there something that God is calling you to do that will make you uncomfortable, and might even cause pain?

EXODUS

Marah was an oasis with bitter water. We have all been to a "Marah":

- A long-awaited, much-needed vacation is ruined because you caught a cold on the plane or picked up a parasite from the local food.
- You meet an admired author, an esteemed colleague or role model and they are rude, abrupt or abrasive.
- You get the job for which you have worked for so long and hard. But it is decided that rather than move everyone around, you will remain in the same cubicle you've been in for the past five years.

You don't need me to make a list for you. We've all been joyous about some event or circumstance, only to be deeply disappointed by the reality. In a dry and desert time, we finally find water, only to discover it is bitter.

In many ways, the grief is exacerbated by the ecstasy. For the Hebrews, the joy of their liberation set them up for the false expectation that, since God had intervened in their exodus, God would ensure smooth paths, abundant food and sweet water. They were God's children, and given their recent past, they anticipated that would mean special privileges in life.

We never feel more like God's children than when life is going well and everything we touch seems to turn to gold. We turn our faces toward heaven and give thanks as we sail joyfully on calm seas. But then the clouds darken, and the waves toss us about. We find our luxury cruise is making us seasick. The bad news is no one has ever died from sea sickness, and as much as you want to simply get off and stand on solid land again, there is only the churning sea in sight. While we may not shake our fists at heaven, we do want to find someone to blame. Where is Moses when we need someone to blame?

Failing that, we blame ourselves, asking "What did I do to deserve this?" We never feel less like a child of God than when life has just taken us high, only to then plunge us to a low. Now, all of this is well known. What I'd like to point out, though, is that even those of us who are standing on solid theological ground still have those thoughts and feelings. We may dismiss them as irrational, but I wonder how they impact how we regard others for whom life is not going so well. In a culture that values success, do we secretly regard those who are poor, hurting or failing as deserving of their pain? If **WE** feel most like God's children when all is going well, do we subconsciously make divine orphans of those for whom life isn't going so well? I don't know, but there has to be some reason for the fact that, while there is more than enough sweet water for everyone, certain groups of people in our society keep getting shoved off to drink the bitter dregs.

EXODUS

We have spent this week with the Hebrews by the spring of bitter waters of Marah. Yesterday, we talked about how those waters might have purged their system of some of the diseases they carried with them from Egypt.

Before we move on in our journey in the wilderness, I want to mention one other thing about the water of Marah. It contained dolomite. Dolomite is used by professional athletes, joggers and tennis players who spend a lot of time in the sun. Is it possible that God was trying to give the Hebrews medication for the desert journey ahead?

God was trying to prepare them for what was ahead, but the water was bitter so the people grumbled and refused to drink. God gave them the sweet water they demanded, but not what was best for them.

The Jews were free from slavery, but that was the easy part. Sometimes solving our immediate problem is the easy part for God. The harder part is the reality that most of our problems are inside of us, and those are much more of a challenge.

God got the Hebrews out of Egypt. As it turned out, the Hebrews kept on grumbling, complaining and rebelling, so it took 40 years wandering in the wilderness before God could get Egypt out of the Hebrews. Next week, we'll look at the story of the manna and what God had to do to change the Hebrews' appetites so that they could be free from the diseases of bondage.

Perhaps one of the ways that we can know if we are making spiritual progress from being a people of bondage to being people of God's promise is how we respond when we encounter bitter water. Do we grumble, or can we drink deeply trusting God? Can we dance the dance of worship and trust even when God offers us bitter water to drink? Can anyone willingly drink bitter water? Is it too much for God to ask?

And Jesus said:

> *Abba, if this cup cannot pass from me unless I drink it, your will not mine be done.*
>
> Matthew 26:42

EXODUS

And so the people of God, newly liberated from slavery through the baptism of the Red Sea, set off from the bitter springs of Marah to journey through the wilderness to the Promised Land. (Exodus 16) I often have thought about three stages in the lives of the ancient Hebrews and how they symbolize the various places where we find ourselves on our faith journeys.

- **Egypt**: In bondage/oppression, we feel as though we have very limited choices. We work hard but don't really enjoy the benefits of our efforts. We look with envy at those whose freedom allows them to make choices we don't seem to have available to us.
- **Wilderness**: This is that in-between place; that place Robert Benson describes as *Between the Dreaming and the Coming True*. It is much better than where we were, but it is still not where we belong. Here we are always living on the edge, struggling, not at home.
- **Promised Land**: Here we have to work as hard ever, but we are at home in the place where we belong. We are at peace, feeling at last that we are where God has led us to be, with both a past and a future.

The next stage of our study takes place in the wilderness. Here we will learn lessons of transitions. The Hebrews were no longer slaves, but they are also not at home. The wilderness seems to be the place where the majority of us spend most of our lives. "The Promised Land" is often spoken of as an idealized place where we only arrive after death.

Understanding this imagery should help us to reframe our seasons of struggle. We are not learning lessons that will make us happier in heaven; we are learning lessons that will make us much more at home in the places where life ultimately leads us. The wilderness is not our home, but the struggles of life are how we get home. Resisting, denying or refusing to learn from them only serves to prolong our time in the wilderness.

EXODUS

> *The whole congregation of the Israelites set out from Elim; and Israel came to the wilderness of Sin, which is between Elim and Sinai, on the 15th day of the second month after they had departed from the land of Egypt. The whole congregation of the Israelites complained against Moses and Aaron in the wilderness. The Israelites said to them, "If only we had died by the hand of the Lord in the land of Egypt, when we sat by the fleshpots and ate our fill of bread; for you have brought us out into this wilderness to kill us with hunger."*
>
> Exodus 16:1-3

It is interesting that the wilderness between Elim, the oasis, and Sinai, the Hebrews' next stop, is called Sin. The proper name of this location and the English word "sin" are not really related, but somehow I feel like they should be connected.

In this passage, we find the Hebrews whining about hunger and remembering their slavery in Egypt with fondness. Notice that they don't talk about the babies thrown in the Nile, or the whips of the taskmasters, or having to make bricks with straw in the heat of the day; no, all they remember are the "fleshpots." The memory of the smell of savory food cooking grew stronger as the rumbling in their stomachs grew louder.

"No," he said, "I'm not out at work. When they make homophobic jokes, I just have to laugh along because I have bills to pay."

"No," she said, "I didn't report him. I'm sure it is how he has treated every young woman who has ever worked for him, but I need him to give me a good recommendation for my next job."

"No, I didn't confront her racism. I'm white like her; I think it is up to people of color to stand up for themselves. Why should I risk my next raise?"

How quickly we forget the pain and degradation of oppression when the cost becomes great. We are heroes fighting for the liberation of all, until we have to suffer a little deprivation. Then, suddenly, the fleshpots of the oppressors begin to smell pretty tasty.

EXODUS

In Exodus 16:4, God promises to rain bread from heaven, and the next morning they awaken to find manna on the ground. The word "manna" literally means "what is it?" For the next 40 years, the Hebrews ate this "what is it?"

Some say that manna was a kind of edible hoarfrost that today is very rare. Studies have shown that a pound of the stuff would provide sufficient carbohydrates for a person to live on for 24 hours. The miracle was not the manna, but the fact that there was enough of it each day to feed everyone.

There seems to be two objectives to this miracle. The first was to teach the Hebrews to walk by faith, not by sight. The manna was sent fresh every morning. You couldn't store it up and rely on your supply while letting others go hungry.

God fed them with a fresh supply every morning. Of course, Jesus tried to teach us the same lesson. **"'Consider the lilies,' Jesus said, 'they neither toil nor spin, yet god provides for them. Pray this way: 'Give us this day our daily bread ....'"**

Jeremiah proclaimed that God's faithfulness was great, morning by morning God's mercies are new.

One Sunday in church I quoted the first verse of the 23rd Psalm: "The Lord is my shepherd I shall not want." Then I said, "That Psalm is among the best known and most widely memorized pieces of scripture. Everyone knows it, but no one believes it." What I meant is that few of us are able to live without wants, longings, anxiety and fear, trusting God with each new day.

It is easy to get angry with our government and leaders exploiting our fears as they have done since September 11. If we really believed Psalm 23, though, we would have a lot less fear to exploit.

EXODUS

Yesterday we looked at the lesson of trust the Hebrews had to learn from the provisions of manna in the wilderness. The other lesson from the manna seems to be a bit more subtle.

In verse 3, notice what happens to the Hebrews the minute they got hungry. They instantly began craving for the fleshpots of Egypt.

God's will for us is health and wholeness, or holiness. To say that another way, to live in the Promised Land, or the "Kingdom" of God, is to live lives that are both whole and holy. That is what God wants for us. It is what we want for us. The catch is that we want it without having to change our lifestyles, attitudes or appetites.

When the Hebrews got hungry they immediately began to crave the tastes of Egypt. Somehow all of the pain and suffering of oppression was completely forgotten.

Manna was God's way of changing the appetites of the Hebrews. They had acquired a taste for things that were not healthy for them. Eventually God would prescribe a strict kosher diet. The purpose of this diet was not that God didn't like pork or shell-fish, though it must have seemed that way to them at the time. We now know that the diet God prescribed for the Jews thousands of years ago spared them many of the diseases and epidemics that wiped out entire nations.

In Exodus 15:26, after their time at the waters of Marah, God's self-identification is as the God who heals, and the promise is made that the diseases that afflicted the Egyptians would not afflict them if they were obedient. By feeding them manna, God was changing their appetites so that the way they would begin to live would be healthier.

It took 40 years for God to get the craving for Egypt out of the Hebrews. How long will it take our appetites to change? How long will it take to change our desires for things that are not good for us? Are we willing to have them changed?

The early Church saw the gift of manna as a symbol for the Eucharist. They believed that, like the Hebrews learned to depend on God for daily sustenance, so the Christians learn to be sustained by Christ's presence.

Is it possible for us to learn to crave for God like we crave for things that are not healthy and life giving? The sooner we do, the sooner we will be able to set up housekeeping in the Promised Land that God has prepared for us.

The wilderness time is important, but how long it lasts is up to us.

EXODUS

In Exodus 16, we see the introduction of new dietary requirements for the Hebrews. In retrospect, we now understand that by adopting a dietary regime different from the Egyptians and other surrounding nations, the Jews avoided many illnesses. Still, at the time, it probably seemed to be a rather arbitrary rule.

In verse 22, Moses introduces another practice that also must have seemed incredibly random to the ancients, a practice that also distinguished the Hebrews from their neighbors. Imagine their surprise when, after years as slaves working for other masters, Moses tells them that on the sixth day they are to gather up twice as much manna as they needed because on the seventh day they were supposed to rest.

The idea of Sabbath is a part of our culture, but it was a radical change for people who live at the margins of starvation. The truly poor of this world struggle seven days a week to eat. God's image was of a community where we shared what nature provided so that all might have enough. That state of "enough" included a rhythm of life in which one day a week was set aside for rest and renewal.

I recently had a conversation with a wonderful woman who is deeply committed to changing the world. She is involved in many progressive organizations but was feeling overwhelmed by all the needs. There just didn't seem to be enough time and she found herself on the verge of burnout. She asked me how I had managed to stay passionate for so long in a seemingly impossible fight. Although I hadn't thought about it much, I realized that early in my career, I committed to keeping a Sabbath. It is perhaps the major reason my relationship has lasted 28 years. I don't work on Saturdays, and 99 percent of the time I spend that day is with Bill.

This is a commitment that can be tougher than it seems since there are always conferences, meetings, weddings or funerals on Saturdays. But Bill works Monday through Friday, and I work on Sundays. Saturday is the only day we can spend the whole day together. Long ago we created a rhythm of life that set one day aside. I'd love to have a weekend, but I don't. However, I have found that one day is enough if you keep it sacred and resist the temptation to go out and pick up manna, even on that day. Perhaps it is the beautiful secret of "enough" that God was trying to teach the ancient Hebrews. Do what you can, and then rest and it will be enough.

EXODUS

As the Hebrews journey from the Red Sea to Sinai, their trip is filled with various challenges that seem to follow a standard pattern. A need arises; the people complain, blame Moses and long for Egypt; and God provides. I'm not sure if there is a lesson for us in this pattern, unless it is that God has had lots of practice being patient with whiners.

In Exodus 17, the Hebrews are thirsty again. In a dry and arid land, like the wilderness east of Egypt, water is a matter of life and death. In this story, the people are about to stone Moses until God points out a rock and tells him to strike it where he will find a spring of water.

In South Georgia they like to say, "You can't get blood out of a turnip." I have no idea where that phrase came from, but it is probably what would have popped to mind if I had felt the Spirit nudging me to strike a rock in order to find water.

Perhaps Moses isn't as much a smart alec as I am, or maybe his thirst was so great that he was willing to try anything. It could be that, by now, Moses was beginning to catch on … Maybe God was trying to use their circumstances to teach them a lesson of trust. That may be why Moses called the place Massah, which means "testing."

Lessons end in tests to assess what was learned. Trusting God seems to be a lesson we must learn again and again. The wilderness is a dry and thirsty place. Centuries later, Jesus discovered this reality on the eastern end of this wilderness. In a place where he was forced to struggle with whom he was and how he would live his life. Ultimately, Jesus struggled with trusting God's way for him.

Notice that, in his dry and desert time, far from whining and believing God had abandoned him, when Jesus told the story (remember he had to be the source) he described it as a place where he had been led by the Spirit. He didn't see testing as a bad thing. Maybe that is because he had discovered that trust was how you get blood out of a turnip.

EXODUS

Our culture is replete with jokes about in-laws.

<INSERT YOUR IN-LAW JOKE HERE>

Fortunately Moses seemed to have married well, at least as far as his father-in-law Jethro was concerned.

After they had been in the wilderness a while, Jethro came to Moses, bringing his wife and two sons back to him. Moses had sent them to live with Jethro while he went to Egypt to face Pharaoh. Obviously Moses thought the task God had assigned him was dangerous. Now, Jethro returns Moses' family to him because, while the wilderness was difficult and tedious, it wasn't exciting. In fact, when Jethro arrives, he finds his son-in-law up to his neck in tedium.

The people brought every minor dispute and conflict to Moses to mediate. Although they may have criticized him and wanted to stone him when they ran out of water, they obviously regarded him as their true leader, and they trusted his wisdom and judgment.

Leading is often an unpopular role, and while it may have its swashbuckling moments, it is largely administrative, management and mundane. When Jethro arrived, he found his son-in-law completely overwhelmed by all the mundane demands of leading such a large number of people. Fortunately for Moses, Jethro had a solution to the problem.

Jethro knew a thing or two about delegation, so he coached Moses on the subject. I'm not exactly sure just where a backwater shepherd acquired his wisdom, but it isn't surprising. Many of the wisest people I've ever known are farmers, laborers and homemakers. I am somewhat embarrassed to admit that this sometimes surprises me. Why should it?

Fortunately, Jethro knew some things I sometimes have forgotten. Maybe there is a shepherd in your family who can help.

EXODUS

Moses' father-in-law, Jethro, saw how he was wearing himself out and, in the process, not serving the people well. Jethro told Moses that he needed to divide the people into groups and then appoint able leaders over each grouping.

Moses had fallen victim to a mind set that seems to challenge many of us. He had come to believe that he alone could hear from God, and with that, his judgment was best. He thought that the people depended on him to tell them what was on the mind of God.

Jethro recognized that this attitude wasn't healthy for Moses or good for other people. The amazing thing about Moses was his ability to listen to the counsel of another and respond positively. Too often we get defensive when someone points out that maybe someone else also might have heard from God.

As someone who works altogether too many hours, I sometimes wonder what I'm trying to prove. I enjoy what I do, but I fear that sometimes I act as if I am the only person God can use. That is idolatry at best. There is only one God, and I am not "the one." We must commend Moses for being able to recognize that reality and letting others share the work that he had been doing.

In the end, Jethro the shepherd taught Moses about God the good Shepherd. In all of Israel's history there was only one Moses, but there have been millions of women and men through whom God has been able to care for people. They may not have had Moses' gifts, but they had their own. Together, they were enough.

We don't need to do everything. When we all do what we can, it is enough in the hands of God.

EXODUS

After about three months, the Hebrews reached the foot of Mount Sinai. This was the place where a race of people who shared common ancestors became a people who shared a common faith.

In Exodus 19:4, we find one of my favorite images for God. Here, and again in Deuteronomy, there is this image of God bearing us up "on eagles' wings." It is an illustration for which most of us have little or no frame of reference, but it is very important to those of us who seek a relationship with the Divine.

In the wilderness, the Hebrews had witnessed firsthand how a mother eagle taught her young to fly. Eagles build their nests at the highest possible location. Both mother and father take turns feeding the young until they have outgrown the comfortable nest that was built for them. Then the baby eagle is literally forced from the nest. As it plummets to the ground, it instinctively and frantically flaps its little wings. The effort has very little effect on slowing down their fall.

Just as the baby bird is certain that it is about to die—the victim of infanticide—the mother eagle swoops beneath it and the youngling's small talons latch onto her wings for dear life. The mother eagle then bears the young high into the sky again. Just as the young eaglet's tiny heart slows a bit, the mother folds her wings and her child is plummeting again.

This process is repeated until the young eagle's wings begin to work. You see, this Biblical image of God bearing us on wings is beautiful, but it is also a statement of how we are taught to use the abilities and resources with which God endowed us.

We'd prefer to claim the image as a promise that God will bear us through the turbulence of life. That may well be what the Hebrews thought was happening when they saw the eagles in nature. The reality, however, is that God desires trust, not dependence. Learning that lesson can cause all our hearts to pound.

EXODUS

Yesterday, we looked at Exodus 19:4: "You have seen … how I bore you on eagles' wings and brought you unto myself."

Before we move on, I want to point out one last thing that seems to go unnoticed. When eagles are teaching their young to fly, it is the mother eagle that does most of the work. Female eagles in that region of the world are almost always larger than the males. For that reason, the mother eagle is the one to bear up the young as they learn to fly.

This is one of the many feminine images for God in the Bible. From the very start, with the Spirit (feminine) brooding over the face of the deep in the opening scenes of Genesis, God is revealed in scripture in feminine terms that for too long have been neglected.

If the Divine is always he/him/father/man upstairs, then masculinity becomes deified in a way that is inaccurate and idolatrous. The obvious result is sexism, misogyny and the systemic inferiorization of women. It is also the root cause of homophobia.

If the Bible had not been written by men, translated by men, and for centuries, interpreted by men, we would have realized centuries ago the real message of the scriptures when it says, "Male and female God created them … in the image and likeness of God they were created." BOTH masculinity and femininity are equally divine. The full witness of the Bible teaches us this even if our culture and religion have been too sexist to hear the Word.

Progressive people of faith must become deliberate and assertive in articulating our trust of the Motherhood of God. Maybe if people understood and experienced God as our Biblically-revealed heavenly mother we would honor more the testosterone-free heroism of compassion and mercy. Maybe if we learned to pray to God our Mother we could live with less fear and care more for the tender creation born from the Womb of the Divine.

EXODUS

After reading Exodus 19:16-25, did you think it sounded just like it was taken right out of "Raiders of the Lost Ark?" I suppose the creators of that movie actually borrowed from this passage. The writer of Exodus couldn't have designed a movie setting with more visual drama. We have a mountain with thunder and lightning, thick clouds and an earthquake. A trumpet blast made the people tremble and "as the trumpet blasts grew louder and louder, Moses would speak and God would answer him in the thunder."

God sent Moses to tell the people that they were not to come up the mountain, or even to look too closely, because they might be struck dead. I don't think God or Moses really had too much to worry about on that account. No one seemed too anxious to get up close and personal with the Mountain God of Exodus 19.

In a recent sermon I talked about Juanita, the 14-year-old-girl who is one of the best preserved mummies of the 15th-century Incas. A study by Johns Hopkins revealed that she was a well-loved young woman. She had been nourished and well cared for all of her life. There was no sign of broken bones or serious disease. This perfectly healthy girl died at 14 because a priest struck her in the head with a spiked club as a sacrifice to appease the Mountain God who had sent a famine on the people.

Today, Christians believe that God's self-revelation culminated in the life, teachings and ministry of Jesus. Still, it appears to me that the average person never got much past the Mountain God of Exodus 19. Fundamentalism requires that we fear God and anticipate that, if we disobey the rules, we will be struck down or, at the very least, sentenced to hell when we die.

It is no accident that this fearsome Mountain God terrifies the people just before the law is given. The Ten Commandments appear in the very next passage. These commands are offered against this backdrop of divine intimidation. The ancient Jews were not threatened with hell; that idea developed much later, when God wasn't as efficient at smiting sinners as religious leaders need "him" to be.

I just wonder what might have happened if, instead of intimidation and fear, our faith had been shaped from the start by the God who welcomes everyone to the mountain for a picnic.

EXODUS

Just in case this question ever comes up on "Jeopardy," the Ten Commandments are found in Exodus 20. There is another list in Deuteronomy 5 that is slightly different.

So let me get this off my chest right from the start: Have you ever wondered why states like Texas—where I live—make such a big deal about the Ten Commandments, but do so little about following them? A marble monument on which the big ten are inscribed stands on the grounds of the Texas State Capital. They are proudly displayed in other government settings as well, with little or no regard that there might be law-abiding, tax-paying citizens who are not Christians or Jews.

That is really not such a big deal to me. I fully support the separation of church and state, but understand those who oppose the separation of state from church. The Ten Commandments certainly played a historically significant role in shaping the legal values that govern our society. Their significance as a religious document aside, an educated culture should know and understand what shaped its identity and values.

I always have believed that the Bible should be studied as literature in the same way that we would study Shakespeare. On a purely literary level, it is a pretty amazing document. So, too, there are some remarkable things about these commandments that deserve even the most adamant atheist's attention. Once we get past the first couple of rules about other gods, the principles laid out in Exodus 20 seek to create a society that is remarkably civil and hospitable for the age in which the document was first produced.

For people of faith, the civilizing principles are offered against a call to set all other gods aside and root our lives first and foremost in the God of Creation and Liberation. Here in the wilderness of life, many gods compete for our devotion and attention, but there is only one God who will call our souls to civility and compassion. There is only one God whose identity is rooted in liberating us from bondage. Other gods—money, success, fame, power, etc.—enslave. The God of Exodus liberates, and then invites, us to live together according to some pretty basic life-enhancing principles. Far from oppressive, these commandments demonstrate God's concern for our on-going liberation.

EXODUS

Thou shalt not take the name of the Lord your God in vain.
Exodus 20:7

The commandments begin with the admonition that we give God the proper place in our lives. To me, this is very similar to Jesus' teaching us to, "Seek first the Realm of God, and all things will add together." (Matthew 6:33) To build a strong and healthy life, we must begin with the right cornerstone: the God of our Creation and Liberation.

As someone who lives in a culture of rampant narcissism, you don't need me to point out what happens when this first principle is ignored and parents make children the little gods of their family life. A plethora of recent studies have shown that the "me-generation" is more unhappy than generations before them. We don't do anyone a favor by indulging their delusion that the universe revolves around them and will bend to their will. The Lake Woebegon world in which "all the children are above average" must ultimately give way to a society where you are just one more car on the freeway and one more body in line at the grocery store.

Far from being a sign of God's insecurity or egotism, the first commandments call us to order our lives with God in first place so that all the other parts will fit together properly. The injunction about taking God's name in vain is not the censorship base for the FCC, but rather an invitation to consider what it is like to live in a world where nothing is sacred.

If the Source of life becomes a profanity then what about life itself? If God is most often invoked to bring forth damnation, then who will bless? If we have so little regard for the Creator, how will we ever care for the creation? This list could go on, but it returns to the original point and purpose of these commandments. None of them are about God, but they are about how we can live a strong and healthy life. That kind of life begins with and radiates from God. While we liberals don't want to impose our faith on others, we need to claim it fully for ourselves and offer it to those who are seeking our help in reordering their lives. No one is served when we try to help our family, friends or society put the wrong foundation stone into place. Sacred living must begin with the Divine. Regardless of the name we use, the One who is our God is our sacred starting place, and unless we reverence our source we will never respect the outcome.

EXODUS

Having grown up in a small town in South Georgia, I remember quite vividly the first time a convenience store other than the 7-Eleven decided to stay open on Sunday. Back then, we had "Blue Laws," which were designed to enforce the moral principle of protecting Sundays from work or commerce.

Of course, those laws were unconstitutional in this country, but they survived for more than 200 years because of how people interpreted the commandment to "Remember the Sabbath and keep it holy." (Exodus 20:8)

I remember my Methodist pastor rallying against the new mall built at the edge of town whose obvious purpose was the moral corruption of our community. He was right, of course, but it had nothing to do with the fact that they were open on Sundays. What he should have been concerned about was that on the edge of town they were building a temple to the true god of our culture and it was bigger than most of the churches combined.

Those who were concerned about the profaning of the Sabbath too often missed the point. To a people who had been enslaved, and whose labors enriched only their masters, God the Liberator was trying to teach a new principle of life. Jesus said, "Humans were not made for the Sabbath, but the Sabbath was made for humans." What an amazing thing that statement says about God. Think about it. From the outset, God cared about our mental and physical health. God understood that we were wired in such a way to need a rhythm of life that included weekly rest and renewal.

While we expect days off and take them for granted, for much of the world, one day is like another. Laboring seven days a week is the norm for those who subsist on what must be eked out every day. God envisioned a culture in which we shared our resources in such a way that everyone could spend one day in rest and renewal.

In subsistence society there is little time for art, or music, or literature. Every resource and all energy must be directed to survival. It was God's desire that all people do more than survive. God's Sabbath vision of life for all people is very different from a world where some must work seven days a week to survive, while we work endlessly to live in comparative opulence. Oh, I know none of us consider our lifestyle opulent, but tell that to the millions of people who live only one meal away from malnutrition or starvation.

For us, the Sabbath rhythm is a summons to balance from a God who cares about us and longs for all people to have enough to set aside one day to enjoy it and be grateful.

EXODUS

Each of the commandments must be understood from the perspective of how they resonate in the heart of God. These rules are not arbitrary or punitive, but rather they reflect a vision of life that includes the care of every person.

The week has run out before we could unpack all of the commandments, but I invite you to do with the rest of the list what I did for the first one. Refuse to think of each as a rule handed down from above to coerce you into behaving upon the threat of hell. Rather, think of them as amazing principles offered from the God of Creation and Liberation whose only desire is a world in which all lives are worth celebrating.

In that light, what do YOU think God had in mind?

- Honor your father and your mother, so that your days may be long in the land that the Lord your God is giving you.
- You shall not murder.
- You shall not commit adultery.
- You shall not steal.
- You shall not bear false witness against your neighbor.
- You shall not covet your neighbor's house; you shall not covet your neighbor's wife, or male or female slave, or ox, or donkey, or anything that belongs to your neighbor.

Ultimately, what this list seeks to achieve is a life in which we are content with what we have and who we are. The list ends with an admonition not to covet that which belongs to our neighbors. While other commandments address behavior, this one is about attitude. It seems to me that God's vision for our life is that we, and all our neighbors, may live together in such a way that, in the end, we have enough and are content for ourselves and happy for our neighbors.

Hey, God is nothing if not an idealist ….

EXODUS

Last week we looked at the giving of the laws known as the Ten Commandments, also known as the Decalogue. Exodus 20 ends with the people cowering because of the thunder, lightning, and the smoke on the mountain. Standing at a distance, they tell Moses, “You speak to us and we will listen, but don’t let God speak to us directly or we will die.” Moses agrees and tells them that God had come “only to test you and put the fear of God upon you so that you do not sin.” (Exodus 20:20)

What seems like a throwaway comment following the giving of the law explains a lot about religions that are rooted in law, rules and regulations. While there are a few more stories to be told in Exodus, much of the rest of the book, and almost all of Leviticus (the following book) is consumed with regulating people’s behavior. The rules seem endless and, frankly, sometimes pointless and petty.

Today, in a scientific world, we understand that certain laws—like dietetic restrictions—were developed to help people avoid certain illnesses and disease. At the time those laws were developed, however, there was no rational justification. The only means of enforcing them was to make them God-given and then to ensure that people feared incurring the wrath of God.

Many of the ancient stories of the Bible seem to serve no other purpose than to keep people afraid of the consequences of making God angry. Exodus 20 offers us an explanation for why natural disasters were interpreted by the priests and religious leaders as “acts of God.” On one level, it was a means of coercing people to do what was right—*thou shalt not steal*—and what was good for them—*remember the Sabbath.* As someone who has been known to don priestly garments, though, I probably also should acknowledge that some of the restrictions offered, then and now, were more about control. Religious leaders have a certain set of values that they think people should live up to, and they have never been reluctant to use fear to control behavior. Often it was God’s reputation that was damaged when religious types decided it was inappropriate for people to dance, or for a woman to show her ankle, or for people of different races to marry, or for the same gender to love.

Using fear to manipulate, coerce and control people is obviously not a technique invented by the U.S. government in the wake of 9/11. At least Moses/Exodus was up front about it.

EXODUS

For the next several chapters, the book of Exodus is mostly a record of a variety of rules and regulations. As with the book of Leviticus, some of the laws sound primitive and vicious by modern terms, while others are remarkably progressive and compassionate.

This section of lawgiving ends with a part in which the Hebrew people receive some remarkable promises. Beginning in Exodus 23:20, God is credited with promising to clear the land of its inhabitants so that the Hebrew nomads can make it their permanent homeland.

Exodus 23:23 says:

> *When my angel goes in front of you, and brings you to the Amorites, the Hittites, the Perizzites, the Canaanites, the Hivites, and the Jebusites, I will blot them out.*

Now, in all my years in the Church, I have never heard anyone talk about how disturbing this passage is. The statement clearly reflects how the Hebrews interpreted the way in which they came to possess the land they inhabited at the time this was recorded. While the author is seeking to credit God for their success and good fortune, what he ends up saying about God is pretty awful.

If we take literally this interpretation of how things happen, we must believe that God is responsible for genocide and the wholesale slaughter of indigenous people. While it was certainly not the intent of the original author, what we have is the attitude that would be expressed for many centuries to follow: people believing that they have some divine right to take the property and even lives of others.

Nowhere in history has this been more horrifically expressed than by our forebearers who slaughtered Native Americans in order to take their lands and then enslaved Africans to enrich them on the land.

Slaughtering people is never God's will nor God's work, regardless if they are Jebusites, Apache, Tutsis or Iraqis. Nothing any priest ever writes can change the fact that God is the mother and father of all people … even if that writing is someday revered as scripture.

Why aren't we outraged about what this passage says about God? Perhaps it is that we still secretly believe God will do the same thing for us in our wars and conquests.

EXODUS

In Exodus, the covenant between God and the people was sealed by blood. To the ancients, life was in the blood, and as Moses sprinkled blood over the people, they were sealed to God as God's own.

Today, blood makes us a bit squeamish, especially for those of us who are city dwellers completely removed from the origins of our food supply. In the movie "Last of the Mohicans" when a deer is killed for the families' food, the hunters stop and acknowledge that the deer had given its life so that they might live.

Our modern life distances us from the realities that, even for vegetarians, the living die so that we might live. It is a cycle that has been so since the beginning. Forgetting it causes us to act as if the only cost for our living is the green paper we give to the grocer. Blood reminds us of the cost of life.

For Christians, this scene in Exodus is a reminder of the wine we drink at communion after hearing the words, "This is my blood, which was shed for you." We don't like to think of drinking blood, but it is an important reminder that our spiritual life is no freer than our physical sustenance.

While I do not believe that Jesus died to convince God to love or forgive us, I do think that the death of Jesus was the price of persuading us that we are loved by God. The blood Moses sprinkled on the people seems like a gruesome ritual. That may be our own cultural arrogance, or maybe the Hebrews felt the same way that day. Perhaps it was intended to dramatically and indelibly impress upon them that they were in a covenant relationship with God.

Given God's physical absence, that seems to be a reality that people of faith in all times tend to forget. The blood of the animals sprinkled on them that day was meant to remind them of the life-giving, and given, covenantal relationship between us and the One who breathed life into us at the very start.

EXODUS

If you have been reading Exodus along with me, you may want to skip the next several chapters. They contain detailed descriptions of the physical space and elements the people used for worship. I can't even imagine that the priests even found these passages very interesting.

Ironically, in Exodus 32, we get to one of the better-known stories in this section of Israel's history. The story of the golden calf is a favorite of Sunday school children. I think Charlton Heston must have enjoyed it, too. In the movie, *The Ten Commandments,* he comes down from the mountain having spent 10 chapters with God to find that the Hebrews decided God must have done him in, so they use their gold to create a god for themselves.

There are enough obvious preacher points in this story that you can probably find them for yourself. What we shouldn't miss, though, is that this story is a good reminder that if we do not work to keep our relationship and covenant with God alive, we all too quickly and easily will create other gods to fill the void.

Moses was gone too long, and like people who neglect attending church, prayer, study or other spiritual disciplines, the experiences of God's presence faded quickly into distant memory. Even liberals need to practice the disciplines of faith in order to keep them alive and our lives full of the Sacred Presence.

It is likely not a coincidence that the idol the people created was out of gold. We all have had work commitments and the worry over money consume us and fill up our hearts. Suddenly there is no more room, even for the One who created us. The problem with this is not that it ticks God off, but that it disorders our lives. Things that become sacred, the source of our love and devotion, are those to which we give our life's energy.

Okay, so I'm a preacher, but it is true that I have rarely ever known anyone to maintain a spiritual balance in their life without being involved in a community of faith and regularly nourishing their soul. Moses was the Hebrews' connecting point to God, and he had been gone too long. Have you? Have you been gone too long from worship, study or prayer? If your relationship is all about your head and not your heart, you better look out for falling tablets of stone.

EXODUS

After discovering the idolatry of the people, it looks like God is going to wipe out the whole nation. In the end, though, the priests/Levites simply slaughtered about 3,000 of them … of course, this was at God's command.

I can't help but wonder why it wasn't the priests who were slaughtered, since they obviously had not been doing their job. Well, as the African proverb says, "Until the lion learns to write the story, the hunter will always win." Since this portion of Exodus was obviously written by the priests, the story was told from their perspective.

Again, this story is used to keep people in line. Fear always has been a tool of the religious to control behavior. Who knows when God just might tell the Levites to slaughter two or three thousand more people? In Christianity, we use the concept of hell for the same purpose. That is the reason that religious leaders have never been able to fully trust the concept of grace. I mean, if people were unconditionally loved by God, what can be used to force them to behave?

The good news in the story of the golden calf is that God doesn't kill them all off, but gives the people a second chance … well, all but 3,000 of them. This pattern is the history of the people of God. We sin, it makes God angry, then we repent, and God forgives. It happens so often that you begin to think that someone in this cycle should wise up. Doesn't God know that we will only mess up again? Don't we know that life is better lived out of a place of a loving relationship with God and one another?

Progressive people tend to think of repentance as a fundamentalist doctrine. The reality is it is strongly humanist to believe that we can change, learn, grow and improve. Of course, there is a great gulf between believing we can do that and actually doing it. That may be why something bad has to happen in our lives before we actually decide it may be time to change directions.

Fortunately, even the ancients, with their primitive vengeful concept of God, had to admit that God was the God of the second … and third, fourth and fifth … chance.

EXODUS

Exodus 33 introduces several ideas that will continue to play a role in the story of the Hebrews for the next 40 or so years. First, Moses set up a tent outside camp and called it a "tent of meeting." There, he would go to meet with God and intercede for the people. This Tent of meeting evolves into the Tabernacle, which eventually became a permanent Temple.

The other thing that happens is that when Moses was in the tent of meeting a "pillar of cloud" would appear over it indicating that God was present. Eventually, this pillar of cloud would lead the people through their journeys in the wilderness. At night a pillar of fire would appear. A more mundane explanation is that in the Tent/Tabernacle when a fire burned it sent a plume of smoke up in the air like a cloud. The fire burning on a mobile brazier would send sparks and light up in to the smoke at night making it appear in the lightless wilderness to be a pillar of fire.

Giving spiritual interpretation to something normal and ordinary is what religions of all brands have always done. After all, Christianity made sacraments of water as well as bread and wine. Seeing God in the miraculous is to be expected. However, if we want to live as a spiritual being in a physical world, we must learn to recognize the divine in the mundane.

Perhaps that trait in Moses is what led to one of the most amazing statements in his astonishing story. In Exodus 33:11, the author describes Moses as entering the tent of meeting where, "Thus the Lord spoke to Moses face to face, as one speaks to a friend."

That kind of relationship with God is unique and remarkable but especially so for the Hebrews who repeatedly emphasize that a face-to-face relationship with God meant death for fragile humans. While we no longer believe in a God who has a physical face, there is something in the most liberal soul that longs for a friendship with the One who birthed us. Perhaps we need to find special places in our lives that can be designated as tents of meeting, and be more sensitive to the Divine in the mundane.

EXODUS

While verse 11 talks about Moses speaking with God face-to-face, the remainder of Exodus 33 is spent with Moses requesting to see God's face. The chapter seems to be three vignettes edited together by a common theme.

Apparently, the people of God struggled with God's physical presence among themselves. In Exodus 33:12-16, God promises Moses that God's physical presence will be with the people and will lead them through their wilderness wanderings. Then, in verses 17-23, there is a rather bizarre and beautiful story of how Moses sought to see the "glory," or the face, of God. What is granted, though, is that Moses is hidden in a cleft of a rock while God passes by, and then Moses was allowed to see God's "back" and afterglow.

After this, in Exodus 34, there is a retelling of the giving of the covenant and commandments. This time, instead of coming down the mountain to find a golden calf, the chapter ends with Moses returning to the people with the stone tablets and a glowing face. The radiance of Moses' face frightened the people, and they asked him to wear a veil until the glow faded.

This event became a significant part of the Jewish religious tradition. It is so noteworthy that St. Paul used it as an analogy in 2 Corinthians 3. While it is impossible to know exactly what this description of a glowing face refers to, we all have had the experience of encountering a friend who "glowed." It is said that new love can have that effect, and a new mother is said to have a "certain glow." There are those rare people who glow because they seem to be so in love with life.

Love, motherhood, life and God all seem closely related to me. Maybe a bit more time spent deliberately seeking the God of love and life would give all our faces a bit of a lift.

EXODUS

When Moses returned to the people, glowing with the covenant and commandments from God, we are essentially at the end of the story of Exodus. The last five chapters describe, sometimes in excruciating detail, the building of the Tabernacle.

That section, as well as the entire book of Exodus, ends with a description of how God's presence filled that new space in the same way that God had been present in the simpler Tent of Meeting. While portable, the Tabernacle is a clear indicator that this phase of Israel's life was going to be more lasting than originally anticipated. What could have been an 11-day journey will take a generation.

We have spent an inordinate amount of time studying the stories of faith in Genesis and Exodus. Obviously, to complete the entire Hebrew Bible, the remaining books will receive much less of our time and attention. With relatively few exceptions, though, the stories that comprise the next 37 books are far less seminal to the Jewish, Christian and even Muslim faiths.

Liberating Word has chosen to focus on the stories more than the teachings, proverbs or poetry, because our Jewish and Christian ancestors in faith were people of stories and of "The Story." For the Jews, THE story was Exodus, told against the background of the patriarchs and, to a lesser extent, matriarchs of Genesis. For Christians, our seminal story was the life of Jesus.

People without a story are orphans. Jesus promised not to leave us as orphans, but to send the Spirit who would teach us. It is my conviction that the Spirit's best teachings still come from providing us new lessons from ancient stories. For historically excluded people like women, lesbians, gays, the poor, people of color and, in our day, liberals, reclaiming ancient stories and hearing them speak to our lives has the power to heal. No longer are we orphans; now, the stories of the children of God are our stories, too. Let's revel in learning them and learning from them.

PENTATEUCH

I have thus far avoided discussing the JEPD theory of the authorship of the Pentateuch or Torah. The first five books of the Bible are regarded as a unit by Jewish readers and are greatly esteemed. They often are referred to as The Books of Moses, and Moses is traditionally attributed as the author.

It is clear, to even the most cursory literary analysis, that the Pentateuch was not penned by a single hand. For example, in the Pentateuch, two major names are used for God, YHWH (or *Yahweh/Jehovah*) and *Elohim*. Some sections of the Pentateuch exclusively use the name *Elohim* for God (Gen. 1) while others exclusively use YHWH. (Gen. 2) YHWH tends to be spoken of more in anthropomorphic terms (walking in the garden and creating with clay, Gen. 2), while *Elohim* is described in more majestic, distant terms (creating by speaking, Gen. 1). Of course, this implies that at least two different authors recorded various stories and that later editors assembled the stories into the Pentateuch we have today. Hence, you have what are referred to as the J and E authors.

The P stands for priests, because huge segments of the books were written by someone highly educated and concerned about the priestly functions of the faith. These later chapters of Exodus are mostly P in source with a couple of the stories standard in the early part of the book mixed in. The D in JEPD stands largely for Deuteronomy with its second giving of the law.

Now, the value of this information rests largely in the possibility that you will someday be a contestant on "Jeopardy." However, while this year-long survey of the Hebrew Testament isn't designed to be a Bible study, it does seem valuable to me that we hear as many voices from the texts as possible.

Fundamentalists and traditionalists insist that Moses was the author of all five books, even the one in which he dies. We, who are liberals or progressives, ought to value the idea of diverse witnesses telling the stories from their own perspectives. Actually, I'm not convinced of the JEPD theory of authorship, but I do greatly value the thought that God speaks through many voices … even the most unexpected. Spiritual maturity is found in hearing other voices without letting those voices silence your own witness of faith.

LEVITICUS

Given my theory that, for most readers, Day Five (or Friday) is the day devotionals are least likely to be read, I thought we'd tackle the book of Leviticus today. Actually, one day is all I want to spend on Leviticus, the third book of the Bible.

The book of Leviticus contains regulations and instructions for both the ritual and lifestyle of the ancient Jews. Only a minority of modern Jews follow all of the laws of Leviticus. For most Christians the rules are no longer in effect. For example, we are free to eat pork or shellfish.

Regarding these laws, the church has been remarkably hypocritical throughout its history. Leviticus has been used when it seems to support their preconceived notions. It historically has been a source of support for slavery and restricting women's rights. Today, fundamentalists still fall back on Leviticus to justify their disdain for the gay and lesbian population.

The selective use of Leviticus probably has caused us to miss the greater truth of the book. While the laws may seem arbitrary and restrictive to us today, a study of the historical context of that day reveals that many of them had value for the survival of the ancient Jews. Even the injunction against men having sex with men was given in the context of a world where procreation was essential for the survival of the species. Like most of the Levitical laws, that one is out of date, but its origin was never just God's arbitrary disdain for gay people.

In this passage, we are reminded of God's overarching intent:

> *You shall keep all my statutes and all my ordinances, and observe them, so that the land to which I bring you to settle shall not vomit you out. ... You shall inherit the land, and I will give it to you to possess, a land flowing with milk and honey. I am the Lord your God; I have separated you from the peoples. You shall therefore make a distinction between the clean and the unclean. ... You shall be holy to me; for I the Lord am holy, and I have separated you from the other peoples to be* ***mine****.*
>
> Leviticus 20:22

It is this last verse that I find so moving. God is saying, with an almost pained voice, "Don't do things that will bring you disease and death. When you feel separated from me, do these things so we can be together again. I want you to be healthy. I want you to be happy. I want you to be **mine**."

NUMBERS

The fourth book of the Pentateuch, or Torah, is called Numbers. Its name is derived from the census with which the book begins and ends. The text says that the starting population number was 603,550. That is quite a crowd, especially when you figure that they only counted military-aged men. There were at least that many women, and a significant number of children and youth.

The book of Numbers describes the adventures and misadventures of two million people who spent 40 years wandering in the barren wilderness between Egypt and Canaan. Envision the entire city of Houston deciding to walk to Dallas and living off the land for 40 years. Those numbers are incongruent with either historic or archeological evidence. But somehow the numbers got mistranslated or exaggerated. Well, the Bible isn't an almanac.

What may be valuable for us is the numbering itself. In a world where it is easy to feel like a single dot in a Georges Seurat painting, it is good to remember that God is like a good shepherd who knows if even one gets lost along the way. It is so comforting that Jesus said that even the hairs of our head are numbered.

God sees each of us as an individual work of art. While remembering that may easier for some of us, it is important for all of us to hear the consistent witness of scripture that we aren't regarded by God as a crowd of dots on a page forming a picture of humanity. The Bible begins its story by revealing God as the artist of creation. Numbers reminds us that we are the work of the Artist's hands. Hopefully this book can remind us that every person we encounter today is also God's work.

Just remember the works of art we often appreciate the least may well be the most valuable.

NUMBERS

The book of Numbers makes for some pretty dry reading, but there are a few stories that deserve our attention. Only five passages from Numbers are read in the three-year lectionary cycle, so many of us haven't heard much of the book … and, frankly, that is just as well.

One of the best known stories is found in Numbers 13. That story is a powerful parable about life. While camped in Paran at Kadesh, Moses sent 12 men to scout the land where they planned to settle. They are referred to as spies, but their mission was neither covert nor military.

The spies were gone for 40 days (are you noting a numeric theme?), and when they returned, they brought grapes, figs and pomegranates. The men also came back with a conflicting report. Two of them, Joshua and Caleb, had glowing reports of a rich and lush future homeland. However, the other 10 men came back with stories of walled cities, strong armies and giants. For the majority, the indigenous inhabitants of the land were so powerful that the Israelites felt like grasshoppers.

Two conflicting visions of the same reality were presented to Moses and the people. The minority report was of great potential and hope that there might be something beyond the dry and barren wilderness in which they wandered. No one denied that it might be difficult and dangerous, but Joshua and Caleb saw a preferable future for the people. Joshua said they were "well able to overcome" the challenges.

The majority report, of course, might have been given by any modern media outlet, because it focused almost exclusively on the bad news and exploited the fears of the people. Of course, given the choice between two reports, the people put all their faith in one that was negative and fear-based. At Kadesh, the people forgot all that God had done for them and utterly rejected leadership that offered an alternative vision of what was possible.

In almost any situation, people of faith are presented with two ways to look at life. Which we choose is always up to us, but our future depends on each choice.

NUMBERS

At Kadesh, the people heard about two visions for their future. Joshua and Caleb saw the abundance and possibilities and called on the people to trust the goodness of the God of the Exodus. Ten of the spies, though, saw the land through the lens of fear and danger. The people put their faith in the bad news.

In Numbers chapter 14, the people suggest they select a captain who will lead them back to Egypt—back to slavery, oppression and bondage. When Moses, Aaron, Joshua and Caleb try to persuade them to trust God, the people pick up rocks and threaten to stone them.

As a result of their rebellion, God decrees that none of them will ever enter the Promised Land. They do not go back to Egypt, but they are doomed to live out the next 40 years of life wandering aimlessly without a home, scraping by and complaining endlessly about their miserable existence.

They came to the edge of the Promised Land, but their fear and negativity kept them out.

This lesson has dozens of applications both in our personal lives and in our lives as the people of God and as a nation.

I listened recently to a television preacher who talked about how our military made us safe and protected the modern state of Israel. It seemed to me like blasphemy for a person of faith to trust in guns and bombs for security rather than in God.

On the money of our nation, you'll find the imprint "IN GOD WE TRUST." Then we spend more of our money on the military than on anything else. If we made a different choice, one that was really rooted in trusting God, we could move the whole world closer to the Promised Land. We could choose a world where there is enough abundance to feed all and everyone has a home. Idealistic? Perhaps, or perhaps it is simply choosing to see reality through the eyes of God.

NUMBERS

Much of the book of Numbers consists of Moses begging God not to wipe out the rebellious and complaining people. In Numbers 14:18, there is a snippet of a Psalm that says:

The Lord is slow to anger,
And abounding in steadfast love,
Forgiving iniquity and transgression,
But by no means clearing the guilty
Visiting the iniquity of the parents
Upon the children
To the third and fourth generation.

Perhaps because the book of Numbers was written by priests, one ongoing theme of the book is that God's mercy requires the intercession of a priest. Moses and Aaron generally remind God to be merciful and compassionate.

It is a primitive view of God, but it is the view that has shaped much theology. For the sacramental church, the mass is a real renewal of the sacrifice of Christ by which people are reconciled to God. Through confession and absolution, the priest intercedes for the sinner. For the more evangelical church, this story finds expression in intercessory prayer by which we persuade God to help people in need.

Our theology about these things often reveals more about us than about God. How different would worship and prayer be if we set aside this primitive understanding of God and claimed the image of the God revealed in Jesus? This God does not need to be persuaded to love us, forgive us or heal us, but rather we worship and pray to place ourselves and others under the waterfall of God's ceaseless mercy and grace.

Bad things happened to the people of the Numbers narrative. In their worldview, those bad things were sent by God and heroic intercessions were required to change God's mind. They may be right, but since we no longer believe that disease is caused by sin, why do we persist in believing that it is God who must be persuaded to love?

NUMBERS

In Numbers chapter 27, the leadership of the Hebrews is transferred from Moses to Joshua. From all the stories we have read, we know fairly little about Joshua. There are no burning bushes, no parting of the seas, no smoke and fire on the mountain in Joshua's life.

Joshua's qualification for leading the people of God rested almost entirely on his ability to look at a situation and see the possibilities. I guess you can say he was the first "possibility thinker." Fortunately, he didn't hear God calling him to build a Crystal Cathedral because glass wouldn't be invented for two or three more millennium.

So Joshua would have to use what was at hand to build a home for the people of God. Let's set aside for a week or so any discussion about the morality of taking land away from indigenous people and giving it to another race. Suffice it to say that the challenges that Joshua would face are just as great as those that faced Moses.

Joshua did not seem to be endowed with the kind of direct line to God that Moses had. Moses was a spiritual leader, and Joshua had to rely on political, military and organizational skills. Still, as we will see, he does pretty well.

As one of only two of the spies who saw the good and believed in the possibility of God working for the people, Joshua was selected to succeed the greatest leader in Hebrew history. I can't help but wonder if Joshua was a natural-born optimist. We sometimes call people "natural leaders," but it seems that effective leadership is a skill that can be learned. What is tougher is learning to have a positive attitude, especially when surrounded by people who are obsessed with the challenges.

It is possible that someone whose natural tendency is to see what is wrong, broken, different and difficult can still choose to empower the positive and the possible. I think Joshua was that kind of leader. He made choices about to what he would give his time, energy and passion. His first reaction wasn't necessarily his last, because the ultimate choice of his life was to trust in the goodness of God, and THAT was enough to qualify him as Moses' successor.

DEUTERONOMY

We probably should have lingered in the book of Numbers for a couple more days, because Deuteronomy is **really** boring. It mostly consists of speeches attributed to Moses, and, as the word "deuteron," (meaning second) implies, much of the material has already been covered. Still, there are some lessons to be learned.

In the speeches attributed to Moses, he reviews the history of the people of God. They are camped once more at Kadesh on the edge of the Promised Land. After 40 years, the generation that had refused to trust God to give them a homeland has all died off, except for Moses, Caleb and Joshua. Before the book of Deuteronomy is over, Moses himself will say goodbye to the people he has led for so long.

The discourses are ostensibly a reminder to the new generation of their history and the core values that form their identity. Historically people of faith understood what we are in danger of forgetting: **anyone who can't remember any further back than their own birth is an orphan.** When we don't know our own story or the story of our people, we are tempted to believe that the story began with us.

The narcissism that is so culturally pervasive has many roots, but one is that this is the first age in human history when elders have failed to pass their stories to the next generation. Children, youth and young adults can tell you all about present-day actors or "American Idols," but have no clue about their grandparents' lives. In the Church, while we may know some of the stories, we lack a sense that they are OUR stories. Lacking that understanding deprives us of a connection to our past and keeps us from assuming our responsibility for our future.

While I hope these daily meditations challenge and inspire, more than anything I hope they help us see that the story of God and God's people didn't begin with us. If we play our part, it won't end with us either. We are a part of something bigger, longer and more durable. It is our story too, even the boring parts.

DEUTERONOMY

Anthropologist Laurens Van Der Post wrote the following about the Kalahari Bushmen:

> *The supreme expression of a people's spirit can be seen in their stories. That is why in so called "primitive tribes," the wisest are always the ones who tell the best stories. These people know what we have forgotten:* ***Without a story, you are not a people.***

While the book of Deuteronomy is set just before the death of Moses, most Biblical scholars believe it actually wasn't written until centuries later. The authors sought to remind the people of their history and their story. Ancient victories are rehearsed, and even the 40 years of wandering was framed as a time when God took care of them. (Deuteronomy 2:7)

The most important lesson of the book, though, is found in what is known as the *Shema* and *Decalogue,* or the great commandment and the Ten Commandments. In chapter 6 verse 4, we read what became the most important and sacred words for the Jews:

> *Hear O Israel: The Lord is our God, the Lord alone.*
>
> Deuteronomy 6:4

That verse has a number of translations, but all agree that it is a statement affirming the radical monotheism of the Jewish faith. While that doesn't seem particularly radical today, in that setting it was the defining trait for the Jews. Even today, millennia later, it remains their most sacred prayer to be prayed twice daily.

For Christians, the next verse became even more famous, because it was quoted by Jesus when he was asked what was most important:

> *You shall love the Lord your God with all your heart and with all your soul and with all your might.*
>
> Deuteronomy 6:7

The rest of the chapter goes on to talk about mnemonic devices the Hebrews might use to remember this core value and to instill it in their children.

Even before the age of distractions, the ancients understood how easily we can forget what is most important. That is why every goal-setting, self-help seminar teaches you to write down your goals. Thousands of years ago, Deuteronomy advised that we write down our core values and always keep them as the focus of our lives.

What would you write for your life?

DEUTERONOMY

Deuteronomy has some strange, and in many cases, punitive laws, like those in chapter 23. Apparently eunuchs and any man whose genitals had been crushed were not allowed to be a part of the family of faith. That also applied to anyone who was born out of wedlock. These people couldn't be a part of the faith; neither could their children, grandchildren, great-grandchildren … for 10 generations.

By contrast, chapter 15 contains some remarkably compassionate instructions on how to treat the poor and those in need. It goes so far as to say that every seven years all debts are forgiven and everyone gets a chance to start over. Even in regards to slaves, there is redemption. By contrast to their neighbors in that day, Jews were commanded by their God to be generous, compassionate and kind.

One of my favorite passages in Deuteronomy is 30:19:

> *I call heaven and earth to witness against you today that*
> *I have set before you life and death, blessings and curses.*
> *Choose life so that you and your descendants may live.*

I like that verse because it is a reminder that almost every choice we make moves us deeper into the river of life, or further out. With each choice, we decide to participate in the flow of God's life or into the stream of death. Simply put, I believe that every time we choose to be generous, compassionate and kind we participate in the Life that is God. When we make other choices, we are rejecting life and, therefore, choosing death.

This passage reminds us that life is nothing more than an accumulation of our choices. Even when pain, tragedy and heartache come, as they do to us all, we still have choices. We can be victims, or we can choose to find the seeds of life. That does not make light of the pain, but it does invite us to find light *in* the pain. Yes, that is difficult to do, but the only option is to let death win it all.

We live in a world that seems to endorse death's agenda: greed, selfishness, fear, prejudice, apathy and so on. Although this ancient book is woefully out of date on many issues, it is still right on when it calls people of faith to make different choices. We are not victims and we are not entitled. We are people with choices.

DEUTERONOMY

In Deuteronomy 31, God speaks to Moses one more time saying, "Your time to die is near." Leadership is then transferred in a sacred ceremony from Moses to Joshua.

In Exodus, we are told that God talked to Moses as a friend to a friend. Now, telling him that it was time for him to die doesn't seem very friendly, but I think it is better than hearing it from a doctor or nurse who hardly knows you. There is no emotion or sadness or drama in the statement. Perhaps it simply is that God is saying, "I have been with you, and now it is time for you to be with me."

What follows in chapter 32 is entitled "The Song Moses." Verses 10 and 11 contain a beautiful image of how Israel is the apple of God's eye. Then Moses describes God as a mother eagle who stirs up her nest forcing her young to fly, and catching them on her wings.

This image appears in Exodus as well, but here it is offered in the context that Moses, their long-term leader, is about to leave them. The Hebrews probably are feeling, as the baby eagle felt forced from its comfortable nest, like the bottom has fallen out from under them.

No one likes that feeling in the pit of their stomach that comes when we feel insecure, uncertain or anxious. In that moment, it is difficult to believe that God our heavenly mother will catch us. The truth is, according to this parable at least, that God is hoping not to have to catch us, but hoping that we will learn to fly.

God wants to live in a covenant relationship of mutuality with us, but, since creation began, has steadfastly refused to enter into a relationship of dependency. Moses led them, taught and scolded them, cajoled them and interceded for them. Joshua was their new leader, but he was no Moses. He wasn't meant to be. The time in the wilderness was over. Now it was time for the nation to learn to fly.

I wonder what would happen if the next time life seems to fall out from under us, we decided to discover what might be possible if we used all the potential God had given us. Inevitably we will pray, "God save me …" Instead, maybe we should pray, "God teach me to fly."

DEUTERONOMY

And so the Torah/Pentateuch ends with a brief description of the death and burial of Moses. Deuteronomy 34 says that, at the age of 120, Moses was led by God to the top of Mount Pisgah, where he looked out over the Promised Land before he died.

This story is a powerful precursor for the sermon the Rev. Dr. Martin Luther King, Jr. gave on April 3, 1968:

> *We've got some difficult days ahead. But it doesn't matter with me now. Because I've been to the mountaintop. And I don't mind. Like anybody, I would like to live a long life. Longevity has its place. But I'm not concerned about that now. I just want to do God's will. And He's allowed me to go up to the mountain. And I've looked over. And I've seen the Promised Land. I may not get there with you. But I want you to know tonight, that we, as a people, will get to the Promised Land. And I'm happy, tonight. I'm not worried about anything. I'm not fearing any man. Mine eyes have seen the glory of the coming of the Lord.*

Of course, the next day, like Moses, Dr. King was dead.

It has been said that true greatness is planting a tree under which you will never sit. Given the direction of our society, that kind of value is more rare and heroic than ever. In both Moses and King, we have leaders who got to see the Promised Land, but never got to live there. They gave their lives trying to get us there, but they themselves never enjoyed the bounty of the harvest.

Every time I try to tackle issues like the death penalty in Texas, or racism in the South, or homophobia in the church, I find myself discouraged by hopelessness. It would be easier to tackle issues that I knew we could win, or at least make progress on, in my life time. Then, the Spirit reminds me that, like these two men, none of us have been assured that we will make it to the Promised Land. Rather, we all have been called to be faithful.

The last verses of the Torah are the obituary of Moses. He was great, and the author sings his praise. I suspect that Moses, after 120 years of seeking to follow God, finally understood that it didn't really matter what people said about him. The only epitaph that really mattered was God saying, "Well done my good and faithful servant." At those words, Moses' eyes truly saw the glory of the coming of the Lord … a friend coming to welcome another friend home.

JOSHUA

For more than a generation, the history of the people of God was largely the history of Moses. It is amazing how autobiographical history can be. It is a tribute to the power of one woman or man to make a difference. Moses, with the assistance of Miriam and Aaron, led the people of God from slavery through the Red Sea and into a covenant relationship with God.

Eventually, Moses led the people to the edge of the Promised Land. That was as far as he could take them. Joshua is the one who will lead them into that land. There is no book in the Bible named "Moses," but the sixth book in the Bible is named for Joshua. Just who is this person who will replace Moses? The Pentateuch and Deuteronomy end with high praise for Moses:

Never since has there arisen a prophet in Israel like Moses.

How would you like to fill those shoes? Moses did what he could to pass the mantle of authority, but, still, it must have seemed a daunting challenge. To make matters worse, 38 years before, Joshua and Caleb had been sent with 10 other spies to reconnoiter the land. The majority came back and filled the hearts of the people with great fear. Joshua boldly proclaimed that, despite all of the challenges, with God on their side, they could easily take the land.

Now it was up to Joshua to prove his assessment. Don't you just hate it when life requires you to prove that your faith is more than just a theory? Who we become in those moments is the truth about who we really are. Tests like these often seem to come after someone we love or admire dies, resigns or leaves.

Now what? Do we have the courage to live with the integrity of our belief, even if it means risking our reputation or assuming larger responsibilities? Joshua was probably tempted to nominate Caleb for the job, but he didn't. Instead he stepped up, took the chance, and proved that God, in fact, could give them the land. Joshua just didn't know 40 years prior that God would do so by working through him rather than Moses.

What about you? Are your convictions strong enough to let God use you to make your values more than theory? Positive thinking is great, but the test is how much we are willing to risk to prove it is true. That is faith.

JOSHUA

Through 40 years of wandering in the wilderness, the people were liberated from their slavery mentality, and they became strong and numerous. Like the Hebrews, most of us spend too large a percentage of our lives wandering between where we were when God rescued us and where God longs for us to be. Although the wilderness isn't where we were meant to live our lives, it does not mean God can't use that time to make us stronger and healthier.

The place where we are supposed to live is the place where God's will is fully realized in every aspect of our lives. However, that does not mean until we get to that point we are on our own. Although it was the Hebrews' own stubbornness and fear that kept them wandering for so long, God didn't abandon them during their time in the wilderness.

Moving into the Promised Land is much harder than one would think. After 40 years, the wilderness begins to look like home. Although you get sick and tired of manna and quail, at least you aren't hungry. Wilderness wandering becomes a way of life. After a while it is hard to remember that life can be any other way. The wilderness seems normal, even fulfilling. Moving into the Promised Land is tough and costly. There is a part of you that wonders if it is worth the effort. Wouldn't it be easier just to let life continue the way it has been for so long?

Perhaps that is the real reason that the task of leading the people into the land fell to Joshua rather than Moses. The people needed new ideas, new visions, new challenges and new leadership. Although Moses could have provided all of that, it was probably easier to receive them from Joshua.

It is amazing how often changes in one area of our lives precipitate our being open to changes in other areas. Perhaps that is why we resist change so fiercely. If we let one thing change, we risk everything else shifting. Imagine how the Hebrews' stress level must have soared when Moses died. Their best connection to God was gone. It probably came as no surprise to them that Joshua was designated to take Moses' place. Maybe they were even a bit glad. Maybe now they could move into the land of promise and get on with their lives.

We can obsess about changes, or we can give ourselves to the possibilities. That attitude just may open the door for more life than we ever imagined as we move from a place of comfortable subsistence to God's glorious challenges.

JOSHUA

Do you remember that Joshua was one of the 12 spies Moses sent to survey the land the first time? Now it is Joshua's turn. Joshua sends spies into the city of Jericho who encounter a woman named Rahab, who we are told was a "harlot."

The wonderful thing about this story is that it speaks of how God used a woman who was a sexual outcast. Fundamentalists often go through all sorts of contortions to make Rahab out to be something she is not. I heard one preacher talk about how "she accepted the testimony of the spies and that transformed her." None of that is found in the Bible. What we have is a woman who typically would be scorned and rejected by religious folk, but who God used in a vital way.

Rev. Don Eastman has a sermon about Rahab entitled, "The Best Little Whorehouse in Jericho." It does seem to be an odd place to find the rescuing grace of God, but maybe the message here is that it is in odd places where God's rescuing grace is best found. The person God uses is not the pale virgin cloistered in some convent. Here is a woman of the world who, because of her lifestyle, has information that the spies needed. She easily could explain away two strange men coming into her house. She was someone who was real, and the spies could trust her with their lives.

Because Rahab "entertained" a great deal, she had heard the story of the Hebrews and was convinced that they were the people of the true God. That is why she risked her life helping them. The other wonderful thing about Rahab was that she wasn't one of these frail and dainty women either. SHE let them down through the window by a rope. Do you know how much strength she would need to lower them with a rope? Then she gives them directions and told them how to do it. This is a woman who knows her way around.

The Bible tells us that when Jericho fell, Rahab and her family were spared. We don't hear from her again, until you run into her in Matthew's Gospel. There she is smack dab in the middle of Jesus' family tree. Saving the spies might have been brushed off as a fluke, but, to make sure we didn't brush her off, God arranges things so that she is a great-great-great-grandmother of the savior of the world.

I guess what this says to us is that if God chooses and uses people like Rahab in such amazing ways, we certainly qualify too. We've probably all messed our lives up enough to be candidates for grace fit to serve the living God.

JOSHUA

I think it is a fascinating parable of life that the Jews traveled hundreds of miles and 40 years into their future to return to where they started. Like their parents standing at the edge of the Red Sea with Moses, this generation, born in the wilderness, is separated from where God has called them to be by the raging water of the Jordan River.

Now, most of the time, the Jordan isn't much of a river, but there are times when it is flooded and dangerous. Naturally, the Hebrews are trying to cross it at just such a precarious time. Isn't that just the way of it? How many times do we face challenges that, incredibly, are like ones we faced before? How many times have we done ordinary things like crossing a river, making a presentation, or writing a paper, but when they are really important the whole thing suddenly becomes a crisis? Murphy strikes again, and everything seems to flood in on us at once.

A normally easy thing suddenly becomes a barrier. For months, the Hebrews had practiced fighting and were prepared for combat. But most of them didn't know how to swim. Remember, they were born as nomads in the Sinai Desert. There aren't a lot of chances to practice your backstroke out there. Besides that, the rushing current would challenge even the strongest swimmer.

So what could they do? The easiest thing would be just to unpack their bags and wait for the flood to subside. Yet God had brought them all this way and waiting didn't seem to be what God had in mind. Could it be that if they had waited that would have given their enemies time to lay traps and plan ambushes?

It is likely that their enemies assumed that the Jordan's flood was protecting them. The Jews felt secure, at least for that moment. To wait would give the advantage of surprise away. Shakespeare wrote:

There is a tide in the affairs of humans
Which taken at the floods, leads on to fortune;
Omitted and all the voyages of our lives
Are bound in shallows and miseries.
On such a full sea are we now afloat
And we must take the current while it serves
Or lose our venture.

We cannot afford to delay when God has led us to a point of decision or commitment. While the challenge may seem great, it is, at times like these, that we must trust that God is greater. Otherwise, what is faith really?

JOSHUA

So, how did the Jews cross the Jordan just as it was flooding? The Bible doesn't explain it, but maybe it was Hymie, the son of the high priest, who persuaded them. You see, Hymie was carrying the front of the Ark of the Covenant. He was the one who had to go first. Maybe the people were willing to try crossing because they weren't all that crazy about Hymie anyway. If the waters swept him away then they would just stay right where they were.

What I'd like to know is what it was that persuaded Hymie to go first. He probably couldn't swim. He was wearing his priestly robes, and he was carrying the ark, which must have been very heavy. Imagine how Hymie must have felt when Joshua gave the order to move out. The river probably seemed faster than ever. There was no sign of it abating. Was he tempted to call in sick that day, or have some other emergency that kept him away?

Or was Hymie like Thomas, who on one occasion, was convinced that what Jesus was about to do was suicidal, but said to the other disciples, "Let us go with him that we may also die with him." Not a lot of faith or optimism in Thomas' approach, but maybe that was exactly how Hymie felt. I suppose there is something to be said for fatalistic obedience ….

The point is that the miracle that allowed the people of God to make it across that which stood between them and God's will for them, required that they be willing to move into the river **before** there was any evidence that a miracle would happen.

So, just imagine the look on Hymie's face when he stuck his toe into the raging water and suddenly the water stopped. How did the miracle happen? Well, how do any miracles happen? On July 11, 1927, there was an earthquake in that area that caused a landslide, which stopped the flow of the Jordan for 21 hours. Did God cause an earthquake upriver back then? Perhaps, or perhaps it was that from God's vantage point, God was able to see that if they responded to the Spirit's nudges and did not delay, they could reach the river just as the river stopped.

At any rate, the point is that often the things that block our spiritual journey are just a different form of the same thing that we've confronted before. To overcome the barrier to growth we must have the courage to move forward, even when the evidence suggests that we cannot succeed. We must be willing to get wet if we expect God to teach us how to swim. Teaching us the principles of growth is what this journey is all about anyway.

JOSHUA

One section in Joshua that has always captured my attention:

> *The LORD said to Joshua, "Today I have rolled away from you the disgrace of Egypt." And so that place is called Gilgal to this day. While the Israelites were camped in Gilgal they kept the Passover in the evening on the 14th day of the month in the plains of Jericho. On the day after the Passover, on that very day, they ate the produce of the land, unleavened cakes and parched grain. The manna ceased on the day they ate the produce of the land, and the Israelites no longer had manna; they ate the crops of the land of Canaan that year.*
>
> Joshua 5:9-12

Notice verse 12: "The manna ceased on the day they ate the crops of the land … " Remember that these folks have been eating manna for 40 years. At last they could at last eat real food. They probably tore up their manna recipe cards and threw them in the fire. Never again would they touch the stuff. Now they had grapes, grain, olives and pomegranates.

It all sounded so wonderful that they must have danced for joy never to have to eat manna again as long as they lived. But have you ever wondered how long it was before someone said in a half-whisper, "You know, manna wasn't so bad. I kind of miss it."

That's the problem with living in the Promised Land. Manna was given to them in the wilderness. All they had to do was get up each morning and gather it. In the Promised Land, they had to learn to tend the crops, pick the fruit, gather the grain and tend the sheep and cattle. They had to hoe, weed, plant and harvest. In other words, they had to learn to live by the principles of the land.

In the wilderness, they picked up the manna. Their clothes never seemed to wear out. Quail would just fly into camp now and then. When they needed water, Moses could find it in a rock. Now in the Promised Land there were crops to plant, orchards to tend, wells to be dug, vineyards to be pruned, and fabric to be woven.

The Promised Land was rich and productive, but it required them to learn the principles of life and to work them. I'll bet after a few crop failures, or a couple of months pulling weeds in the hot sun, manna started sounding better.

As children, our parents took care of most of our needs. To be spiritually mature, we must begin to learn the principles of God. I wonder if Joshua had as tough a time weaning Jews off manna as God must have getting us off our spiritual Gerbers®.

JOSHUA

The Hebrews crossed the Jordan, won the battle for Jericho, and began to make their home again in the land of their ancestors. Once all the fighting was finally over, Joshua gathered the people and invited them to consider their choices now that they had a permanent home. As we finish our journey with the Hebrew people, look at Joshua 24:14-15:

> *Now therefore revere the LORD, and serve God in sincerity and in faithfulness; put away the gods that your ancestors served beyond the River and in Egypt, and serve the LORD. Now if you are unwilling to serve the LORD, choose this day whom you will serve, whether the gods your ancestors served in the region beyond the River or the gods of the Amorites in whose land you are living; but as for me and my household, we will serve the LORD.*

Ultimately, the choice is ours. We can serve the same gods we served when our souls were in Egypt—that is when we were slaves to the market masters. We can serve the Gods we served beyond the river—that is back when we were wandering and our lives had no real meaning and purpose. Or we can serve the God who created us, delivered us and led us to this point.

Living life by the purposes and the principles of God will not be easy, but, as for me and my house, Joshua said we have decided that the Promised Land is the only place to live, so we will serve the Lord. But quitting the manna and living spiritually mature and responsible lives is a difficult choice.

A recent article suggested that the fact that people were delaying having children was having an impact on charitable giving. The explanation was that couples with children often have to delay gratification in ways single people do not. Rather than buying new shoes for themselves, they spend money on shoes for their children. Having pastored for many years a mostly lesbian and gay church with few children or grandchildren, I recognized that there might be some truth to that finding. Denying yourself something so that the needs of others might be met is a learned skill that does not come naturally.

Practicing spiritual values like generosity, mercy and compassion require a depth of maturity that sometimes only comes by making choices that are better for others than for ourselves. Sacrifice is an action that has been taken only by the rarest of souls. In a prosperous culture such as ours, it seems even rarer. Study after study has demonstrated that the poor are consistently more generous than the rich or the middle class.

Choosing to serve God rather than self is apparently no easier today than it was for the ancient Hebrews. It is also no more common.

JOSHUA

At the end of the book of Joshua, we read of his death and burial as well as the re-interment of the bones of Joseph that the Hebrews had brought with them when they left Egypt. Then, in Joshua 24:31, we read:

> *Israel served the Lord all the days of Joshua, and all the days of the elders who outlived Joshua and had known all the work that the Lord did for Israel.*

This verse is an introduction to the next phase of Hebrew history that the Bible records and an anticipation of things to come. Tomorrow we move on to the book of Judges—the two centuries between Joshua and the selection of the first king. At that point, though, there were still a few living who knew Moses and had firsthand experience in the wilderness.

Those who experience something firsthand have a different perspective and perhaps different values from those who either hear about it in stories around the campfire or read about it in history books.

I recently visited again the National Holocaust Museum in Washington. At the end of the journey through that amazing space, there were two older women who sat at a table talking to people about their experiences as Holocaust survivors. The number of those who survived is rapidly diminishing, and soon there will be none who lived to remember the Holocaust, only those who refuse to forget the history.

As I walked past these lovely women, there were some students talking to them, so I didn't stop. But after seeing displays of the atrocities that the Nazis committed and the German people permitted, I wanted to stop and ask them about current issues and their opinions on water boarding, Guantanamo Bay, Abu Ghraib, or secret interrogation camps on foreign soil where we can do things to people that are illegal on American soil, or the complicity of silence by both the press and religious leaders.

Israel's history changed once all the elders were dead. I kept thinking of who we would become once our elders are gone and no one remains to remind us of who we can become when our highest value is security and self-preservation.

JUDGES

And so we arrive to the seventh book of the Bible, which is called Judges because of the system of government that was exercised during that era. The tribes each settled in their own small region and were led by their elder or family head. The regions where they settled also were inhabited by the people who had been dwelling there when the Hebrews suddenly "returned" after 400 years in Egypt. Although there might have been enough land to share, humans have never been very good at that, and this particular patch of ground in the Middle East seems to bring out the worst in the human race.

At this point, I probably simply need to state the obvious. As I have written these meditations, I have tried to find ways the scripture speaks to our own lives. I also have tried to honor the Jewish understanding of the stories, since this portion of the Bible is obviously their book. It is also important to avoid the anti-Semitism that has too often plagued Christian interpretations of Hebrew scripture. However, the twin evil of our historical abuse of indigenous people must also be acknowledged.

The book of Judges tells a number of stories (like the one in the first chapter) about how the various tribes managed to defeat the people who dwelled in the land when they arrived. The concept of the judge is that, when there was a challenge that was too great for one or two tribes, a "judge" would arise who would unite and lead the people. Each victory is described in terms of God's help and each defeat interpreted as God's displeasure.

This was the writer's, and probably the people's, understanding of how the universe worked. They saw taking the homes of indigenous people as a moral, even God-supported, act. While I am aware that it is arrogance on our part to evaluate their beliefs by modern values, I also am fearful of allowing to stand unchallenged the historical view that might makes right.

Let's face it; we preemptively invaded Iraq because we could. We had the might. Europeans conquered the "New World" because, collectively, they had the might to do so. The continent of Africa was colonized as if those who had lived there for centuries were just one more asset to be exploited and enslaved. All three of these examples—and many more—were carried out in the name of the conquering God of the Bible.

If you are reading this devotional, faith is obviously important to you. What must be equally important is for us to be ruthlessly honest about the things we say, believe and do in the name of God. We can see how the ancients might have been mistaken … but can we see how we might be?

JUDGES

The book of Judges is a book of history, and like most history, it is largely biographical. It contains the stories of the people under the leadership of 14 different judges. We know almost nothing about most of them, but there are a couple whose names are familiar and who deserve our attention. There are a few who could be considered true heroes, like the third judge. This judge is most remarkable because in an age and region replete with sexism and misogyny, the third judge of Israel was a woman named Deborah.

The story of Deborah is told in prose form in Judges 4 and in poetry form in chapter five, which is likely the older account. It is quite possible that a songwriter sought to memorialize the great victory of Deborah in song. Even in English, it is easy to see that the poem has a great deal more passion and power than the retelling of the story that is found in chapter four. It appears that chapter four was written after the period of judges had ended and was intended to explain some of the detail the poem missed.

The poetry of chapter five is among the most ancient surviving pieces of literature known to humankind. It is of significant enough literary importance that it deserves our attention on that basis, if no other.

King Jabin was a minor Canaanite king when those people co-inhabited the land with the Hebrews. As long as there was a united people, there was little he could do, but when Ehud died, and the people again did their own thing, they were at his mercy.

That was particularly scary because the leader of his army was a commander named Sisera. Ancient legends call Sisera one of the fiercest warriors that ever lived. He is supposed to have killed all his enemies by the time he reached age 30, including the enemies of his king. He is portrayed as a gigantic man whose shout could knock down a wall and whose stare could cause wild animals to flee. It took 900 horses to pull his chariot, and when he went swimming, the fish that got caught in his beard could feed a host of hungry people.

Obviously, Sisera was a pretty fearsome foe. Most of that is ridiculous, but if you don't understand what's happening here then you've never had an enemy you feared. It is easy to endow them with much more strength and power than is theirs. This aggrandizing of Sisera made his defeat by a woman even more extraordinary.

Deborah had to resist the downward pull of her own culture that tried to limit who she was and what she could do. Then she had to fearlessly face a fierce enemy. Her greatness was not in her ability to wield a sword, but in her confidence and faith. In the end, that is what makes every hero great and what can make each of us heroic.

JUDGES

While reading the book of Judges, you will find examples of the kind of thing that makes English teachers pull their hair out. Chapter five ends with a great heroic poem, but look at how abruptly chapter six begins:

> *The Israelites did what was evil in the sight of the LORD, and the LORD gave them into the hand of Midian seven years. The hand of Midian prevailed over Israel ... Thus Israel was greatly impoverished because of Midian; and the Israelites cried out to the LORD for help.*
>
> Judges 6:1 and 6

Even if you know nothing about the Hebrew's history during this period, you notice that the opening sentence of chapter six is a constant refrain. It would be easy for us to wonder just what kind of thick-skulled heathens were the Jews. It seems that the same thing happens to them over and over, but they just don't get it.

We have to remember, though, that this book is written in retrospect. It is easy enough from that perspective to see patterns that are painfully obvious. It is not nearly so easy to recognize those patterns when we are in the middle of them. If you can look back over your life and recognize patterns, you are one of the lucky ones. You are lucky because you have, at least, the beginnings of self-awareness, which is a vital ingredient for recovery and healing. If you can't recognize them, take my word that not seeing them does not mean they don't exist. (I bet a convention of your exes could identify them in two minutes.)

The people of God repeated an extremely dysfunctional pattern in their community life, but it was only later that, looking back, they recognized it as the source of much of their trouble and pain. They were reaping a bitter harvest, but they never seemed to connect that harvest with the seeds they sowed. Notice how verse six talks about how they were impoverished by the Midianites. Think for a moment about areas of your life where you feel impoverished. Now, it probably is not difficult to trace the cause. You may know instantly who/what is to blame, but is it possible that you need to trace the roots of that poverty back further until you discover the part of it for which you are responsible?

In verse one, it is clear that whatever pains the Midianites caused, it was the Hebrews who were ultimately responsible. Blaming someone for our problems certainly makes us feel better; however, the only growth that will come from the situation comes from recognizing the role we played. We can't do anything to change the people we blame, but there is always something we can change in our own lives.

JUDGES

As always, God rescued the Hebrews. God did not wave a magic wand. Just as when God rescued them from Egypt, God looked around for a woman or man to work through:

> *Now the angel of the LORD came and sat under the oak at Ophrah, as Gideon was beating out wheat in the wine press, to hide it from the Midianites. The angel of the LORD appeared and said to him, "The LORD is with you, you mighty warrior." Gideon answered him, "But sir, if the LORD is with us, why then has all this happened to us? And where are all his wonderful deeds that our ancestors recounted to us?" Then the LORD turned to him and said, "Go in this might of yours and deliver Israel from the hand of Midian; I hereby commission you." He responded, "But sir, how can I deliver Israel? My clan is the weakest in Manasseh, and I am the least in my family." The LORD said to him, "But I will be with you ..."*
>
> Judges 6:11-16

Gideon responds by asking the most ancient theological question: "If God is with us then why are these bad things happening?" We could talk about this question, but maybe we should save that for when we get to the book of Job. What deserves our attention here is the technique of evasion Gideon used. It takes a thousand different forms, but the essential element is that God makes a demand and we answer with a theological distraction. That's how the woman at the well responded to Jesus.

Gideon began his encounter with the messenger of God with a theological discussion, but, like Jesus, this messenger doesn't get drawn into an abstract discussion. Gideon's second strategy is also common. He pleads his insufficiency. He comes from the smallest clan, and he is the youngest person in that clan. It is easy to suddenly become modest when we are being asked to do something that might be uncomfortable or costly. How can I tithe, God; I'm one of the poorest members of this church? How can I get involved in justice work; I'm one of the busiest people I know. How can I speak up against homophobia/sexism/racism; I've got too much to lose.

Notice that God never calls strong people to lift heavy burdens, smart people to solve complex problems, or bold people to confront tough challenges. God simply calls all people to do the work of justice and grace, and then promises to be with us.

JUDGES

Do you remember the Sunday school story about Gideon putting a fleece before the Lord and asking for a sign?

> *Then Gideon said to God, "In order to see whether you will deliver Israel by my hand, as you have said, I am going to lay a fleece of wool on the threshing floor; if there is dew on the fleece alone, and it is dry on all the ground, then I shall know that you will deliver Israel by my hand, as you have said." And it was so. When he rose early next morning and squeezed the fleece, he wrung enough dew from the fleece to fill a bowl with water.*
>
> Judges 6:36

This all sounds rather arrogant on the part of Gideon, and, in fact, it was. You may be wondering why God didn't turn Gideon into a fleece. The difference is that now Gideon is not testing the call of God on his life; rather, he is testing to make certain that he has correctly ascertained the call of God on the life of the nation. Many lives were at stake, so God was patient with Gideon's desire to be sure. Or maybe God was saying to God's self, "That's okay, Gideon. You test me now, but very soon the testing is going to be on the other foot."

At any rate, this legend that was passed down is an example of the magical thinking practiced by a people who had no scientific concept of how the universe operated. Even by Jesus' day, when he was tempted to put God to the test, rather than cite the story of Gideon, he quotes Deuteronomy 6:16 with its commandment that we are not to put God to a test.

Still, I have known modern disciples who decide to "put out a fleece" to see if they can determine the mind of God. As often as not, they got fleeced. Jesus described the Holy Spirit as being like the wind. Genesis talks about the "breath of God." While there have been many times when I have longed to hear God shout directions, in my own experience, God's guidance is the softest of whispers, like a gentle breath on the ear of my soul. I'd love a fleece to show me what to do, but, most of the time, I just have to settle for a gentle breath … that and the principles of compassion, justice and grace that God has tried to teach me all my life.

JUDGES

Then Gideon and all the troops that were with him rose early and encamped beside the spring of Harod; and the camp of Midian was north of them, below the hill of Moreh, in the valley. The LORD said to Gideon, "The troops with you are too many for me to give the Midianites into their hand. Israel would only take the credit away from me, saying, 'My own hand has delivered me.'"

Judges 7:1-2

Gideon is about to go to battle against 135,000 Midianites with an army of only 32,000 Hebrews. Now that takes a great deal of courage … or stupidity. (No wonder Gideon kept testing the Lord to make sure that he had this right). God told Gideon that he has too many soldiers (no wonder God tolerated Gideon's testing). In the end, Gideon had to have complete confidence in God and in his ability to hear from God.

God tells Gideon to let anyone who is afraid to go home. I wonder what Gideon thought? Was he confident that his soldiers were brave and loyal and true and no one would leave? Or was he more in touch with human nature so he was sure that the only ones left would be he and his dog? Whatever he thought, 22,000 of them jumped ship, leaving Gideon with just 10,000 soldiers.

"Bad news," I'm sure he thought, "but with God on our side we ought to be able to still pull it off somehow." Just about the time he was convincing himself that he could still make it work with a smaller band of really brave soldiers, God gave him worse news: He still had too many soldiers.

Like most leaders, he was convinced that the more people he had on his side, the better his chances of winning. That wasn't God's strategy, though. God wanted to be sure that forever and ever people would know that this battle was won God's way, not the normal way.

First, everyone who was frightened was allowed to leave. Now, if the truth were known, EVERYONE in their right mind was frightened. The ones who left probably weren't any more scared than those who stayed. The ones who stayed, though, were committed. Their dedication and hope was greater and stronger than their fear.

God would rather have 10,000 dedicated, hopeful people than 32,000 people who give up when the challenge grows tough. In the end, the other 22,000 take up room and resources, but provide very little in return. That probably should advise how we define success and strength.

God wasn't through thinning Gideon's ranks yet. This time, Gideon was to send his men down to the river to get a drink of water. All of those who leaned over and lapped water like a dog were to be sent home, and those who drank water from cupped hands he would keep. Only 300 were allowed to stay.

The principle behind this decision seems to be that for soldiers in a state of war to stick their necks out and put their faces in the water meant that they were not prepared for an attack. Those who drank from their hands were on the lookout, protecting not only themselves, but their fellow soldiers.

Not only is God looking for people who are called and committed, but God also is looking for people who are wise and prepared. Notice that drinking from your hands didn't require any great talent, but it did require them to be alert to what was going on around them and to remember, in all circumstances, who they were.

Gideon is left with just 300 soldiers to face the Midian army of 135,000 soldiers! It is clear that brute force is not going to do it. Still, the battle is a rout because of the psychological warfare of Gideon and the 300 soldiers. The cunning of this victory should always serve as a reminder that God's ways are not our ways. Jesus called us to be as cunning as serpents and as innocent as doves. What that means to me is that we should use our wit and wisdom to serve God, but never against others to benefit us.

When you are picking people with whom to work, live and serve, pick them like God did. Don't choose on the basis of outward strength, beauty or charm. Spend your time with people who are deeply committed, whose positive commitment is stronger than their fear. Pick people who are not stuck in having to do something the way it has always been done before. Pick people who are willing to try new possibilities. If we keep doing what we've always done then we'll keep getting what we've always gotten.

Finally, pick people who are willing to allow God to supply the missing ingredient. If they have to have every "i" dotted and every "t" crossed, they probably haven't made their plans big enough. Choose to spend your life with people who are willing to figure God into their formula.

While you are busy picking this kind of person, it might be a good idea for us to work at being this kind of person, too.

JUDGES

There is one more famous judge who deserves our attention before we move on. His name was Samson. Like almost every hero of the Bible or in real life, Samson was a deeply flawed human. There are two lessons to be learned from Samson. The first is that all humans are flawed, and often their great flaws are also their great strengths. We somehow are able to rationalize our own shortcomings—after all, we are "only human"—but we expect perfection from our leaders.

I used to be a Methodist minister. Traditionally, in those days, Methodists moved their pastors every four to six years. Despite flaws, Methodist pastors actually have a history of longer average tenures than Baptist pastors. In a conversation with a Baptist colleague many years ago, he explained, "In the Methodist Church, when people begin to discover their pastor is human they think, 'Well, we only have to put up with our pastor only two more years then he/she will move.' In the Baptist church, when a congregation discovers you are human, they try to make you disappear by chipping away at you until you are gone."

I don't think chipping away at leaders is a skill confined to the Baptists, nor do I think it is purely a Christian practice, though it has been said that the Christian army is the only one who shoots its wounded. We expect our leaders in every area to be flawless, which is not an expectation God has for us. Throughout the Bible, God calls, and uses, deeply flawed humans like Samson.

The other lesson is that you and I have to quit using the fact that we are "only human" as an excuse. It can't excuse our bad behavior because, by definition, humans have the capacity to learn and grow. It also can't excuse us from serving God. After all, when was the last time you saw God call a cow or a crow? Humans are the only creatures called by God to serve the greater good. Sorry; God calls you flaws and all and doesn't even ask you to get a haircut first.

JUDGES

The story of Samson and Delilah is well known. In fact, in 1949, Cecil B. DeMille directed the famous movie, *Samson and Delilah,* starring Hedy Lamarr and Victor Mature.

Samson is a strong man who serves as judge/leader for more than 20 years. He rescues his people from the oppression of the Philistines, but he is remembered for none of this. Rather, the story that is recounted and remembered is how Delilah seduced him into revealing the source of his strength, which was his long hair.

What is missed even in that is the fact that he had long hair because of a vow that he made. It wasn't his hair that magically gave him strength but the covenant he made and ultimately broke. It is a heroic fable whose moral is that we are always weakened when we break our vows, go back on our word or violate our own core values. A moment of pleasure may be the lure, but the consequences are much greater than we know, even if we are not caught. The strength of light and life drains from us and makes us vulnerable.

Samson is blinded by the Philistines and imprisoned. While held captive though, his hair grows back and he regains this strength. When his captors have a party, they attempt to torment Samson as they make him entertain for the party, but Samson seizes two pillars and brings the building down around their heads.

What of this story is factual, we do not know. Perhaps what the storyteller was trying to do was to use the collapse of a Philistine palace that killed many of their leaders to redeem Samson's reputation. In the end, Samson was once more their hero, even at the cost of his own life.

It is amazing how death can redeem a person's reputation. Critics fall silent, and people suddenly can only remember the good. People almost superstitiously refuse to speak ill of the dead, treating them with respect and acknowledging the good of their life. I wonder if, as people of faith, we ought not to treat living people a little more like they will be treated when they leave our presence and enter the presence of God. Maybe if we did, we'd bring a little more heaven on earth.

RUTH

Wedged between the story of the Judges and the books that tell about the era of the Kings is a little book named after its leading character. Before we move on, perhaps we should pause to look at the life of Ruth.

In our Bible, Ruth's placement is explained by the opening verse: "In the days when judges ruled …" In the Hebrew Bible, however, the book is placed among the books of writings and is categorized as literature, not history. That is probably a more accurate placement because it is a beautiful story, even if it is not important history.

The book of Ruth begins with the story of a woman named Naomi. Because of a famine, she moved to Moab with her husband and two sons. Although they found food, they also found great grief. First her husband died, and Naomi was left to raise two boys. The sons of Naomi grew up and married women from Moab, but after ten years, her sons also died.

There is no explanation for the deaths of these three men, but the grief Naomi felt must have been overwhelming. Not only had she lost three people that she loved, but the prospects for a woman of that day left without husband or sons were pretty grim. Begging and prostitution were almost the only options for a woman without a husband, children or grandchildren. On top of that, she also was a foreigner in Moab.

Jeanette Foster wrote a book about the subtleties of the lives of women in the Bible that male biblical scholars have traditionally missed. She suggests that, because this book focuses on the lives of Naomi and Ruth rather than Boaz, the Book of Ruth just may have been written by a woman, which would make it the only one in the Bible. There is no evidence of that theory, but then there is no evidence that a man wrote it either. Certainly, it begins with a great deal of compassion shown for the situation in which Naomi and her daughters-in-law find themselves. Such compassion was certainly not typical of male writers of that day. It is a good reminder of our need to listen to seldom heard voices, because in them we might just hear the word of God.

RUTH

Naomi heard that, once again, Bethlehem had food. The famine that had driven her away was over; she could go home again. She and her widowed daughters-in-law packed up their few personal belongings and set out. Along the way, Naomi decided that what was best for these two women was for them to do what she was doing herself. Although she had lost everything else, she decided that it was unfair for her to cling to Ruth and Orpah and ruin what was left of their lives. Naomi put aside her own pain and need and tried to send the women off to live with their own families where Naomi thought they would have a better chance of starting over.

When we are in pain and struggling with a sense of loss, it is easy enough to become consumed by that struggle and completely forget the needs of those around us. In order for us to stay spiritually healthy, we, like Naomi, eventually must be able to look beyond our own personal needs and struggles to help someone else.

Now, in addition to that bit of self-help insight, there is an interesting piece of theology in this passage. Notice that Naomi tried to send away BOTH daughters-in-law. Orpah goes, but Ruth insists on staying.

What would have happened if Naomi had been more persuasive, or if Ruth's love for her had been less tenacious? You see, the major point of the book of Ruth is that she, a foreigner, becomes an ancestor of great King David, and of his even greater son, Jesus. If Ruth had returned to Moab, that lineage never would have happened. Or would it have happened anyway?

This opens up all sorts of questions and should remind us to be very aware of the power of our decisions. Ruth never knew that she was used by God in such a powerful way, but her decision could have made a major difference in the history of Israel and the world. Or would it?

What decisions will you make today that will change the course of your life? Did you pray about it first?

RUTH

No voice from Heaven stopped Ruth from leaving Naomi, despite Naomi's insistence. All that keeps that from happening is Ruth's love for Naomi, which brings us to the most famous passage in the book of Ruth:

> *Then they wept aloud again. Orpah kissed her mother-in-law, but Ruth clung to her. So she said, "See, your sister-in-law has gone back to her people and to her gods; return after your sister-in-law." But Ruth said, "Do not press me to leave you or to turn back from following you! Where you go, I will go; Where you lodge, I will lodge; your people shall be my people, and your God my God. Where you die, I will die—there will I be buried. May the LORD do thus and so to me, and more as well, if even death parts me from you!" When Naomi saw that she was determined to go with her, she said no more to her.*
>
> Ruth 1:14-18

For lesbian and gay people, this passage is important for a number of reasons, not the least of which is that it has always been honored as a classic statement of love and fidelity. Millions of times this passage has been read at weddings, but never acknowledging these words were spoken by one woman who loved another.

In her vow, Ruth says that she is willing to leave her people and her faith. That is more than just the love of a daughter-in-law for a mother-in-law. Her vow is as deep and profound an expression of committed love as can be found anywhere. Her willingness to risk everything tells of her devotion and of the kind of person Naomi must have been.

What did Ruth find in this Hebrew woman that made her determined to give up her people and her god to embrace the Jewish people and Yahweh as her God? We shall never know, but what we do know is that the love between two people of the same gender is as sacred and powerful as any love described in the Bible.

Eventually Ruth has a son by Boaz who becomes the ancestor of David and, ultimately, Jesus. Yet, even after she is married, Ruth did not leave Naomi. Naomi lives with them and even serves as a nursemaid for the new baby. When the baby is born, Ruth takes him to Naomi, not to Boaz.

Whether Ruth and Naomi had sexual relations is of little consequence to this point. It seems that heterosexuals are the ones who seem so obsessed with the sex lives of lesbians and gays. I don't think that even the more energetic of us spend more than one percent of our week having sex. The other 99 percent is spent loving, fighting, struggling, growing, dreaming, hoping and simply living.

Nothing in the Bible indicates that Ruth and Naomi's relationship wasn't as blessed and sacred as any other, and, in the end, that is much more valuable than any license from the state or the approval of any fundamentalist preacher or priest.

RUTH

This week we begin to explore the portion of the First Testament covering the time that monarchs ruled the Hebrews. While it has worked well to this point for us to go book by book and chapter by chapter, that strategy is not so effective going forward. From the beginnings of everything in Genesis 1, through the stories of Ruth that took place in the days of the judges, the Bible has followed a *relatively* chronological order. With the next 31 books, however, there is a lot of overlap and even repetition. What follows the book of Ruth are three books, each written in two volumes. The two volumes of Samuel tell the story of the prophet Samuel and Kings Saul and David. The next two-volume book is called Kings, and we find the story of the third King, Solomon, along with various kings who followed him after the nation split in two. The book of Kings also records the stories of the prophets Elijah and Elisha.

Next are the two volumes of Chronicles, which tell about the reigns of David and Solomon and those who followed until the fall of the nation. The challenge, of course, is that there are more than a dozen books at the end of the First Testament that contain the words and stories of the prophets, many of whom lived and worked during the era that these books record.

So, I just wanted to warn you that it will be confusing if you think chronologically. Although this is only inspirational to Old Testament scholars, let me give you a thumbnail of history that will help you through the rest of the First Testament:

- Samuel was the last Judge and also considered the first major prophet.
- Saul was the first King.
- David was Saul's successor.
- Solomon was David's son and successor.
- After Solomon's death, the nation split. The Northern Kingdom was known as Israel and the southern as Judah.
- About 225 years after the divided kingdom, Israel is conquered by the Assyrians and then the Babylonians. About 250 years after that, Judah is conquered by the Persians, the Greeks and the Romans.

Now I am supposed to say something inspirational to make your day better … Well, if it makes you feel better, you now know more ancient history than the fundamentalists who drive you crazy …

1 SAMUEL

1 Samuel 1-2

Samuel was dedicated by his mother to the Lord. The first three chapters of the book of Samuel tell the story of her great faith and the prophet's boyhood. By chapter four Samuel has grown up, and in the next three chapters he acts as the last Judge of the Hebrews. They had been beaten by the Philistines who had captured the Ark of the Covenant. This was a very grave spiritual crisis because the ark was the center of their faith and their connection to the God who, through Moses, led them out of Egypt.

Samuel gathered all the people together and set up a stone that was called Ebenezer. It served as a marker for the power of God in their midst. (1 Samuel 7:12) Having lost the ark, they needed a touchstone of faith to renew their confidence in themselves and their trust in God. Samuel set it up as a place where they could come to remember who they were and whose they were. It was a reminder, a memorial of what God had done for them and who God had been to them.

In the old Christian hymn "Come Thou Fount," written in the 18th century by Robert Robinson, the second verse says, "Here I raise my Ebenezer, hither by thy help I come, and I hope by thy good pleasure safely to arrive at home." The modernizing of that hymn has deprived present generations of pondering just what an Ebenezer was. I suppose those who create modern hymnals knew that no one was going to bother to read I Samuel 7 in order to understand.

Funny, isn't it, that we Google™ anything these days, but it is probably too much to ask that we moderns actually go in search of the spiritual meaning of something. The quests of our lives seem to all be for money, entertainment and pleasure. Maybe what we really need is an Ebenezer. Maybe each of us needs that peculiar place, stone, or symbol of God's presence with us that is not valued or even recognized by others. Perhaps rather than purging the word Ebenezer from our vocabulary, we need to find Ebenezers in our lives. If you don't have a place or a touchstone that marks your renewed confidence in yourself and your trust in God then don't bother with Google™. That isn't the kind of search engine you need.

1 SAMUEL

In 1 Samuel 8 we find that Samuel has grown old, and, while he appointed his sons as judges over the Hebrews, it just wasn't working. They somehow lacked the spark or charisma or authority of their father. So the elders of the tribes came to Samuel and told him that they needed a king.

The single ruler of the nations around them was what they assumed gave those people their unity and power. They were 12 disparate tribes who only came together when there was an attack or some other crisis. The model was that God was their sovereign, and they didn't need an earthly ruler to tell them what to do and how to live. The people decided that they knew better and went to persuade Samuel that they needed a king.

In the text, written by priests, there is a great struggle against the people's demand for a king. God ultimately acquiesces but clearly isn't happy about it. It is possible that the priests were the ones who were unhappy because, with God as the ruler, the priests had greater power. Or maybe they were defending God's reputation since the first person chosen to be king didn't work out so well. It is even possible that Saul was a much better king than the record shows. After all, history isn't so much what happens as it is the interpretation by those who recorded the story of what happened.

All of this is a reminder that we can't use the Bible as an Ouija™ board or one of Gideon's fleeces. We have to read it with open hearts and questioning minds. We have to constantly remember the historic and social context, as well as the values and biases that informed the author. We also must remember that we weren't the audience for whom the story was recorded. With all of that in mind, we read about Saul with scant concern for the historicity of the story, but with the ears of our spirits open to the Voice of the Spirit.

I'd like it better if the Bible was indeed the kind of road map the fundamentalists try to make it out to be. Instead we are left to our own devices, struggling to hear the faint Word of God to be heard amidst the words. As a result, we, like the Hebrews, end up making mistakes. Perhaps if they had been able to hear God's voice more clearly they wouldn't have demanded a king … or perhaps they would have recognized that God was at work even through an all too human king named Saul. Not only do we not have a clear map, we often are not even sure we have arrived at the right destination. That is why they call this journey faith.

<u>1 SAMUEL</u>

1 Samuel 9

The recorders of history are not kind to Saul. They clearly favor his successor David, so Saul is described as a ruler who betrayed his own values, consulted witches and sunk into paranoia. What is fascinating is the first description we are given of Saul who was described as the most handsome man in the land and who stood a head and shoulders taller than those around him.

> *He had a son whose name was Saul, a handsome young man. There was not a man among the people of Israel more handsome than he; he stood head and shoulders above everyone else.*
>
> 1 Samuel 9:2

This physical description is amazing. One wonders how important his physical appearance was in his selection. The text suggests that the choice was God's, but then goes on to trash Saul as a king. Is the author suggesting that, like the rest of us, God can fall for a tall, good-looking man or woman?

Perhaps this is all a historic parable, a warning to us as much as to them. The higher road advocated by Samuel and the author was for the people of God to allow God and God's principles to rule their lives. However, rather than choosing the wisest woman or man in the land, or the most profoundly spiritual, the people chose to have their lives ruled by the best looking.

It is easy to ridicule that choice except that many, if not most of our values, choices and decisions today are made on precisely that basis. Our decisions are not ruled by what is wisest nearly as often as they are by what has been sold to us by advertisers using "pretty people" to convince us. Our choices are far more often governed by marketing than by what is most profoundly spiritual. How did you pick your last car, what you are wearing, or the lifestyle you live? We are told the definition of "beautiful," "sexy," "successful," "proper" or "cute." Our lives are more ruled by those who say taller and handsome is better than they are by God who values most the poor and those in need.

The Hebrews may have chosen their ruler badly, but I wonder if we do any better in picking what rules our daily decisions.

1 SAMUEL

1 Samuel 13

In 1 Samuel 10, Saul is anointed as the first king of Israel. However, the main star of the chapter is still Samuel. In verse 6, there is a rather bizarre prophecy that says when the Spirit came upon Saul, he would "be turned into a different person." This sounds like some sort of superhero's transformation, but it may simply be an ancient description of the fact that the person selected as king was schizophrenic.

Chapter 11 describes one of Saul's early military victories, and chapter 12 tells about Samuel laying down his office as the last judge of Israel. Then I Samuel 13 begins with a verse that is fragmented in the ancient manuscripts. The New Revised Standard Version of the Bible renders it this way:

> *Saul was ... years old when he began to reign; and he reigned for ... and two years over Israel.*

The footnote says that the numbers are simply lacking in the Septuagint. The translators of many versions simply fill in the numbers. For example, the bestselling King James Version translates this passage:

> *Saul reigned one year; and when he had reigned two years over Israel.*

That sentence makes no sense, of course, but it is one of the clearest examples of the fact that, because we lack access to the original manuscripts or the tools to interpret ancient extinct languages, we rely on others to decide what we read and how it is nuanced. Just as the priests who tell Saul's story shaped it, so the value and theology of the most faithful translators ultimately shape how we understand the English version of the Bible that we read. If we could read the original manuscripts in their original languages, though, we still would read them through the lens of our own experiences, understandings and beliefs.

None of this is said negatively, but simply offered as a reminder of the fact that we must hold scripture reverently but loosely in our hands. When you see anyone firmly grip the Bible and wave it like a club while telling us what it says, it is likely that they have forgotten this lesson. The Bible is "inspired" or, literally, "God breathed." You grasp it much as you do the wind.

This 13th chapter of 1 Samuel begins by shooting a hole in many people's theory of the Bible's infallibility. That chapter also describes the "sin" of Saul that caused his priestly biographers to turn against him. Before a battle, they are waiting on Samuel to show up and make the "good luck" sacrifice. Samuel is late, so Saul makes the sacrifice himself. Saul learns the hard way not to intrude on the territory of priests and preachers. They have a stake in making sure no one else thinks they can access God or God's word without help. We would do well to remember that, even as you read these daily interpretations by this preacher.

1 SAMUEL

1 Samuel 14

Jonathan was the first born son of Saul and the heir apparent to the office of king. While he doesn't get a lot of air time in sermons, there is a great deal about Jonathan in the Bible. He is a fairly unique person, in that the authors of this portion of the Bible say almost nothing negative about him. Even when he makes a mistake, it isn't his fault.

In chapter 14, we are told that, for some reason, Saul orders all of his army to spend the day fasting upon penalty of death. Jonathan and the group he led came upon a honeycomb, but the troops restrained from eating any of it because of Saul's orders. Jonathan, however, dips his finger in the honey and tastes it. The text says that it was because Jonathan had not heard his father's orders to the troops, which is certainly possible. Or maybe he simply disagreed, because in verses 29-30, he argues against his father's commandment.

Ultimately, Jonathan's guilt is discovered, and Jonathan hands himself over to be executed. (v. 43) Saul, being a man of his word, agrees that he has to die. However, the people all rise up and insist that Jonathan be spared:

> *So the people ransomed Jonathan and he did not die.*
>
> 1 Samuel 14:45

There was something about that text that made me read it over and over. Perhaps it simply was the realization that this is the mission statement of the people of God. Our job is just that simple: to ransom the guilty so they will not die. Yes, maybe that speaks of our fight to end capital punishment, but, over the years, I have found that death comes in many ways other than lethal injections. What about all of those people whose guilt and shame squeezes the life out of them by never letting them take a free breath?

Jesus tried to tell us that we had "power on earth to forgive sins." (John 20:23) The trouble is the guilty are the ones who need forgiveness … and usually they are the last people we want to ransom. Isn't it a good thing God didn't feel that way about us?

1 SAMUEL

1 Samuel 15

Often after we have read a really tough or judgmental Gospel lesson in church, you almost can hear the question at the end of the rubric when the liturgist says, "This is the Gospel of hope." That is pretty much how I feel about this chapter of I Samuel. I know that the author is simply telling the story as he had learned it and been taught to understand it, but I have to say that I just don't buy it.

The story is told as an explanation of the sin that Saul committed that resulted in God's rejecting him and picking David. Saul's "sin" was that he spared the king of the Amalekites and didn't slaughter all their sheep and cattle. Old Samuel, who retired several chapters ago because he was too old, just won't die, so when he heard what Saul had done, he went down to Gilgal to confront him.

Saul repents, but there apparently is no forgiveness for him. Samuel grieves for him, but the chapter ends in hopelessness. Samuel never saw Saul again, and the last sentence says, "And the Lord was sorry that he had made Saul king over Israel." (v. 35)

There is so much wrong with the theology of the chapter that I don't know where to start. Again, what we have here is not "the Word of the Lord," but an accurate account of how the author understood what happened and why. If there is any word from the Lord in this chapter it may come from pondering if God ever looks upon our lives with regret.

I have no doubt that, like any healthy parent, God's love for us is unwavering, but I'm not so confident that how we live our lives is very pleasing. Are we ever a disappointment to God? I suspect for all of us, the answer is too often yes, because the truth of how we live our lives is often a disappointment to ourselves. The good news is today is a new day, and all that can change. The warning of this passage may be that the day will dawn for us all when that is no longer true.

1 SAMUEL

1 Samuel 16

The story of Saul's sin is told in chapter 15 as a backdrop that the prophet Samuel is going to anoint someone else as king over Israel. In chapter 16, God sends Samuel to the house of Jesse the Bethlehemite. Jesse is the great-great-grandson of Ruth, and he has several sons from whom Samuel can choose as king over Israel.

In the end, Samuel rejects them all, based on a criteria God gave him:

> *Do not look on his appearance or on the height of his stature, because I have rejected him; for the Lord does not see as mortals see; they look on the outward appearance, but the Lord looks on the heart.*
>
> 1 Samuel 16:7

One after another, Jesse's strapping sons are rejected, until at last they send for the youngest boy named David who is out tending sheep. From this point forward, in both Jewish and Christian history, the image of the Shepherd King becomes very important.

The statement about how God evaluates a person given in light of David's selection is a deliberate contrast to what had been written about Saul. David is described later as short of stature, ruddy of complexion, and comely in appearance. I happen to think that short, red-headed people make good leaders (the author's bias), but the physical description of David isn't offered as his qualification. In fact, the writer of I Samuel seems to think God should offer a disclaimer.

So, Samuel anoints the shepherd boy as ruler. Because Saul will continue on the throne for many more years, they tell no one, however, as it wouldn't have been a healthy thing for David if Saul knew that the prophet already had chosen his successor. This event in Chapter 16 isn't talked about again until Saul is killed in battle many years later.

What does happen, though, is that David increasingly acts like one who has been anointed by God. No one knows except him, Samuel and his family, but the anointing transforms the shepherd boy in almost every way. We are left to wonder how our lives might be changed if we were to understand that we have been chosen and anointed by God.

Personally, I believe God calls and anoints us all. However, there have been only a handful of lives that have been lived out in 24/7 awareness of that anointing. David didn't need Saul to hand his crown over to him any more than Jesus needed Herod or Caesar's crown. Both lived their entire lives aware that they belonged to God, and the world was never the same. What might change if we could at least live that way on Wednesdays?

1 SAMUEL

1 Samuel 17

Chapter 16 ends with David playing his harp to ease the torment of King Saul. It is offered as an explanation of how the shepherd boy from Bethlehem ended up in the palace. Then chapter 17 describes the famous story of how David took on the Philistine giant Goliath.

There is much about this young hero's tale that could speak to us. Given its threadbare nature, I want to note verse 38 where Saul tried to dress David in his personal armor. You will remember that the author described Saul as a head taller than any of his fellow countrymen, and David as a mere boy. David tries on the armor but discovers immediately that it doesn't fit and would encumber him in his confrontation with Goliath. David is wise enough to reject the King's armor. Unfortunately, few of us are that wise.

In our conflicts, we almost always try to fit ourselves into places and positions where we do not belong. We often take up weapons that do not fit our hands. We act in ways that are not, or should not be, part of our nature. The result is often disastrous, because our pride causes us to try to take the results into our own hands.

Jesus called us to forgive, turn the other cheek, go the extra mile, and love our enemies. Those weapons leave us feeling naked and exposed, but they also allow for the Spirit of God to work on our behalf. They are small stones in the face of the weapons of giants, but we are not spiritually designed to wield the weapons of our enemies. The trouble is that if we had been in David's place, we would have probably worn the armor of the King or died trying … which is almost always the result.

1 SAMUEL

Over the course of the rest of 1 Samuel, we hear three themes:

1. David's rise to power. His music comforts the king, and he is the heroic victor over Goliath. He becomes a military leader and has great success on behalf of both Israel and Saul.
2. David's success only makes Saul afraid of him and paranoid about him. He and Saul have a number of conflicts, and it appears, at times, that Saul is determined to kill David.
3. The other theme that is powerfully present but almost always neglected is the love affair that Jonathan and David carry on.

Now, I am not suggesting that David and Jonathan were gay lovers in the way that we understand that, but 1 Samuel 18-20 tells an amazing story of deep devotion and love. Despite Saul's fear that David will steal the throne from his son Jonathan, the men do love one another. Jonathan betrays his father to save David, and David spares Saul out of love for Jonathan.

Chapter 18 begins with the statement that "the soul of Jonathan was bound to the soul of David" and then goes on to describe Jonathan stripping and putting his clothes on David. In chapter 20, verses 12-16, we hear again a great covenant of love between the two men ending with these words:

> *Jonathan made David swear AGAIN by his love for him; for he loved him as he loved his own life.*

If there is any doubt of the love between these two, one only needs to read 1 Samuel 20:30-35. There Saul rails against Jonathan and his love for David. It is the kind of speech many lesbian or gay people have heard from a parent who learned that they loved someone of the same gender. Saul even blames Jonathan's mother, using words like perverse and shameful. Despite all of this, though, Jonathan still gets up from his father's table to go and again warn David.

Verse 23 describes how the two men fall into one another's arms, weeping together and kissing one another. We do not hear from Jonathan again until chapter 31 when we are told he and his father Saul were killed in battle. When David learns of this he is reported to have said, "I am greatly distressed for you, my brother Jonathan; greatly beloved were you to me; your love to me was wonderful, passing the love of women."

A reading of this text always leaves me wondering why fundamentalists only take parts of the scripture literally and fail to take huge chunks seriously. This love story has never really been told by the Christian church. I wonder how many families might have treated their lesbian or gay children differently if it had been truly addressed. Please read it for yourself, since obviously the church isn't going to read it to you.

2 SAMUEL

2 Samuel 1-5

The book of 1 Samuel ends with the death of the first Hebrew King. The entirety of 2 Samuel is a record of the reign of David.

Chapter one is a description of David and the people grieving the death of Saul and Jonathan. The last seven verses are a song, attributed to David, recording his lament over the death of his king and his beloved Jonathan.

In chapter two, David is anointed as king over Judah, which is the largest of the 12 tribes ruling over half the territory claimed by the Hebrews. No mention is made of his prior anointing by Samuel. David ruled over Judah for seven years while various sons of Saul led the other tribes. Eventually, the events led to a civil war described in the first verse of chapter 3: "There was a long war between the house of Saul and the house of David; David grew stronger and stronger, while the house of Saul became weaker and weaker."

Finally, in chapter five, David is made ruler over both Israel and Judah. The chapter begins with an acknowledgement that they are all of the same flesh and bone. I suppose that should be the basis for all peacemaking. Nationalism divides us along artificial borders and makes us enemies who fear one another. If our starting point was always that we are all of one race—the human race—and one family—God's—the outcome almost always would be better.

David was 30 years old when he became king over the reunited nation. He then ruled for about 40 years. This was probably the period of greatest military power for the nation. David's first act after uniting the nation was to capture the city of Jerusalem. Verses 6-16 describe how Jerusalem became the capital of the nation, and chapter six describes how it becomes the spiritual center.

The term and concept "Zion" is introduced here. It originally referred to the fortress from which the Jebusites defended Jerusalem. Eventually, it came to refer to the city and even the nation. In modern times, Zionism became the ideology that advocated for a homeland for the Jews. This, of course, became very important after the Holocaust of World War II. Our almost universal guilt over the treatment of the Jews led to a movement that, at times, has come perilously close to committing a holocaust for the indigenous people in Palestine. Bloodshed that begun in David's day and continues in ours because the world cannot seem to remember that we are all one race and all one family.

2 SAMUEL

In chapter six, the Ark of the Covenant was brought into Jerusalem with great ceremony and celebration and Jerusalem became known as the city of David. At the end of the celebration, David danced so exuberantly before the Lord that he danced right out of his clothes. This action embarrassed the queen. David's wife Michal, who was Saul's daughter, came out and rebuked him, but David was having none of it. He said that if his passionate worship was an embarrassment then she would just have to be embarrassed.

David's public exuberance for God is a reminder that just because we are smart, important and successful doesn't mean we can't be passionate in our faith. Or maybe more to our point: just because we are liberal, sophisticated and intellectual, doesn't mean we shouldn't love God with all our heart, soul, mind and strength.

It seems to me that this is where progressive Christianity breaks down. We more often approach faith with our heads than our hearts. We value the intellectual integrity of liberal theology, but discount the exuberant worship and devotion of fundamentalism. Again, this is a dualism that renders both liberal and conservative faiths less effective.

We are emotional beings, and worship that is purely intellectual is defective. Our hearts also must be a principal connecting point to God. We may never dance out of our clothes like David, but if our love for God is real, even the most inhibited of us will feel our feet tapping now and then; we will feel our hearts swell with gratitude; our eyes will mist with tears as we consider how much we love and are loved. If you can't go to church and find your heart more full than when you arrived, you need to change churches or work actively to change your church. If you can come into the presence of the living God and not be deeply moved, then you may be worshipping a different God from David.

For today, relax and let yourself FEEL how much you love God … who knows, you just might sense your clothes getting a little less tight.

<u>2 SAMUEL</u>

2 Samuel 9:1-13

The ninth chapter of 2 Samuel begins with David asking, “Is there still anyone left of the house of Saul to whom I may show kindness **for Jonathan’s sake?**” Although years had passed, David obviously still missed his friend. Casting around for a way to express his grief, he discovers that one of Jonathan’s sons, Mephibosheth, was still alive.

David gives instructions that Mephibosheth is to be cared for, and he is invited to eat at the king’s table for the rest of his life. Then the text ends with an after note about Mephibosheth: “Now he was lame in both his feet.” This passage is one of the few places in early scripture where differently-abled people are treated with honor and respect. Later, Jesus will model a tenderness that is rare in a cultural age when most people were barely able to provide for themselves.

In addition to bearing the distain that was both subtly and overtly heaped upon those with disabilities, Mephibosheth was a member of a family that had waged a civil war against David. Saul’s grandson might have seen himself as his father’s legitimate heir, and David might have had every reason to eliminate a potential rival for power. Insecurity is the determining force in how we deal with people far more often than compassion and grace.

I often have wondered if the real source of our discomfort with differently-abled people isn’t rooted in insecurity. When we interact with people who have a disability, we encounter a powerful reminder of our own vulnerability. Each of us is an accident away … our own physical ability literally hangs by a neurological thread. Our reactions are much more about us than about them.

David invited a disabled member of a former rival’s family to sit at his table. Here is someone who can’t help him at all, but he is welcomed unconditionally. Did David feel uncomfortable? Did he have reservations? I’m sure he did, but notice that he didn’t give in to his fears but acted out of his better self to do what is right. Almost always that is what great people do. They feel the same fear and insecurity as the rest of us, but they make more noble choices. It is what great people do; it is also what good people do.

2 SAMUEL

2 Samuel 11

Yesterday we talked about the grace and nobility of David. Then ironically, and almost immediately, we encounter what is perhaps the low point of David's life. The story of his affair with Bathsheba is well known. The powerful monarch saw something he wanted and took it. He acted without regard for the effect on anyone else.

In the end, Bathsheba becomes pregnant, which means that David's sin soon will be revealed since Bathsheba's husband, Uriah, was away in battle and couldn't have fathered the child. David brings Uriah home, hoping that he will sleep with his wife and everyone will assume the baby was his … just born a little early. However, Uriah will not accept the comfort of family and home while his fellow soldiers are fighting in the field, so David's plan fails.

What is interesting about this story is that it is told at all. Moses is the great leader of the Hebrew people, but David is the great king. He is the one through whom God makes an everlasting covenant. So why wasn't this story purged from the scripture? It is told with sufficient detail that one must assume either it is fabricated or one of the principals is the source. In the story, the ultimate victim is Uriah whom David allows to die in battle to cover his shame. Uriah is also the only hero in this story. He lives his life with simple integrity, which only serves to highlight the lack of that quality in great King David.

Time and again over the course of my life, people have applied lessons that I have taught or sermons I have preached to how they live their lives. Time and again, I have been chagrined when others have taken seriously the spiritual principles and practices that evade me. Perhaps it is David who tells this tale to his biographers as a way of honoring Uriah and in hopes of bringing healing to his own soul. For me, spiritual survival has required that I exercise honesty about my own failings. If I had the courage of David, though, I'd know that true and consistent honesty could lead to spiritual health, not just survival. This is a lesson David learns, but even for him it didn't come easily or without a price.

2 SAMUEL

2 Samuel 12

At the end of I Samuel 11, David marries Bathsheba who is pregnant with his child. Chapter 12 begins with the story of who might be the bravest man in the world. The prophet Nathan confronts David about his sin. He is a brave man because he is confronting the king who was, at that very moment, one of the most powerful men in the world.

Nathan tells David the story of a rich man who took a poor man's only lamb. When David is outraged by such selfish greed, Nathan then turns the story back around upon the king revealing the analogy that David is that rich man. "You are the man," Nathan thunders at the king. Despite the depravity of his sin, one must credit David with his ability to hear the word of rebuke and respond by repenting. Rare is the person who can hear any word of rebuke without becoming defensive or taking the offensive.

Over the years, I have discovered that people who confided secret failures often became my enemies. Almost always those who have attacked or maligned me have been people about whom I knew truths that they did not wish to become public. David did not run the prophet Nathan through with a sword when he was confronted, and he did not later need to assassinate him with secret poison.

David genuinely repents, and the Psalm that is numbered 51 is often credited to him and this season of repentance:

Have mercy on me, O God,
according to your steadfast love;
according to your abundant mercy
blot out my transgressions.
Wash me thoroughly from my iniquity,
and cleanse me from my sin.

Regardless of the true authorship of that psalm, David's greatness as a person of faith was not in his sinless life, but in how he dealt with his sin. It is an amazing testament of scripture that the Bible doesn't seek to preserve David's reputation, but acknowledges that true virtue is being able to turn one's life around when we have gone astray.

A sinless life is a sign of spiritual delusion. The true sign of spiritual maturity rests in being able to hear a word of reproof without needing to defend yourself or attack the messenger. In this, the Bible understood David was a true leader.

2 SAMUEL

2 Samuel 13-18:33

Beginning in chapter 13, we read a long convoluted story about how David's older son Amnon rapes his half-sister Tamar. David was angry about the rape but did not punish his son. Tamar's brother Absalom bides his time but, eventually, has Amnon murdered. As a result, Absalom has to flee, leaving David to grieve over the loss of two sons.

Ultimately, David allows Absalom to return to Jerusalem and forgives him. In verse 14:25 we have another description of physical beauty. Absalom is described in such detail that the writer records how much his thick luxurious hair weighed when it was cut each year. The point of this description was primarily to explain that many in Jerusalem were smitten with Absalom largely because of his physical beauty. Absalom also panders to the people for several years and thus "stole the hearts of the people of Israel." (2 Samuel 15:6)

All of this leads to an outright rebellion by Absalom against King David who has to flee his own capital. In the ultimate battle described in chapter 18, we learn that Absalom had not cut his hair in a while when we read that his hair got caught in a low-hanging branch, which led to his death.

In 18:33, David learns of his son's death and weeps deeply, saying, "O my son Absalom would that I had died rather than you my son, my son!" The heart-wrenching grief of a father reminds us of pure love. When Joab arrives in chapter 19 he rebukes David, saying that his grief makes the soldiers who are loyal to him think they are worth nothing; after all, didn't Absalom try to kill them all? Still, David didn't love Absalom for political gain, nor even because he was cunning and beautiful. David loved him because he was his son, and nothing Absalom ever did changed that love.

If a flawed human like David could so love an erring child, why do you sometimes doubt God's love for you? Regardless of what has happened in the past, you are God's daughter or son, and NOTHING can change that. I think this is the real reason the Bible calls David "A person after God's own heart."

2 SAMUEL

2 Samuel 24

Most seminaries require students to take what is called "Systematic Theology." The idea is that those who teach and preach should hold for themselves a theology that is coherent and free of contradictions. It seems to me that fundamentalists would always fail Systematic Theology. In part, though, it isn't their fault. They claim to take the Bible as the "infallible, inerrant word of God," yet the Bible itself is full of contradictions and, well, just plain oddities.

Chapter 24 of 2 Samuel is a good example. It begins by saying that God told David to take a census of the people because God was angry:

> *Again the anger of the Lord was kindled against Israel, and God incited David against them, saying, 'Go, count the people of Israel and Judah.*

We aren't told what ticked God off, nor why David taking a census is an expression of that anger. The text is clear, though, that the idea for the census originates with God. However, in verse 10, we find David repenting of having done so:

> *But afterwards, David was stricken to the heart because he had numbered the people. David said to the Lord, "I have sinned greatly in what I have done. But now, O Lord, I pray you, take away the guilt of your servant; for I have done very foolishly."*

So, if God incited David to do this, why is David repenting? If it was wrong, shouldn't God be the one repenting? Is the author trying to protect David by blaming God, or is David simply the fall guy for God's foolishness?

Fortunately, WE are not fundamentalists. We don't have to try and create a systematic and coherent theological understanding from this text. Thus freed, we are able to see the passage for what it is: an expression of the author's systematic theology.

You see, the author does not have a dualistic view of life. Rather, he believes that God is in control of everything. Therefore, although what David did was wrong, God was the power behind that choice because God is the power behind every choice. This leaves God the one ultimately responsible for "inciting David" to do wrong.

That idea is unacceptable to us; however, it should also serve as a warning against some of our expressions of piety. While we want to worship God and offer God our praise and adoration, what are the implications when we credit God with being all powerful and "in control?" Systematic theology means that, if we believe God is in control of everything, God ends up being responsible for wars, epidemics, child suffering AND our own greed and apathy. Maybe that is the great lure of fundamentalism.

1 KINGS

1 Kings 1

The book of 2 Samuel ends with an account of 70,000 people dying in Israel because of a pestilence of some sort. The explanation for the plague was that David had sinned by holding a census of the nation. There is no explanation of why exactly counting people antagonized people, but apparently that was the only thing the author knew of that David had done that might have been to blame for the disaster.

It is always a dangerous thing to attribute to earthly events a heavenly cause. Still, that doesn't seem to slow us down. Even those of us seeking to break free of our fundamentalism still have those thoughts from time to time; otherwise we would never ask the question "Why?" in prayer.

The book of 1 Kings begins with the words, "King David was old and advanced in years …" One might think that is redundant. However, we all have known people who were old and not advanced in years, and a few people who were advanced in years but never old. Apparently, David was both, though he was only 70.

There is this strange phrase about how the King could not "stay warm." They find a young virgin to come and sleep with him, but the text notes even she could not keep him warm. The whole text is just a euphemistic way of saying that David needed Viagra®, but, since they didn't have any, they thought a young, pretty girl might do the job. She did not because the text concludes, "But the King did not know her sexually." (1 Kings 1:4)

It is difficult to tell who exactly had the toughest time talking about this, the author who used the euphemism or the translators who don't make it clear what is meant. My guess is that the people with the toughest time are the preachers who have tried to approach this text. It seems that talking about sex is taboo for religious folk. Outside the church everyone talks a great deal about sex, but somehow religious people get tongue tied. You may find all this sex talk in a devotion to be odd … which is the trouble.

You see, when human sexuality is excommunicated, it becomes something profane rather than something normal, natural and even sacred. It is as if we are keeping what we do secret from God. Have you ever wondered why God made sex so much fun (at least when it is done well)? God could have made us like animals that go into heat and are compelled to mate. Human enjoyment of sex is separated from procreation. If it were not, there would be lots more babies, the elderly would never have sex, and lesbian and gay people would be out of luck. God made sex fun and isn't surprised or embarrassed by it. Church and the Bible are not places for sexual euphemisms that insult the One who gave sexuality to us as a gift.

1 KINGS

1 Kings 1:11-2:10

In his old age, David is manipulated by Nathan and Bathsheba to ensure that Solomon becomes his successor. Apparently, Adonijah, David's oldest son after Absalom's death, had begun to assume leadership of Israel. While Adonijah and his friends were partying, Solomon was anointed and proclaimed the royal successor. When Adonijah and his followers heard this, they proclaimed their loyalty to Solomon, though the text notes that they only did this out of fear.

In chapter two we hear David's final instructions to his son Solomon. One would hope that this exchange would be inspirational and instructional, not just for David's heir but for all those who follow. What we get, though, is essentially David's hit list. He takes Solomon aside and gives him a list of those who need to be taken care of and disposed of after his death.

The text concludes, "Then David slept with his ancestors and was buried." (1 Kings 2:10) The life and reign that began so gloriously seems to end with a whimper and a sigh. As a boy, David single-handedly took on the giant Goliath, and exercised great love and grace. In the end, he tells Solomon to kill his brother, and Joab who had served him and Israel so well, and even a priest who David has sworn to protect.

We are left to wonder if David actually gave these instructions to Solomon or if the author, seeking to protect the reputation of Solomon, attributes the motivation to David. It appears that, upon David's death, Solomon decided to consolidate his power by eliminating rivals. This seems a more congruent explanation than blaming the idea on David; however, the writer of the story is clear that the end of David's reign and of his life were not glorious. The writer makes public David's sexual dysfunction and then simply lets him fade away.

David tells Solomon that he is going "the way of all the earth," which is true. However, I have been privileged to know women and men who did not simply fade away, but who used the energy of their lives to make a difference almost until the end. Many of my peers want to retire so they can relax and play, but some want to retire from having to make money so they can use their time and talent and energy to make a difference. Many are those who make a good beginning of their lives, leaving college with energy, resolve, vitality and passion. Great souls manage to stay fully alive all of their days, and, when they die, those who write their life story don't note that their souls needed Viagra®.

1 KINGS

1 Kings 3

So Solomon begins his reign by unifying his hold on power. First, he executes any enemies, real or potential. Then he begins to make strategic alliances with the nations surrounding Israel. His first strategic move is to marry the Pharaoh's daughter. Hundreds of years have passed since Moses led the people out of Egypt. Solomon would marry hundreds of women, many for strategic purposes, but this woman was notable to the writer.

In the third verse of Chapter 3, we read of the defining moment in the story of Solomon. He was regarded by history as one of the wisest people who ever lived, and here we find the source of that wisdom. In a dream, God allows Solomon to ask for anything he wanted. Solomon asks for wisdom. This request so pleased God that God says that since Solomon did not ask for long life or wealth God would give him those things too.

That seems to be more than a parable of life. We all know people who spend their lives seeking to be happy. Some think happiness will come once they have enough money or success. Still others think that finding the right person will make them happy. The truth is that happiness isn't a goal that can be attained, but rather **happiness is the by-product of a well-lived life.**

Solomon asked for wisdom, and his wisdom brought him success and prosperity. Had he pursued other things, they may forever have proven elusive and just out of reach. Even when he had attained them by external standards he may have remained dissatisfied and anxious. Living wisely allowed Solomon not only to attain the other things he might have wanted, but allowed him to use his long life and prosperity well.

This is the truth of what Jesus meant when he said, "Seek first the reign of God within your life, and all these other things will be given to you as well." (Matthew 6:33)

So, be honest. If tonight in a dream God agrees to give you anything, would you have the courage to ask for wisdom, or would you still be tempted to ask for that million dollars? … And we wonder why true happiness is so elusive.

1 KINGS

1 Kings 3:16

According to the Bible, Saul, David and Solomon each reigned for exactly 40 years. Obviously, that is unlikely and speaks more to the symbolic significance of the number than to the actual historical length of their reigns.

At any rate, Solomon's reign was about the same length as his father's, but, unlike David's, his reign wasn't as exciting. Or as my grandfather used to say about me, "Solomon was a lover, not a fighter." I think that was my grandfather's acknowledgement that even as a kid, I was gay. Solomon wasn't gay, but he was determined to marry every eligible woman in the Middle East.

The first story about Solomon's reign is one of the most famous. It is the account of two mothers claiming the same child. Unable to decide between the competing claims, Solomon ordered the child cut in two, with half to be given to both mothers. Of course, the real mother immediately abandoned her claim in order to save the life of her child, thus Solomon discovered the truth.

The story is told as an example of the legendary wisdom of Solomon. It is also an important parable about life. How often have we been willing to "kill the baby," the relationship, or the progress, or the hopes and dreams of others, rather than to admit we were wrong or simply let someone else "win?"

I'm sure the "fake" mother must have been horrified when, after the heat of the moment, she realized how far her need to be right had taken her. It is quite likely that this poor woman had lost her own child and perhaps had even convinced herself that this other baby was really hers. When being right becomes our highest value, it is amazing the lengths our own minds will go to support us. That is why one recovery facility always had over the fireplace the question, **"Do you want to be right or be well?"**

1 KINGS

1 Kings 5

Solomon was not a mighty conquering warrior like his father David. Through a multitude of marriages, though, he managed to secure relative peace and prosperity for the nation. As a result, he was able to use the resources of the country for purposes other than weapons and wars.

The fifth chapter of 1 Kings begins with the description of Solomon's greatest accomplishment, a great temple he built that became the epicenter of the Jewish faith and identity for centuries. Until that time the holy place of their faith had been in a tent called the Tabernacle. The most sacred relic was the Ark of the Covenant, which held the sacred tablets on which the law was recorded.

The description of how the temple was constructed in this chapter is pretty outrageous and strains credibility. The Bible sometimes seems to have trouble with numbers because the writers used them symbolically and we take them literally. According to the text, Solomon used 30,000 timber cutters, 70,000 laborers, and 80,000 stone cutters. No construction project in human history would compare to those numbers, which may have been the point of such extraordinary figures.

The sixth chapter explains that all of this took place 480 years after the exodus from Egypt. Biblical scholars have long argued over this date, which is a bit silly. Again, the writer was not a historian, nor was that the message the text seeks to communicate. The point was that the Hebrews, even five centuries or more later, still derived their identity from the great liberation of God.

The writer describes the great temple and its construction in detail. It was glorious! However, the seventh chapter contains an even more detailed and glorious description of the temple that Solomon built for himself. At first, you might think that this is offered as a criticism of Solomon and his lavish lifestyle—building a greater house for himself than the one he built for God. If you read the chapter, though, you see that what we have is an ancient version of Robin Leech. The author is no critic, but seems smitten by the lifestyles of the rich and famous.

Then, as now, there was a reticence to criticize those who live in excessive luxury while the hungry grovel at their door. In fact, only Jesus seemed to have the courage to describe such a scene and condemn it with eternal judgment. Jesus' words were quickly forgotten, though, and "Christian nations" and "Christian people" alike have made heroes and idols of those who make excess a virtue. Some things never change … but that doesn't make them right.

1 KINGS

1 Kings 8-9

After an exhaustive description of Solomon's palace, the author describes the dedication of the temple. It is a beautiful scene, as the Ark of the Covenant, with its ancient stone tablets, is processed into the temple. Solomon speaks and then prays. The lengthy prayer reviews the components of the law that the author obviously thought were important.

The place is filled with a cloud, perhaps smoke. To the people, it represented the "shekhinah," or glory of God. "Shekhinah" is a feminine Hebrew word that literally means "the presence of God." Shekhinah is practically the same as the Greek word "parousia," also a feminine word, meaning presence. Too often that word has been interpreted as the second coming, and fundamentalists, with their apocalyptic vision, have tried to make it the way it was to be understood. What a difference between Tim LeHaye's understanding of this promise and how Jesus and the ancient Hebrews seemed to understand it.

The Divine feminine presence is the greatest expression in the Hebrew Testament of God's covenant. What could surpass God's willingness to be with us? Christianity, of course, understands Jesus as an incarnational expression of God's presence: "Emmanuel, God with us." Before his death, Jesus promised that, in his absence, we would be given another presence. Again, the description of the Spirit is a feminine one.

Has all of this been ignored because too many Christians need a vengeful God who comes to wipe out unbelievers and punish sinners? Even the bloody apocalyptic book of Revelation ends with this tender feminine image:

> *Behold the dwelling of God is with mortals. God will dwell with them as their God and they will be God's peoples and God will personally be with them; God will wipe every tear from their eyes and death will be no more.*
>
> Rev. 21:3-4

What more tender image could we long for than for our heavenly Mother gently stooping to wipe tears from our eyes? Even the ancients of Solomon's day knew that when Mother arrived, all would be well.

1 KINGS

1 Kings 10

Chapter 10 begins with a description of how Solomon was visited by the Queen of Sheba. The whole story is a little strange, but the monarchy of Ethiopia, which was finally deposed in 1974, claimed to be descended from the love child produced from this encounter.

The Queen of Sheba apparently was very impressed because she gave Solomon many gifts, including 120 talents of gold, which, if it is to be believed, is the equivalent of hundreds of millions of dollars. Verse 14 says that Solomon accumulated billions of dollars of gold in a single year.

While this was a prosperous time in ancient Hebrew history, there is nothing to suggest that anything like this wealth ever existed. Like the pyramids of ancient Egypt, such extraordinary wealth historically leaves a record. Still, the author seems determined to communicate to us that Solomon was the most successful and prosperous ruler of that day and in Hebrew history. Okay, we get the point, even if the facts don't support such accumulated wealth.

There are strains of ancient tradition that see prosperity as a sign of God's favor, though the Bible also repeatedly makes clear God's favor rests upon the poor. Jesus himself identified with "the least." Still, it appears that the author of the book of Kings is setting us up to think of Solomon as a superhero of sorts. In the Qur'an, he is literally described as a prophet with supernatural powers over nature.

In the next chapter, though, we begin to watch the fall of Solomon. It is as though the author wants us to appreciate the heights of his success first. Or perhaps the writer just wanted us to get a balanced picture of this human that achieved the greatest success, but whose choices ultimately were the seeds for the nation's destruction.

What might be a helpful reminder in this is that no leader, star, pastor, idol, mentor, teacher, hero or parent is perfect. Oh, we say that all the time, and on one level we understand it. We know those we admire are human, but we don't want them to be "too human." Actually, we don't want them to be as human as we are.

The truth is, for every human, our strengths and weaknesses are two sides of the same coin, and the bottom line is we don't get one without the other. Somehow we can understand that when we look in the mirror, but we don't do so well when we look at the portraits of leaders or heroes … or partners for that matter.

1 KINGS

1 Kings 11

And so, in the 11th chapter of Kings, we come to the end of the life and reign of Solomon. For that matter, we reach the end of the golden age of the Hebrew monarchy.

The opening paragraph gives a summary of Solomon's many marriages. Verse three says he had 700 wives and 300 concubines. Again, that number strains credulity. Solomon would have had to get married every six weeks to have accomplished that many unions. Still, the point was he had a lot, which is a remarkable description of the "Biblical model of marriage." Nowhere does the Bible condemn or disavow Solomon's polygamy. Only New Testament deacons are told they should have only one spouse.

What incurs God's anger with Solomon are not his many wives, but the fact that he let all his wives bring their gods with them. The radical monotheism of Israel was what held the 12 diverse tribes united as a nation. By allowing other gods to be introduced into the culture, Solomon sowed the seeds that ultimately led to a loss of unity that eventually made the nation vulnerable to marauding and conquering neighbors.

This, too, is a powerful parable for a nation and an individual. I recently had to ask a friend to stop using the word "god" in expletives, at least when I was around. Now, I am not a fundamentalist in my understanding of the commandment about "taking God's name in vain." In fact, I don't even think profanity is what that injunction is about. However, I am clear that if SOMETHING is not held sacred in your life, soon nothing is held sacred.

I believe that for life to work well it needs to be ordered, and while I oppose hierarchy in many forms, it is clearly how life works in lots of ways. Or to say it as Jesus said, "Seek first God's reign in your life and everything else will fall into place." (Matthew 6:33, *Piazza Paraphrase*)

Solomon allowed the very cornerstone of the nation's faith to be undermined, and all too soon, it began to crumble. Perhaps we Americans would do well to stop allowing politicians to use fear to introduce the god of "security." When worshipping at that altar causes us to abandon our core values—like civil liberties and intolerance for torture and resistance to preemptive unprovoked war—greater damage is done than any terrorist could ever do. The same is true when prosperity or success causes us as individuals to abandon who we are or what we hold sacred. Even Solomon's wisdom failed him when it came to this.

1 KINGS

1 Kings 12

So, with the death of Solomon, which is very succinctly recorded in 1 Kings 11:41, the downside of his being a lover rather than a fighter became apparent. Had Solomon been a fighter, he would have killed off some of his enemies. Instead, he married their daughters and moved them and their households to Israel. There, they set up altars to their various gods, brought in priests and created holy places all over the country.

The country began to unravel as soon as their longtime leader was dead. Rehoboam was his father's designated successor, but when he went to Schechem to be consecrated as the new king, a delegation met with him to seek relief from the burdensome taxation his father had imposed to finance his opulent construction.

Rehoboam had done nothing to earn his position in life, so he responded with no sensitivity or grace, only with a sense of entitlement. As a result, when an old enemy of Solomon's named Jeroboam returned from exile in Egypt, the 10 northern tribes revolted and made Jeroboam their king. Thus, the nation was divided. The 10 tribes in the north formed a nation called Israel, and the two tribes in the south were called Judah, after the larger of the two tribes.

The trouble was Jerusalem and the great temple (with its Ark of the Covenant) was located in the south, so Jeroboam had to create a new capital and faith centers at which the local people could worship and offer their sacrifices. It wasn't just a political or geographic division, but also a spiritual division. The writer of the book of Kings interprets the events in verse 19: "So Israel has been in rebellion against the house of David to this day." The phrase "house of David" was, of course, a reminder of the covenant God made with David and an indication that the rebellious tribes were not covered by that covenant. The writer of the story is, of course, a priest in Judah.

Both sides had their arguments, but in the end, the nation was divided, weakened, and eventually, destroyed. It is a powerful reminder that, regardless of who is right and who is wrong, violence ultimately damages, and often destroys, BOTH parties. The money that nations have spent on war and "defense" in just the first eight years of this century could feed and educate every human on earth. The winners are as diminished by that choice as the losers because we are made less human every time we are less humane.

1 KINGS

1 Kings 13

The 13th Chapter of 1 Kings contains one of the saddest and most bizarre stories in the entire Bible. It is the tale of two prophets, and, while there are great lessons to be learned from it, the story itself has so little significance that one wonders why it is there. The original author apparently included this story simply as evidence that God really did try to get Israel to repent and come back. The story was told, and then the writer concludes that, since Jeroboam wouldn't repent, he and his family are doomed to be cut off and destroyed.

The next several chapters give brief accounts of the reigns of the kings of the two kingdoms. Then, in chapter 17, we are introduced to the prophet Elijah, and the kings' stories recede and are seen in the light of the life and ministry of Elijah and his successor, Elisha.

Elijah is one of the most important characters in Judaism. This is symbolized by the fact that Elijah and Moses appear to Jesus on the mount of Transfiguration. Malachi predicts that before the messiah comes, Elijah will return. Because of this prediction, John the Baptist is often held as a prophet like unto Elijah.

What is interesting is that Elijah appears out of nowhere. There is no introduction or preparation. He is identified as "Elijah the Tishbite," though no one knows what or where Tishbe was. We don't know who he is or who his people are, but he shows up to confront Ahab and Jezebel, who are considered the very worst of the many bad rulers of Israel. Their great sin was that they introduced the worship of Baal among the people and many apparently turned away from the true God.

In the Bible, Baal is one of the few gods significant enough to be named. Every time I hear that name, I think of our 21st century gods who have recently found millions of followers in this country. Like Israel, we still claim our faith history, but the truth is we worship at many other altars, i.e. Capitalism and Security. Where is the prophet who will rise up to lift their voice against the sacrifices we make to these modern gods?

Capitalism is a more sacred and universally held doctrine in this day than Christianity. No one dares to question it or the power capitalism holds on our society. No one dares to even wonder aloud if there might not be another way. And Security … if recent years have taught us nothing else, we have seen that there is nothing Americans won't sacrifice for the illusion of Security. When the wealthiest and most powerful country in history lets its own people go hungry, accepts torture of teenagers and labels terrorists, you know the gods we really worship are not related to the God that Jesus served.

1 KINGS

1 Kings 17

Elijah confronts Ahab and his queen Jezebel and is told by God to get out of town. Then as now, confronting entrenched power is never the work of those who are risk adverse. If you value what those in power think of you, then you can't be a prophet, which says a lot about our culture's worship of celebrities … but that's another *Liberating Word.*

Elijah flees and makes camp by the brook Cherith. In an arid land, sources of water are major points of reference. Elijah also has just prophesied a terrible drought over Israel. There at the Wadi Cherith, Elijah is fed by "ravens." I have tried to figure out what on earth was symbolized by the ravens. While that has been the popular translation of the story, I think the more logical explanation is that the word could be translated "Arabs." Elijah crosses to the far side of the Jordan and is fed by the Arabs, the Bedouins who practice a strict ethic of hospitality.

What is fascinating is that the translators, and most scholars, found it more palatable to believe that birds brought Elijah bread and meat every morning and night rather than to accept that outsiders might have been used by God or done acts of generosity and kindness to a stranger. This is just one of many examples of our capacity to deny the humanity of those who are different, those who disagree or those of whom we don't approve. We'd rather believe in magic than to change our minds about a person or a group of people.

Whether this prejudice was first recorded by the original author, subsequent translators, or the multitude of preachers who have told this story, make no mistake that prejudice has shaped how scripture was recorded, translated and understood. All too often scripture has been used as a haven for prejudice and bigotry, and as the defender of discrimination.

Yet to every prejudice we must ask these questions: Did God create this person/these people? Who didn't God create? Who doesn't God love?

If that is ALWAYS our starting place then how we understand the scripture and life itself is very different. If we pick up the Bible believing that we are right, loved and approved, and "they" are not, we will always have to resort to magical thinking, because THAT is never the view of God.

1 KINGS

1 Kings 17:8

Speaking of prejudice …

In this story, we have a widow to whom Jesus references in Luke 4:25-30 (and citing this reference almost got Jesus thrown off a cliff). Actually, He dared to use examples from the lives of Elijah and Elisha in which God sent the prophets to assist outsiders. In this story, a non-Jewish widow feeds Elijah using what little she has left. This offering of meal and oil is blessed so that it will not run out because of her willingness to feed someone else who is hungry too.

There is great power in this parable and in the fact that Jesus thought it was important to remind "insiders" that God is God for the "outsiders" as well. This story infuriated his hometown listeners, much in the same way Americans don't want to hear about al Qaida, or even Muslim people, who are tender, compassionate and generous people loved by and used by God.

Nationalism then and now creates an "us vs. them" that allows us to dehumanize "them." We create an artificial dynamic by which we need not regard "them" as fully human, let alone as children of the One God, parent of us all. Ultimately, Elijah heals this outsider woman's son and raises him from the dead. Jesus, in an act of courage or foolishness, asks his hometown insider listeners if they didn't think there were lots of insider widows to whom the prophet might have gone. Weren't there plenty of OUR children God might have healed, yet Elijah healed one of THEIR children.

Jesus didn't make this story up. His listeners already knew the tale. Jesus just had the temerity to ask the question that challenged their worldview and confronted their prejudice. Many of his parables did that. As we read this story from 1 Kings 17, perhaps we would do well to think of all the people in our worldview who we don't believe deserve God's healing and providing love … at least don't deserve it as much as we and our own children deserve it.

Jesus seemed to think this was one healing story with a lesson we shouldn't forget. Have we?

1 KINGS

1 Kings 18

In this chapter, we find the story that is the apex of Elijah's prophetic career. Here he confronts Ahab the apostate king of Israel and goes up against all the priests of Baal in a "Battle of the Prophets" on Mt. Carmel. This is a story worthy of reality TV, if ever there was one. You probably remember how it goes.

The prophets of Baal set up an altar with a sacrifice to their god, and Elijah sets up an altar and sacrifice. Both sides are to call down fire from heaven to consume the offering. The 850 prophets of Baal go first while Elijah stands by taunting them. At one point, Elijah encourages them to cry louder, saying that maybe their god is taking a nap or on the toilet … at least that is how the Living Bible translates verse 27.

Of course, in the end, there is not even static electricity on Baal's altar. Elijah, the consummate showoff/showman, has them pour buckets of water over his altar over and over until the water was running everywhere. Then he prays a simple prayer, and, of course, fire rains down from heaven, consuming the offering and the altar and lapping up the water.

So spectacular was this display of power that Elijah seizes control of the situation and has all the prophets of Baal arrested and executed. Then Elijah prays, and the drought ends, which is a witness not only to the true God, but against King Ahab and his queen Jezebel.

Wow! This great victorious display of might by God is an example of how we all want God to act … at least every now and then. Who of us hasn't wanted to call down fire from heaven on the heads of evildoers (or at least the creep who cut us off in traffic)? Even good liberals like us want God to punish polluters, warmongers, torturers and bigots. If God would just take them out, the world would be a better place.

Then we come to the Gospels. Apparently, when Jesus' disciples want to call down fire from heaven Jesus rebukes them. It seems that, at least according to Jesus, grace doesn't allow for fire-callers. That isn't the job description of a disciple of Jesus, which is a shame, because I had several juicy targets in mind. Please don't tell Jesus.

1 KINGS

1 Kings 19:1-9

Elijah's great victory over the prophets of Baal on Mt. Carmel apparently really ticked off Queen Jezebel. She decides that it is time to get rid of this meddlesome prophet once and for all. Powerbrokers almost always find a way to eliminate prophets who say uncomfortable things. Usually they can be discredited, ridiculed or embarrassed into silence.

Looking back on how Rev. Jeremiah Wright was treated by the media, you realize that "Jezebel" simply has updated her methods. Oh, I didn't agree with everything he said, though when you took time to hear the context and the total statement much more of it made sense than we were led to believe. So, even if Wright's words were outrageous, have you ever wondered why he needed to be utterly discredited and destroyed? Wouldn't it have been sufficient just to ignore him? After all, thousands of preachers are routinely ignored in this country every Sunday. Something he said obviously threatened someone. Maybe what he said threatened us all. Conservatives/fundamentalists hated that he questioned our nationalism and nationalistic hubris. Liberals/progressives were terrified that he might endanger the election of their candidate. Wright had to be destroyed.

Jezebel threatened Elijah, and, despite his brave show on Mt. Carmel, Elijah fled into the wilderness where he sat down and whined to God. (v. 4) His courage had run out. Elijah was exhausted with no more self-confidence, and apparently, not much faith left either. The battle left him emotionally depleted and spiritually vulnerable. He ran and hid, asking God to simply take his life.

Prophetic ministry is hard. You want to be loved, appreciated and approved. It takes a lot out of you to say uncomfortable or unpopular things. It is not easy to stand against the stream of popular opinion. We get addicted to approval as a child, an addiction few people have the strength to resist. We prefer to be on the winning side or to be a part of the majority. Yet the majority, the crowd, the mob has lynched innocent people, trampled the rights of minorities, executed Jesus and elected utterly incompetent leaders. Jesus calls us to play out our lives to an audience of One.

This story reminds us, though, that even when we win, the inner cost is high, so high that, like Elijah, we are easily threatened and would rather die than rise up to fight again. Yes, Elijah knew firsthand the power of God, but exhaustion leaves even a prophet vulnerable to self-pity.

1 KINGS

1 Kings 19:9-20

The battle on Mt. Carmel left Elijah exhausted, depressed and feeling vulnerable. It is in that state, though, that he discovers and offers what is perhaps his most enduring spiritual lesson.

Hiding out in a cave, he continues to whine to God about how faithful he has been, but how abandoned he now feels. (v. 10) Then he gets this sense that the presence of God is with him. At the mouth of the cave, he witnesses a great wind, so strong a wind that it causes landslides. But he also knew that God was not present in that wind. He experienced from his refuge an earthquake, but God was not to be found in that show of power either. Eventually there is a fire, but again, there is no sign of God.

Then Elijah experiences something profound. After all the sound and fury, the Bible says there was a "sound of sheer silence." Sit with that phrase for a moment: ***a sound of sheer silence.*** In his loneliness and despair, the word of the Lord came to Elijah only when he was able to hear the sound of sheer silence.

In a sermon on this text, Rev. Andrea Castner Wyatt wrote:

> *Does Simon and Garfunkel's song, "The Sound of Silence," hold any special meaning for you? They could be singing about Elijah, that night! "Hello, darkness, my old friend, I've come to talk to you again. Because a vision softly creeping left its seeds while I was sleeping. And the vision that was planted in my brain still remains within the sound of silence." Elijah rests and heals. The sound of silence has a different quality now, for silence is also a place of renewal, vision restored, hope re-awakened. American poet, Mary Oliver, could be describing Elijah that night: "little by little, the stars begin to burn through the sheets of clouds, and there is a new voice which you slowly recognize." The prophet begins to listen, in a new way. Elijah recognizes a new voice in the silence, a voice deep within himself, a holy companion who will never abandon him. And he knows it is time to get up.*

We are a people who fear true silence more than wind, earthquakes and fire. When we have unanswered or unanswerable questions we fill that silence with argument, debate, magical thinking, and even irrational explanations. We prefer even bad solutions and explanations to silence. The lesson in this text is that when we have come to the end of all our resources and we are feeling all alone, the sheer silence may be the only place where we truly can hear the voice of God.

1 KINGS

1 Kings 19:15-21

Depression, despair, paranoia and burnout followed Elijah's great victory. However, even that state is not without grace. In fact, it is into that state of "sheer silence" that the voice of the Lord comes and Elijah gets the next work he is to do. He must go and anoint a new king over Israel and anoint Elisha who will someday be his successor.

How often have we all felt too tired, sick or depressed to go back to work, but since we didn't have any choice, we went anyway? While this isn't always a good idea, it is amazing how often the act of "getting back to work" is the best possible therapy. Sitting around wondering or worrying can take us on a downward spiral. God doesn't act as therapist to the depressed Elijah, but simply gives him his next assignment.

In a sense, that may have been the best therapy of all. God was demonstrating that Elijah's life wasn't finished. Sometimes depression follows a great defeat, but it can also follow a great victory. Many of us handle defeat with grace, but have no clue how to act after we succeed. Many Americans have prospered beyond their expectations only to find themselves in a deep angst and even despair.

What Elijah needed was a purpose, a cause, a mission. He needed a reason to get back up and go back to living. Making money and acquiring wealth is the only thing that gets many people up in the morning. No wonder a downturn in the economy can send an entire nation into a malaise. Money is the only means many of us have to keep score. It is how we know if we are succeeding or failing. Only when it is too late do we discover that even if you win the rat race, you are still a rat.

God understood that Elijah's life needed a divine purpose if it was to have meaning and power. So does your life! Rick Warren has sold more than 30 million copies of *The Purpose Driven Life*. That is testament to our instinctive awareness of this truth. Unfortunately, reading that book didn't help most of us deprogram from the purpose of life we have been sold by advertisers. We still live as if the only purpose we have is to work harder to earn more money to buy more and better things.

Purpose is imperative, but we have to be delivered from the demonic purposes that have infected our souls through our worship at the altars of Capitalism, and turn our souls to discover the purpose for which we were created. If you are feeling dissatisfied, discouraged or even despondent, be grateful! Those feelings are proof that your soul is still alive and knows there is something more to life. Now go find what it is.

1 KINGS

1 Kings 20

The next several chapters shift from the story of Elijah back to the end of the reign of Ahab. Ironically, the authors consider him to be one of the worst in a long line of bad kings. Still, his story is told in surprisingly great detail. He reigned for 22 years and apparently wasn't so bad that God wouldn't help him. He had some success that was credited to God.

This leaves me wondering if God uses someone despite the fact that they were not a "good person," but whose success advances the cause of the people of God. Or is it simply that the author of this history couldn't imagine that Ahab could have ANY success apart from God's blessing/will?

I have to admit that I sometimes struggle with this myself. When I awake on a beautiful morning my heart wants to thank God for the gift. As a young Christian, I was taught to live with gratitude for all of the blessings of God. I always have felt sorry for those who felt blessed, but had no one to whom they could express their gratitude. It feels to me as though expressing praise or gratitude to God for my blessings is natural and right and enhances the total experience. It is almost as if I have been twice blessed.

The trouble is, if I awake on a glorious morning and praise God, should I also curse God when I awake on a terrible day? I mean, if God is the source of the blessings of my life, then isn't God also responsible for the challenges and pains of my life? I'm uncomfortable with that, but that theology is at least consistent. The dualism of the good coming from God and the bad coming from the devil is not logical to me. So, if dualism isn't an option, and if making God responsible for both the good and the bad isn't the answer, then shouldn't we consider God is not the source of either? That is actually the most logical explanation to me, but I'm uncomfortable living with ingratitude for my blessings.

The truth is that, in life, rainy days are often greater blessings to more of the earth than bright, blue, cloudless days. My limited knowledge and understanding actually disqualifies me from claiming what are blessings and which are not. Do I dare have enough faith and trust in God to live a life in perpetual gratitude?

The historian of Ahab seemed to believe there were times God blesses even a bad person. I happen to believe that all of us are such a mixture of good and bad that if God didn't bless bad people then all of human life would simply be abandoned.

1 KINGS

1 Kings 22

King Ahab of Israel and King Jehoshaphat of Judah decided to work together to push back the Syrians. This might have been the beginning of a new partnership and even reunification, but as the very first battle begins, Ahab is hit by a stray arrow that finds its way through a gap in his armor.

It would be fascinating to read a history of the impact of incidental and accidental events on human history. How much of our own life has been shaped by accidental or incidental events? We might be able to identify some of them, but many have passed unnoticed until after the impact has been felt. The archer who simply let his arrow fly may have had no idea that the king was even in the battle, and probably never knew that he might have dramatically changed history.

That, of course, is a parable about most of the arrows we release in life. We may never know our impact. Unfortunately, that is as negatively true as it is positively. That is why we need to discipline our lives to release more cupid arrows of love than arrows of war/anger/resentment.

Ahab's life ends, and so does the book of 1 Kings. The book actually ends with a few sentences about Ahaziah, the son of Ahab and Jezebel. His reign apparently was short, and the author certainly shed no tears over him. His summary was "like father (and mother), like son."

Few of us have famous, or infamous, parents. Still, I am dismayed by how much our parents continue to shape our lives, even long after we have lived more years apart from them than we did with them. Increasingly, I hear my mother or father speaking through my mouth, especially in dealing with my children. It seems the human tendency is to either demonize or deify our parents, when the truth almost always is that they were a blend of good and bad, healthy and unhealthy. Perhaps if we really understand and accept that, we would come closer to understanding and accepting that about ourselves.

Only as we accept our faults and weaknesses can we work on them. Only by embracing and celebrating our strengths and gifts, do we have the confidence and self-esteem to be honest about our faults. Both sides of that are often "gifts" from our parents. Accepting honestly the gifts and the curses of our heritage with humor and humility seems to be as tough for kings as it is for subjects.

2 KINGS

2 Kings 1

The first chapter of 2 Kings is one of those passages that makes me feel sorry for fundamentalist preachers. I mean, there is a reason this never appears in the lectionary cycle, and you very well may never have heard a sermon on it.

Apparently King Ahaziah, son of Ahab and Jezebel, was in an accident just a couple of years after he became king. He fell and was injured severely enough to be confined to bed. He sends servants to the priests of a false god to find out whether or not he will recover. This action irritates Elijah's god—who I am reluctant to call the true God. Elijah confronts the king's servant and tells him to ask the king what he is thinking consulting a false god. Elijah then tells him to assure the king that he will, in fact, die without ever getting out of bed.

Well, the king decides to summon Elijah, so he sends a captain and 50 soldiers to fetch the prophet. Unfortunately, Elijah is not easily fetched. He calls down fire, and God incinerates the 50 and the captain. The king tries a second time with the same result. Not a quick study, the king sends another captain and 50 more men. This third time, though, the captain is smarter. He is very humble and begs Elijah not to kill him, but to come with him to the king. Elijah goes, and he says to the king exactly what he had said to the servant. Sure enough, the king dies.

Now, I would like to say that this is a parable about how dangerous it is to try and mess with men (or women) of God. It would be nice to let people think we could call down fire on them. Apparently, the author wanted people to think twice before they took on the religious authorities. Unfortunately, this is one of those passages I'm glad to simply dismiss. I just don't believe God fried 100 people just to prove Elijah was important, and then let him go and repeat himself.

I do believe that then as now many people WANT a God who will send a prophet to burn up the wicked and reward the good. Even sending Jesus hasn't seemed to convince Christians that this isn't how God operates.

2 KINGS

2 Kings 2

It is sad that the last recorded act of Elijah is incinerating 100 soldiers sent to fetch him and then pronouncing the death sentence of the king of Israel. In this chapter, we find the very elaborate story of Elijah's death … well, of his ascent into heaven.

There is no more magical character in the Bible than Elijah. He makes Dumbledore seem like an amateur. It seems only fitting that he doesn't simply die of old age. Instead, God sends horses and a chariot of fire to pick him up, and, like Dorothy in Kansas, they all get caught up in a whirlwind and presumably swept up to Oz … or some other place in Technicolor.

Again, I'm glad I'm not a fundamentalist, because I'd have to try to explain this story literally. Fortunately, I don't. Rather, like the wonderful story of Dorothy's trip to see the wizard, I can enjoy the story and listen for lessons along the way and assume that Elisha had gotten a bump on the head when he saw all of this.

So, without the benefit of believing in magic, as literalists seem to do, just what is meant by "chariots of fire?" Some have suggested that this is the First Testament's witness to UFO abductions, which, if you have to take the story literally, makes about as much sense as anything else.

To me, it is a symbol that the ministry of Elijah did not end, but is a part of the repertoire of heaven. It was anticipated that Elijah would return to prepare the way for the messiah, and John the Baptist fulfilled that role. Both were prophets who were unafraid to speak truth to power and to confront evil in the common life. The work of both Elijah/John was not the final Word from God, but prepared the way for that final word: grace.

It is said that if your only tool is a hammer then everything looks like a nail. Elijah and his prophetic ministry were tools in the hands of the Spirit. We need prophets to rail against modern evils that oppress the poor and those at the margins. That ministry didn't die, but it isn't the only tool in the Spirit's toolbox … or, given some of my lesbian friends work preferences, perhaps we should picture Elijah on the Spirit's tool belt.

2 KINGS

The story of Elijah being swept up into heaven was important because it marked a dramatic moment for transition from Elijah to his successor Elisha. The prophetic mantle is literally passed, which is where this phrase comes from in our culture.

As Elisha got ready to say goodbye to his mentor, Elijah asks him if there is anything he could do for him before he leaves. Elisha asks for a double portion of the great prophet's spirit. Elijah says that is a hard thing, but that if Elisha is able to see him when he is taken away then his wish will be granted.

Elisha is asking for the heir's portion, which might sound greedy unless you remember that Elijah wasn't universally beloved by those in power. He spent his time running and hiding just to stay alive. Was that really what Elisha wanted? As Elijah said, he asked for a hard thing.

Not many of us volunteer these days to do hard things. We enjoy our free time and our comfort. If we gain a little praise and respect then we think we are successful. No wonder there are so few prophets any more. Then, as now, the goal of the prophet is not popularity, approval or affection. Prophets have to be willing to challenge people, especially the people of God:

- We live in a world where thousands of people die of starvation every day. They do not die because there isn't enough food; they die because some of us have too much and all of us share too little. Where are the prophets who should be harassing us to do better?
- We live in a world where our ease results in the destruction of God's creation because we aren't willing to inconvenience ourselves by driving less, recycling more, or reducing our consumption. Our public leaders are still preaching that we can have it all, without regard to the world our grandchildren will inherit.
- Where are the prophets calling for higher taxes because that is the only way everyone can have healthcare, education and a promising future?

Well, now you know why there aren't many prophets. What was Elisha thinking?!?

2 KINGS

2 Kings 2:23-25

So, Elisha's wish was granted. The mantle is passed, and the next era of history will focus on the powerful ministry of this prophet of God.

Unfortunately, one of the early stories of the life of Elisha causes him to be widely ignored by most contemporary preachers. According to the story, the prophet is heading to Bethel when some small boys come out and begin to tease him because he is bald. Elisha seems especially sensitive about this, which I fully understand. He reacts by cursing the boys in the name of God. The result was two she-bears emerged from the woods and mauled 42 kids.

Now, I have to admit that I have wanted to have that power a few times, not so much with children, but with critics. I mean, is it so wrong to want a couple of bears to maul people who dare to criticize the prophet of God? I guess it is wrong, which is why you don't hear this text read in the common lectionary. It is another case where I'm glad I'm not a fundamentalist.

Perhaps some kids did tease Elisha, and perhaps some bears did attack the children. I'm not surprised to see those two events connected by people; after all, even if the implications are horrendous, we all need for tragedy to have meaning and context. What this story says about God is terrible, but apparently it is better to have a God who kills children than deal with meaningless and random tragedies.

If you have been to many funerals for children or those who died prematurely, you know that this falls into the "some things never change department." In an attempt to bring comfort, people talk about God "taking" a loved one, or even "needing another angel." Most of us are theologically sophisticated enough to reject that type of thinking, yet almost none of us are immune from trying to make sense of tragedy. It is a natural coping mechanism. What we must resist, though, is the temptation to make God into a deity of child-mauling she-bears.

2 KINGS

2 Kings 4:1-7

This chapter in 2 Kings recounts several miracles performed by Elisha. First he makes a poor widow's jar of oil into an oil well that produced enough to pay her debts as well as to feed her family and the prophet. This story is very popular in my state of Texas where oil has provided for a lot of families' financial needs and where some folks think it is a sign of God's favor. Still, what does a bottomless oil jar really mean to the rest of us?

In our day, there is a strain of teaching in some of the more evangelical, and a number of predominantly African-American, churches that generally is referred to as "the Prosperity Gospel." It is very popular in certain mega-churches, including the largest church in America, Lakewood Church in Houston, Texas.

I actually like Joel Osteen and have long admired much of the work done by that congregation under his father's leadership. As someone who grew up very poor, I also understand the great appeal of preaching that proclaims health, wealth and success to be the will of God for our lives. But as someone who has buried hundreds of young men who lost their health but not their faith, and as one who honestly can say that the best people I have ever known were among the poorest, I have to disagree with this theology.

In the magical thinking of the author of 2 Kings, the widow's unending fount of oil was a sign of God's favor. However, in the Gospel, I watch in reverence as Jesus praises the faith of a widow who gave away her last two mites. He did not lay hands on her and make her poverty go away. This woman, who was Jesus' hero, left the temple financially poorer than she came in, but her life apparently was blessed in ways that money could not measure. We are left with the feeling that Jesus felt sorry for those of us who use money to keep score, and who think that financial prosperity is how God blesses a life. You might get that message from this story of Elisha, but you'll never get it from the One who was born into abject poverty and buried in a borrowed tomb.

2 KINGS

2 Kings 4:8-37

Following the account of Elisha making the widow's oil reproduce, there is a rather long story involving a prosperous Shunammite woman. She was kind and supportive of the prophet, and one day, he tells her that she will have a son, which she does. Elisha is credited with this, but I suspect her husband at least had some responsibility. As I read the story, though, I wondered if this was the author's way of telling us that Elisha was the one who got the woman pregnant. You see, in those days it was assumed that the failure of a marriage to produce children was ALWAYS the woman's "fault," hence Henry VIII kept marrying new women, when he was probably infertile. In these miraculous biblical pregnancies, since I don't believe in magic, I always wonder if it was God working in the woman's body, or permitting her to get pregnant with another man. I know, that disturbs a lot of our traditional thinking and even disregards one of the "big ten" (commandments). But the alternative leaves us with a God who plays favorites and randomly violates the laws of the universe, laws that the Creator wrote, like women get pregnant through sex with fertile men.

What does it say about us that our faith has more room for God working magic than it does for God approving unconventional sexual relationships? Today this unnamed woman of great faith might have had artificial insemination, in vitro fertilization, or an anonymous sperm donor. That wasn't an option for the widow. So was it more ethical for her to die childless, in a culture where having children was understood as the only means to eternal life, rather than to get pregnant in some way other than by her husband? I'm really just wondering …. Unless you believe God worked magic here, it is a question this story raises.

Unfortunately, the son born to the Shunammite woman developed a headache and apparently died. This woman of faith refused to take death as the final answer. She can't believe God answered her prayers only to take her son, so she sent for the prophet. Elisha returned with her and performed what appears to be a form of CPR and mouth-to-mouth resuscitation:

> *Then Elisha got up on the bed and lay upon the child, putting his mouth upon his mouth, his eyes upon his eyes, and his hands upon his hands; and while he lay bent over him, the flesh of the child became warm.*
>
> 2 Kings 4:34

The boy then awoke, sneezed seven times, and lived. I don't quite know what all of that means. I do have a feeling about it, though. It feels like a call to us all to be willing to become more physically involved in others' lives, especially in the lives of those who are hurting. Who knows what might come to life? I do know this won't happen by magic.

2 KINGS

2 Kings 4:38-44

The third and fourth miracles of Elisha in this chapter are culinary ones. First, some men were eating stew and, for some reason, decided it was poisonous. The cook apparently wasn't following a recipe and threw in some strange ingredients. That is the kind of cook I am, and my family and friends can bear witness to times when the results were unfortunate. My youngest daughter, who is the most finicky, often thinks I am trying to poison her with spices.

So, let's return to the story. Elisha took some flour, threw it into the pot, and the stew became safe to eat. Was it a miracle, or did Elisha just know his way around the kitchen? Just last night at my house, we had a wonderful meal of spaghetti made from leftover meatloaf that had been too salty to eat. It was tasty, but certainly did not qualify as a miracle. Perhaps it was just a lesson.

Finally, the chapter ends with a story of Elisha causing food to stretch enough to feed 100 people, with some left over.

Reading these stories, it is clear that the writer was trying to stress Elisha's importance to the reader. The stories are similar to those told about Elijah, and except for the bottomless oil jar, they all have very logical and natural explanations. The last miracle appears to be a precursor of a miracle Jesus was reported to have performed, though, of course, Jesus did it on a much bigger scale.

The question we must honestly struggle with is what we believe about these miracles. It is perfectly conceivable that the author was simply trying to burnish Elisha's memory and reputation. Prior to our more scientific age, supernatural explanations often were offered for natural events. Now we can objectively examine the stories about Elisha, but I wonder if we have the courage to do the same with the stories of Jesus. Our investment in magic seems much greater when it comes to Jesus.

I am not suggesting that miracles don't happen, because I know there is still much about the universe we do not know or understand. What I am asking is if we have the courage to let go of our need to believe in magic. It is easier to struggle with this now than to wait until we get to the Gospels. I wonder why that is?

2 KINGS

2 Kings 5

In this chapter, we find the best known of all of Elisha's miracles: the healing of the Syrian general Naaman. This may be better known than the others because Jesus referred to this specific miracle in his first sermon. (Luke 4:27) Earlier I mentioned that this is the sermon that nearly got him thrown off a cliff by his hometown congregation. As Jesus knew, the remarkable thing about this miracle was that God used Elisha to cure one who would have been considered an enemy of Israel. It is not remarkable that God healed Naaman; it is surprising that such as story was preserved and repeated.

Naaman has leprosy, and a "servant girl" suggests that Elisha could cure him. "Leprosy" referred to a wide variety of skin diseases, and it is unlikely that Naaman had Hansen's disease, which is the label we generally call leprosy today. Whatever the ailment, Elisha decided that it could be cured with seven baths in the Jordan. General Naaman is insulted by this prescription, but eventually is cured when he does what the prophet suggests.

Of course, Naaman wants to reward Elisha, but the prophet declines his gifts. At the end of the story, note the postscript. One of Elisha's assistants, Gehazi, decides that Naaman ought to make a donation, and if Elisha wouldn't take it then Gehazi would do so. In the end, Elisha finds out and Gehazi ends up with Naaman's leprosy.

In his book, *The Faith of the Outsider: Exclusion and Inclusion in the Biblical Story*, the Old Testament scholar, Frank Spina, explores the insider-outsider motif in the Bible. He dares to point out that much of the Biblical story is based on what scholars call the "scandal of particularity." This is apparent from the special relationship God has with the Hebrews, all the way through to the idea that "there is no other name under heaven by which humans must be saved." (Acts 4:12)

Despite the preponderance of this insider/outsider theology by biblical writers, stories like this seem to be the Spirit's work, scattering hints of another truth. In the end, this story describes the blessing of an outsider who came to God by faith, and the cursing of an insider whose greed got him in trouble.

In his first sermon in Nazareth, Jesus not only cites this story, but has the temerity to ask his listeners if they thought that there were no lepers in Israel so God had to heal a Syrian. The question almost got him killed. Suggesting that God loves others at least as much as us isn't any more popular today. How many prayers for Saddam Hussein do you suppose have been prayed in American churches?

2 KINGS

2 Kings 13-17

There are one or two more chapters of miracles worked by Elisha before the story shifts dramatically. For the rest of the book of 2 Kings the author talks mostly about Elisha and the kings of Israel and Judah. It seems that all the kings of Israel are either incompetent or evil, and that is true of many of the kings of Judah as well.

The author provides a brief commentary on the series of 19 or 20 kings who ruled over the separate countries until they were conquered. Elisha serves God for 60 years, though little is recounted about his later years. His death is recounted in 2 Kings 13. As Elisha is dying, King Joash of Israel comes to weep over him. He calls Elisha "the chariots of Israel and horsemen of Israel," which is what Elisha had called Elijah as he was taken up into heaven. The statement is meant to express the belief that the true strength of the country came not from its armies, but from his spiritual leadership.

Elisha isn't taken like Elijah, because his death is meant to prepare the reader for the fact that Israel is about to fall. Still, Elisha can't be allowed to simply die without one last sign of his spiritual power and greatness. Elisha's funeral is interrupted by a band of marauding Moabites. One of them is killed and thrown into the grave with the prophet, but, when his body touched the bones of the prophet, the Moabite was resurrected. Factual history aside, it is true that many of us have been "resurrected" by the "bones" of the great saints who have gone before us.

Eventually, we come to 2 Kings 17 where, in the absence of Elisha, the northern tribes of the nation of Israel are ultimately conquered by Assyria. Verse 24 gives an explanation of how the king of Assyria brought people from other conquered lands to settle in the northern kingdom where they began to intermarry with the Hebrews who lived there. This story is the account of the origins of the people known as the Samaritans and offers as an explanation of why the Jews of Judah distain their "half-breed" cousins who lived to their north.

Again, the writer interprets the events because, well, he was the one who paid for the pen and ink, and his account was preserved. We must be grateful, because without this account, we would know little or nothing of these days. Still, we also must read the stories remembering the values and bias of the writer. That isn't to say 1 and 2 Kings are not "inspired," but to say that God is able to speak to us through stories that were written by humans. That is a good thing to remember, because, if we begin to discard or disregard all humans who have biases or values different from our own, we will miss much of what God has to say to us. After all, that seems to be how God works.

2 KINGS

2 Kings 18

Elisha is dead and Israel conquered. The writer of the Kings and Chronicles now turns his full attention to the southern kingdom called Judah. The story of the reign of Hezekiah is described in fairly significant detail. Some scholars would argue that after Saul, David and Solomon, Hezekiah is the most important of the First Testament kings.

Hezekiah took the throne at the age of 25, and reigned for 29 years. He is one of the kings mentioned in the genealogy of Jesus with which Matthew's Gospel opens. In addition to this account in 2 Kings, 2 Chronicles 29-32 offers a similar record of his reign, filled with lavish praise. Isaiah 36-39 offers yet a third account, including a word of judgment that is closer to the account in 2 Kings than the unconditional praise of 2 Chronicles. The funny thing is that the author of 2 Chronicles refers the reader to Isaiah, preferring to let the prophet be the one to criticize. (2 Chronicles 32:32)

There was apparently a great revival of faith in the land during the reign of Hezekiah. According to the account in 2 Chronicles, he renovated the temple and re-consecrated it. Hezekiah renewed the observance of religious holidays, like Passover, and he called the people back to their faith. He himself listened to the prophet Isaiah and sought the guidance of God. He tore down the worship centers of other gods in the land.

The result was that God gave him great military victories. Hezekiah was able to repel the Assyrians and retake the territory traditionally belonging to the Jews. The writers are clear that, because Hezekiah was a righteous man, God blessed his military efforts. I believe that those two things were clearly connected; however, I'm not so sure that God was the one giving Hezekiah victory, at least not in the way the writers understood.

While I do not question that Hezekiah was sincere in all his religious reforms, it was also the most political savvy thing that he could do. He watched as Israel fell, and he must have known that, in part, the tribes to the north lost their unity and common sense of purpose when they lost Jerusalem, the temple and the Ark of the Covenant. When the nation divided after the death of Solomon, the northern tribes lost their spiritual "headquarters" and they were weakened as a federal nation. Hezekiah's religious reforms united Judah and gave them strength.

And so it is for us. I don't think God blesses the devout more than those without faith, but I do believe our faith gives our life a strength that comes from better integrating our body and soul and spirit. In that, God gives us certain victories, too.

2 KINGS

2 Kings 20:12-21

According to the author, Hezekiah seems to be the exception to the string of bad rulers for both Judah and Israel. While the southern kingdom (Judah) survived almost two centuries longer than the northern kingdom (Israel), Hezekiah's reign seemed to be the apex of that time. Toward the end of his days, the prophet Isaiah came to him predicting a gloomy future:

> *Then Isaiah said to Hezekiah, "Hear the word of the Lord: Days are coming when all that is in your house, and that which your ancestors have stored up until this day, shall be carried to Babylon; nothing shall be left, says the Lord. Some of your own sons who are born to you shall be taken away; they shall be eunuchs in the palace of the king of Babylon." Then Hezekiah said to Isaiah, "The word of the Lord that you have spoken is good." For he thought, "Why not, if there will be peace and security in my days?"*

Hezekiah's response seems to be a startlingly frank disclosure of how most political leaders apparently think. When the summer heat makes the ozone-laden air toxic, and the kids are not allowed to play outdoors, I just want to scream at politicians, "Have you no children or grandchildren?" Politicians reign as if the future is inconsequential so long as business and industry prospers while they are in office.

We run up deficits by cutting taxes on the rich while spending recklessly on the military, borrowing money from China to buy oil from autocrats in the Middle East. Run up a deficit, and let our children pay our debts …

We attacked Iraq because the political leaders hated Saddam Hussein and saw a political climate that would allow them to act. These "leaders" seemed to care less that the war would manufacture generations of terrorists that their own children and grandchildren would have to face. "Who cares, so long as there is peace and security in **MY** days?" Hezekiah asked.

He, too, practiced an outward form of religion that unified his power and allowed him to use military force against his enemies. In the end, he didn't really care what would ultimately befall his nation or his children after he was gone. While it is not said as a criticism of him by the author, Hezekiah's statement says all I need to know about the kind of person he really was and the kind of person so many of our current-day political leaders really are. If they are not willing to plant trees under which they will not sit, then they have nowhere to lead us.

2 KINGS

2 Kings 22:14-20

After the death of Hezekiah, there are two kings over Judah about which nothing said is good. Manasseh became king at the age of 12 and reigned for 55 years. Amon only reigned for two years before his own servants killed him. Since he took office at the age of 22, we are left to assume he died at age 24. He then is succeeded by his son Josiah, who was eight. Talk about your teenage fathers …

Still despite the young age when he became the ruler, Josiah was a good king. He repaired the temple and apparently in the process, rediscovered a book of the law, which is often believed to be a section of the book of Deuteronomy. When it was read to him, he was deeply moved (Kings 22:11) and called the people to return to being faithful to the law.

In verse 14, we meet a prophetess named Huldah. She predicts the destruction of Judah, which her male counterparts also had predicted, but she affirmed that King Josiah's life and reign would be blessed. Huldah also is referred to in 2 Chronicles 34:22, though we are told almost nothing about her or her life. In fact, we are told more about her husband. What is remarkable, of course, is that here we find a woman speaking for God in an age of incredible sexism.

She must have been quite remarkable for the king to have sought her out when there were many other prophets in Judah he might have consulted. This fact may speak volumes about the true character of Josiah. He was brave enough to listen to someone who was marginalized. Huldah was so gifted that even the avalanche of historic sexism was unable to cover up her life and ministry.

What we have is an image of the conjunction of political and positional power as well as inner and spiritual power. Huldah says, "Tell the man who sent you," (v. 15) with scant regard that "the man" was the king. She drew her authority from her relationship with God and had already determined for herself that she would not be defined or controlled by any man, and that included the king. This courage of self-definition is as rare as the voice of God plainly spoken.

What would it take for us to throw off the oppression of others who define us and tell what it means to be "a man," "a woman," "a lesbian," "a lawyer," "a pastor," etc? What courage would it take to define ourselves and find our own voice? Only you can answer that, but I am convinced that doing that is critical if God is ever to speak to us and through us with power.

2 KINGS

2 Kings 23

Following the prophecy of Huldah, the uniquely recognized woman prophet of Judah, there was a season of great renewal. The nation returned to the radical monotheism that historically had been both the hallmark of the Jewish faith and the unifier of the Jewish people. The writer is unrestrained in his praise of King Josiah and his reformation. It is clear, of course, that the priest who is writing this text greatly appreciated the religious fervor by which the king led. Nothing whatsoever is said about Josiah's military or political leadership.

The account of Josiah's death in 2 Kings is different from the account in 2 Chronicles, but, in both places, it appears that he does not die peacefully as the prophet had foretold. He apparently picks a strange fight with the Pharaoh of Egypt, resulting in his death. His death is interpreted as a sign that he had displeased God by getting involved in this fight. No warning shot, he was just dead.

I suppose one lesson in this is that good people do often make mistakes that cost them dearly. Even being good and righteous and holy doesn't guarantee that you are wise, or even smart. Or maybe it is just a reminder that just because we are good people doesn't mean we can't be wrong, and that all our goodness doesn't insure us against consequences.

Whatever the lesson, this was a terrible ending for a good man. The interesting thing is that, while this story is written many years after Josiah's death, the author doesn't make his end the summary of his life. That takes a maturity of grace. I mean, think about how hard it is to remember all the good with relationships that have come to a bad end. A person makes a terrible mistake, and suddenly they are defined by that mistake and all the good of their life seems forgotten. How often have I seen people leave a church because of something someone said or did? Years of good are forgotten by a single act.

Josiah came to a bad ending. The judgment of history, or at least the scripture, was that his destruction was his own fault. The best of us make bad choices and that is an important thing to remember when we are being critical of others. It is also important to remember this example of scripture that refused to disregard all of the good just because of a bad ending.

We all make bad decisions, but that doesn't make us bad people. That is also true of others, which is something people of grace should remember.

2 KINGS

2 Kings 24-25

The end comes very quickly in this account of history. It is almost like the scroll on which the author was writing was about to run out, so he describes the reign of Jehoiakim and the conquest of Judah in just a few words. The small nation had survived more than two centuries longer than Israel, their cousins to the north. But, in the end, they fell too. The Babylonian king Nebuchadnezzar was just too powerful.

The theologians and prophets declared that it was God's judgment upon the nation, but historians say that Judah was just one of the many small states to fall to a series of empires that arose in this age. The Assyrians, Babylonians, Chaldeans, Persians, Greeks and then Romans all came to dominate that region of the world.

The author describes the destruction of the temple, Jerusalem and Judah in the last chapter of 2 Kings. Artisans, scholars, priests and leaders are either killed or taken into captivity back to Babylon. In the prophetic book of Daniel, we read about some of Nebuchadnezzar's captives. For now, though, this period of history has come to an end. The slaves that Moses led out of Egypt have lost their independence. No longer does a king rule from the throne of David.

This part of both 2 Kings and 2 Chronicles seems abrupt and sudden, but that is the way of endings. Despite the prophet's repeated warnings, no one quite believed that it could happen. That is true for us as mortals, just as it is for nations. Perhaps it is impossible to actually believe that death really comes to us. Like Judah, we get lots of warnings but continue to live as if it really doesn't apply to us.

Judah and Jerusalem's end is also described at the close of the book of the prophet Jeremiah. He tells the story, but it is in the book called Lamentations that the feelings of this event are most fully captured:

> *How lonely sits the city that was full of people*
> *How like a widow has she become, she that was great among the nations ...*
> *She weeps bitterly in the night, tears on her cheeks;*
> *Among all her lovers she has none to comfort her...*
> *Judah has gone into exile because of affliction and hard servitude*
> *She dwells not among the nations but finds no resting place.*
>
> Lamentations 1:1-3

So, the history of the Hebrews moves from Exodus to exile. Both are states of the human soul, and like them, many of us know more of the emptiness of exile than we do of the joy of exodus. Still, in both Exodus or exile, the Jews remained God's children. In the pages ahead, maybe we will learn to detect God's presence even in the exiles of life.

CHRONICLES

So far, we have read through the first 12 books of the Bible and have been taking our time as we look at the stories that shaped the faith of the Hebrews and of Jesus. Since our plan is to finish the First Testament by the end of the year, we'll move more quickly through the next 27 books. With just five more books of history, moving at a quicker pace will be fairly easy. In fact, why don't we tackle two books today?

Following our study of 1 and 2 Kings, we come to 1 and 2 Chronicles. We can pass over this information quickly because we have studied it all before. In fact, most of it closely parallels the information found in the books we just finished.

Most of us have probably made New Year's resolutions to read the Bible from cover to cover. Unfortunately, 1 Chronicles is one of the obstacles where many became discouraged and quit. The first nine chapters are genealogical tables that would cure the most virulent insomniac. The author then focuses on the period in Hebrew history during the reigns of various kings. He mentions King Saul, the first king of the unified nation, but only notes that his reign ended badly because he was not faithful to God.

David gets a bit more attention, though curiously, his record is whitewashed. This version of David's life leaves out the sordid tale of Bathsheba, as well as David's other failings. This fact is rather interesting considering the author starts with Adam and ends with Israel being conquered by Nebuchadnezzar. It just goes to show that making a story long doesn't necessarily make it complete.

Clearly, the writer wants us to think well of David and regard his, and Solomon's subsequent reign, as the apex of the nation. It undoubtedly was that by almost any measure, but greatness is always accompanied by faults and failings. As Freud tried to teach us, repressing the bad only weakens the good. Recounting the reigns of these two great kings without noting their faults and failings only makes them into artificial caricatures.

That seems to be a lesson for us all to learn. Denying our faults, failures and weaknesses never makes us better people, only more artificial.

EZRA

So Kings and Chronicles end with the fall of Judah at the hands of Nebuchadnezzar. We will return to various points in this history when we look at some of the Psalms and the prophets. The books of Ezra, Nehemiah and Esther are all set in the time after the conquest, a period often referred to as "The Exile."

Ezra was a priestly scribe who apparently led about 5,000 exiles from Babylon back to Jerusalem. In that day (458 BCE) such a move would have been considered a mass migration. The book describes the return of the people, the rebuilding of the temple and the restoration of Jewish faith and practice. It was this later act by Ezra that caused him to be greatly esteemed by Jews in subsequent generations.

I suspect Ezra wasn't universally revered in his day, however. When he returned to Jerusalem, he discovered that many of the citizens who had remained had married outside the faith. He literally had a fit:

> *When I heard this, I tore my garment and my mantle, and pulled hair from my head and beard, and sat appalled.*
>
> Ezra 9:3

He then demanded that the marriages be annulled. In chapter 10, he makes a list of the offending priests whose marriages were annulled and whose wives and children were sent away. And, remember, Ezra is one of the "good guys."

It is a classic example of what is so often bad about religion. Ezra is a good person, a leader and liberator, a person of great faith and moral devotion. He does historic good for thousands of people, but his particular brand of religion blinded him to what was most important in life. Ezra was a man who believed that the rules were the highest objective good, elevating them even above love, relationships and family. This seems to be the most significant correction that Jesus came to bring.

To Jesus, there was no rule greater than love. The grace that Jesus taught as a devout Jewish rabbi wasn't in contradiction to his religion; it was foundational to it. Followers of Jesus have often made the same mistake that Ezra made putting the form of faith before the substance of it. I have comforted hundreds of people over the years who were cast out of their faith because they were lesbian or gay. Many were cast out of their families at the insistence of the church.

In a world of chaos—like the one in which Ezra lived—rules and regulations offer order and control. Love is messy. If you are not careful, you just might find yourself in a relationship that doesn't live by the rules. While Ezra would annul it, I don't think Jesus would have done that. Jesus was a lot less afraid of the chaos love causes.

NEHEMIAH

The last three historical books of the First Testament (Ezra, Nehemiah and Esther) are in the period called "The Exile." After the conquest of Judah, thousands of citizens apparently were taken away into exile by their conquerors. Ezra recounts the return of many of those exiles and the conditions they found. The book of Nehemiah continues the story. In fact, in the Jewish Bible, Ezra and Nehemiah are combined into one book.

Ezra was a priest who led exiles back to Jerusalem and used his heroic status to restore the practice of the traditional Jewish faith. Nehemiah followed Ezra home 12 years later and apparently served the Persian king Artaxerxes as the governor of the land.

I've always loved the story of Nehemiah for several reasons. First, he was someone who took on a tough task and, in many ways, a thankless job when he might have continued a life of luxury and ease. Nehemiah somehow had risen in the Persian court to become the cupbearer of the king. I've never been exactly clear what a cupbearer did, but it certainly couldn't have been too stressful.

Nehemiah became depressed after he learned the desperate condition of the city of his birth. Noticing his mood, the king asked him what was wrong. This inquiry alone is a testament to how highly Nehemiah was regarded. Why would a king care about a mere servant's mood? Further, when the king discovered the reason, he gave Nehemiah a leave of absence and the resources with which to return to the city and begin the restoration process.

This story is a parable about how the way we live our lives can make allies of enemies. There are many with whom we may disagree who can be partners in areas of service. What a foolish thing to dismiss people who may think or vote differently than we do on certain issues when they might be our allies for larger more important causes.

Nehemiah is also a model of one who was willing to set personal comfort, luxury and success aside for the greater good of the people. For every Wall Street billionaire and Harvard legal tycoon, there are women and men who choose to use their education, energy and influence to help the poor and marginalized. Our job is to remember and honor them while the media makes heroes of the others. It is also our job to follow their example as well as Nehemiah's.

NEHEMIAH

Nehemiah returned from exile in Persia and led the rebuilding of the walls and temple of Jerusalem. My fondness for him and his story may rest in the fact that, like him, much of my ministry has been unexpectedly spent building and rebuilding. I also should probably confess that I appreciate the fact that Nehemiah is a Biblical hero about whom no bad is spoken, despite the fact that he was a eunuch.

Traditionally, a eunuch was a castrated slave, which is possible. However, Jesus pointed out that there are those who are *made* eunuchs and those who are *born* eunuchs. (Matthew 19:12) I hardly think he was speaking of those very rare men who may be born with a genital birth defect. Rather, I believe he referred to those who, by nature, do not have sexual relationships with women. Episcopal priest Tom Horne suggests that Jesus was referring without judgment to homosexuals. Slaves who served the queen or women of the royal house would much more likely have been the latter type of eunuch since men who had their testicles removed could not reproduce but could still rape the queen or princesses. Nehemiah 2:6 makes it a point of placing him in the presence of the queen.

This is more than can be explored in a devotion, but what is significant is, regardless of the "type" of eunuch Nehemiah was, he would have been regarded by many in his religion as "unclean" and unacceptable. There was a law that banned eunuchs from the inner courts of the temple. Later in the prophecy of Isaiah, eunuchs and those at the margins are promised a special name and a special place. (Isaiah 56:3-5)

Regardless, Nehemiah knew how many, perhaps most, who shared his faith felt about him. Despite that, he would not allow their view to block his relationship with God and his compassion for those in need. The bulk of the first chapter of Nehemiah is his prayer of intercession on behalf of the people.

Nehemiah refused to be defined by his sexuality, by his job as cupbearer of the king or by the opinions of religious authority. Central to his life and his identity was his relationship with God. Everything else radiated through his life from that core. This relationship gave his life purpose beyond his vocation, and beyond his cultural identity. It also gave him courage and determination to defy the judgment of others and live into the vision God had given him. How else would a marginalized slave become the leader who would rebuild the city? How else will we become all that God dreams for us?

NEHEMIAH

The book of Nehemiah is a record of how he led the people to rebuild the city of Jerusalem. Chapter 2 ends with a moving call to the people:

> *I told them that the hand of my God had been gracious upon me, and also the words that the king had spoken to me. Then they said, "Let us start building!" So they committed themselves to the common good.*
>
> Nehemiah 2:18

Amazing things are possible when a leader calls people to commit themselves to the common good. It has been a long time since we have had that kind of leadership in this country, I'm afraid.

The one thing about the book of Nehemiah that should not be neglected is the fact that much of it is a record of all the opposition that he faced. Obviously, the enemies of the Jews did not want them refortifying the city. They accused him of betraying his patron, the king, and tried to twist what they were doing to make it seem disloyal and unpatriotic. (Nehemiah 4)

When that didn't work, they tried to make the people so afraid that they would betray their own values and turn against the project. (Nehemiah 5) Finally, when neither of those tactics stopped him, the enemies tried distraction. They called him to come down from the wall and negotiate with them. To that, Nehemiah replied:

> *I am doing a great work and I cannot come down. Why should the work stop while I leave it to come down to you?*
>
> Nehemiah 6:3

In the days following the events of September 11, 2001, I often thought about this story. As tragic as those malevolent attacks were, no terrorist organization could muster the military might to destroy the United States. What disturbed me, though, was how easily they managed to divert us and distract us. They couldn't defeat us, but they could make us change how we lived. They made us divert trillions of dollars from education, healthcare and social services to militarism. Worst of all, they made us abandon some of our most profound core values and revert to preemptive warfare and torture.

While it would be easy enough to simply blame our leaders in Washington, the truth is we were the ones brought down. The towers were not all that fell that day. What it meant to be an American fell, and, given the witness of much of the Church in this country, what it meant to be Christian came down too.

Nehemiah understood that there were many roads to defeat, and being distracted from the greatness to which God calls all people is one of the swiftest routes down.

ESTHER

The book of Esther describes events that took place after 465 BCE. The first wave of exiles returned to Jerusalem, but the story of Esther concerns events in the lives of those who had not returned. Whether they had not been allowed to return or they had become so settled in Persia is difficult to tell. If Mordecai and Esther's lives are any example, it appears that some of the Jews gained a great deal of success in the land of their enemies.

In the book, after a series of challenges, Esther becomes Queen of Persia, and her cousin Mordecai becomes the prime minister. Together, they use their positions to save the Jews who were still in Persia from being massacred. Their bravery is celebrated on the Jewish holiday of Purim.

The best known part of the story is when Esther doesn't want to risk her position and, perhaps, her life to intervene. Mordecai says to her, "Who knows, but perhaps you have come into this kingdom for just such a time as this." (Esther 4:14) Esther is deeply moved and decides to do whatever it takes to save her people, even at the cost of her own life.

Preachers love this story and this text because it gives us a chance to ask our congregations to ponder if perhaps we have been placed where we are in life "for just such a time as this." It is a healthy question for us all to ask, because surely our lives have more value than pleasure and profit, but it is up to us to discover that value. Esther had gained much, and, though it was tough, she risked it all. Mordecai's challenge was powerful, but, clearly, it simply evoked who Esther really was as a person.

That may be the problem for us. Esther was beautiful. She was so beautiful that the king, who could choose to marry any woman, married her. As a result, she literally had it all! Such position, power, wealth and comfort are addictive. It is so addictive that it often keeps us from doing what is right because the price seems too high. Esther enjoyed what she had but obviously wasn't addicted, because she did what was right. And no preacher, no matter how effective, can motivate us to pay the price of giving up our addictions. That is something only we can do. It is an internal battle we must fight. When we come to "such a time as this" what we do and how we live may be helped by external encouragement, but it will be determined by our true internal identity.

JOB

Today, we come to the section of the First Testament that contains the literature of the Jews and early Christians. The book of Job is considered by many scholars as the oldest book in the Bible. That, of course, makes it one of the oldest preserved writings of humankind.

While I cannot substantiate the age of the writing, I do know that the subject of this book is one of the oldest struggles for people of faith: *Why do bad things happen to good people?* This ancient story seeks to offer a kind of explanation, but not really an answer.

The book, which appears to me to be a parable, begins with an introduction to Job's character. According to the parable, God is bragging to Satan about what a good servant Job is for God. Satan says, "Of course he is righteous. You've given him everything he wants or needs, so of course he serves you. Let bad things happen to him, though, and he'll turn against you." God says, "Okay, prove it." Thus, Job begins a season of great suffering in his life.

Now, this story might not be quite so bad if Job had just been the only pawn God and Satan played with, but his livestock and family were killed along with him. The death of innocents seems totally incidental to the point of this parable, though, which is the problem with so much of religion … but don't get me started.

The main portion of the text consists of the discourse between Job and his three friends concerning why Job had been so punished, and it ends with God answering Job. The Lord blessed the latter days of Job more than his beginning, and he lived a long 140 years. Many scholars believe the end was added much later in an attempt to redeem God's reputation. To me, it doesn't help.

Actually, though, if you look at it as a parable, which allows you simply to set aside the irrelevant parts, the story is a powerful reminder that when we are suffering and asking why, we are just the latest in the common history of humanity. Apparently, we always have wanted our suffering to mean something, and the message of Job is that sometimes, it just doesn't. When we try to give it artificial meaning, as this author did, we almost always end up making a monster out of God. In Job 40:8, God asks, "Will you condemn me to justify yourself?" If history is any indication, the answer is yes.

PSALMS

The word, Psalms literally means "song." You could say that this was the hymnal of Jesus and the ancient Jews. Many of the Psalms are attributed to King David, though it is unlikely he wrote any or all of them. However, some may well have been commissioned by him or during the time of his reign, so, in that sense, I suppose they are songs of David.

It would be well worthwhile for us to examine the Psalms one by one. However, there are 150 Psalms and we must hurry on if we are to finish this survey by the end of the year. Today, let me introduce you to the whole body, and then we will look at a couple of specific Psalms that are favorites of mine.

Like almost all of the Bible, the Psalms were sung or spoken, and eventually recorded in Hebrew. It was eventually translated into Greek, then Latin and then into English. As a result, it is stunning that the Psalms have retained their poetry or beauty. The series of translations have resulted in some numbering challenges. Ultimately, the Protestant Bible has sought to use the Hebrew numbers, but in the Greek Bible (upon which the Catholic and Orthodox scholars originally relied), the Psalms were sometimes combined or divided differently.

Unless you have a Bible with an Apocrypha, you probably don't have Psalm 151 in your Bible. It is ascribed to David after he fought Goliath. This is what it says:

I was small among my brothers,
and the youngest in my father's house;
I tended my father's sheep.
My hands made a harp;
my fingers fashioned a lyre.
And who will tell my Lord?
The Lord himself; it is he who hears.
It was he who sent his messenger
and took me from my father's sheep,
and anointed me with his anointing-oil.
My brothers were handsome and tall,
but the Lord was not pleased with them.
I went out to meet the Philistine,
and he cursed me by his idols.
But I drew his own sword;
I beheaded him, and took away disgrace from the people of Israel.

This Psalm was left out of the canon by some scholars because they believe it was originally written in Greek, not Hebrew. Then it was found in the original language with the Dead Sea Scrolls. So you see the Bible that fundamentalists worship was much more a product of chance and opinion than they like to believe. On the other hand, given the age of the Bible, how often it has been translated and mistranslated, and how badly it has been interpreted by religious leaders, I think the fact that we ever get any good from it is proof of Divine inspiration.

PSALMS

Psalm 42

Almost everyone is familiar with the 23rd Psalm. In fact, it is probably the best known song or piece of poetry in the world. It is remarkably beautiful and powerful given its familiarity and how far we are removed from its origins.

One of my personal favorites is Psalm 42. It has been popularized by the Christian chorus built on the psalm's opening words:

As the deer panteth for the water, so my soul longeth after thee.

It is a beautiful image, made all the more endearing to me because a literal translation would use the word "doe." It has been suggested that this may be the only psalm recorded whose author was a woman. It seems to be the song of a woman who is struggling with depression but finding the strength not to despair: *Why are you downcast O my soul, Hope in God, for I shall yet praise the One who is my help and my God.*

The song weaves back and forth between sadness and hope, and the author resolutely returns to choose hope, regardless of the circumstances or how she was feeling:

Deep calls to deep at the thunder of your cataracts;
and all your waves billow over me.
By day the Lord commands steadfast love;
and at night a song is with me, a prayer to the God of my life.

Psalm 42:7-8

The beauty of this woman's faith is that she doesn't trust and praise God because she has slain the giants threatening her life; rather she trusts and praises God despite the fact that she has not. True faith is like a star; it is best seen when the night is darkest. This woman has great faith because she expresses her devotion and trust, even in the midst of her own discouragement.

Sometimes when my own faith seems to have evaporated, I recite the words of this ancient wise woman who I call Sophia. At times, I let her faith be mine. When I cannot pray or praise, I read her words and I let her do it for me.

Maybe that is where you are today, or maybe you know someone who is there. Why don't you give them this Psalm to help?

PSALMS

What a shame we don't have time to explore the psalms more thoroughly. Saints through the ages have found the Psalms to be a great source of strength and inspiration. On the cross Jesus cries aloud the opening words of Psalm 22: *My God, my God, why have you forsaken me?* It is possible that, like many of the devout of his day, Jesus had committed all the psalms to memory and recited them under his breath in that time of torture. At that moment, the psalm must have reflected what Jesus was feeling, or perhaps it was an accurate description of his own spiritual reality.

Of course, the Gospels give us a context for that verse, but I wonder what those who read the words for centuries must have thought it meant. In fact, as beautiful as the psalms are, there are a number of places that give me pause. I'm always amazed while reading a beautiful, uplifting passage when suddenly the whole thing goes off the rails. It happens again and again in the Bible. The people begin praising and worshipping God, but then they apparently open their eyes and look around. It is as if they are reminded of how they had been conquered and oppressed by their enemy. All they can think to say expresses that pain and anger.

There are many vengeful passages in the psalms. The most famous of course is found in Psalm 137:9: *Blessed are those who take your babies and dash them against the rocks.* (Try quoting that next time a fundamentalist insists that the Bible is the literal word of God.) That Psalm begins by describing how the Jews taken into captivity sat down by the rivers of Babylon and wept. It isn't a song of faith or hope but the record of such absolute and utter despair that they felt like doing to the enemies the worst they could imagine. You don't read Psalms like this for inspiration or hope, but you need to remember the context in which they were written.

I actually think the author of this Psalm was probably a very good and devout man who records the lowest moment of his life when he was at his absolute worst. Sister Helen Prejean asked us to think about how any of our lives would be judged if all that was ever seen was that moment when we were at our absolute worst.

Maybe the psalmist was holding up a mirror to remind us of our own capacity for evil, vengeance and even violence. Maybe that is what Jesus meant when he warned that if we commit these things in our hearts, we have responsibility for them. Maybe if we all remembered our own worst times, we'd be a little more merciful with others at their worst … at least most of us don't go around bashing babies for Jesus.

Psalm 51

For some reason, my Systematic Theology professor required all of his students to memorize Psalm 51. He preferred we learn it in Hebrew or Greek, but English was acceptable for those of us who had not taken the Biblical languages. Fortunately for me, I was allowed to memorize it in English. It was not only easier to memorize, but I have retained it long after my knowledge of ancient languages faded.

This psalm is ascribed to David as a song of repentance. He sang it after his liaison with Bathsheba. To be more accurate, David repented after the prophet Nathan confronted him about his sin with Bathsheba and after their conceived child had died. One wonders if he would have ever repented if he had not been caught or if tragedy had not struck. Oh sure, there are times when our conscience just won't leave us alone, but imagine how often it does.

Think of how often we rationalize our behavior, values, words or deeds. Maybe it will help to remember all those times other people have acted rudely, or irresponsibly, or selfishly, or cruelly, without even knowing they had done anything wrong. Then assume that they have just as often thought the same of you and me. It is tough for us to repent when we are so self-absorbed that we never even know we've sinned.

Maybe that is why my professor had me memorize this psalm. Perhaps he thought it might be an accurate and healthy exercise to cry out every day with David:

> *Have mercy upon me, O God, according to* ***your*** *steadfast love; according to your abundant mercy blot out my transgressions. Wash me thoroughly from my iniquity and cleanse me from my sin ...*
>
> *Create in me a clean heart, O God and put a new and right spirit within me, Do not cast me away from your presence and do not take your Spirit from me. Restore to me the joy of your salvation, and sustain in me a generous spirit.*

I know that we liberals have tried to escape the way fundamentalists have used the concept of sin to control behavior they don't like. I also know that we liberals still sin. We are still thoughtless, unkind, self-absorbed and arrogant. Maybe if we regularly prayed this prayer of Israel's most successful king, we might be more aware of our own need for God's help in assuring that we have a right spirit of joy and generosity.

Today, challenge yourself to memorize Psalm 51.

PROVERBS

Just as the book called Psalms is an anthology of songs by various authors, the book called Proverbs is a collection of short pithy sayings that, although often credited to Solomon, have numerous origins. The book of Proverbs is referred to as "wisdom literature" along with several other books including the book of Job, Ecclesiastes and Song of Solomon, as well as several apocryphal books.

The proverbs contained in this book cover a wide range of topics, including social evils and concern for the poor. My personal preference is found in Proverbs 11:25, which says that *the liberal soul shall prosper ...*

Of course, I don't think the author was using the word "liberal" the way I do. Actually, though, I think progressive/liberal causes would be well served by linking the word *liberal* to the word *generous.* If fundamentalism is a more fear-based philosophy of life, then liberalism ought to set us free to be more generous, optimistic and hopeful.

This collection of proverbs ends with two chapters of wisdom from Agur son of Jakeh and King Lemuel. Ironically, no one has a clue about either of these people. As a gay man, I'm amused by the fact that it appears that chapter 31 isn't really the wisdom of King Lemuel, but of his mother. She warns him against "giving his strength to women" (v. 3), which could be a euphemism for sex. Then she warns him against strong drink. (v. 4) I do appreciate that she tells him that he is to stand up for the destitute, the poor and the needy. That is advice I wish mothers always gave to leaders, though I'm not sure the message would be heard.

It is in King Lemuel's mother's advice that we find the description of the "virtuous woman." (vv. 10-31) While this passage might be interpreted today as sexist and oppressive to women, there is still some wisdom that might help women push back against the sexist way the "beauty industry" tries to force women into its mold—a mold designed by and for men.

Charm is deceitful and beauty is vain, but a woman who loves God is to be praised. (v. 30)

The fact that this book of the Bible ends with a large set of teachings for women is worthy of attention in an age that often regarded women as property. Here is a mother, using her son's position, to give advice to young women. To these women she also teaches that virtue is caring for the poor. (v. 20) Hence we end the book of Proverbs with the word of a woman who is liberal in more than one sense of that word.

ECCLESIASTES

The word *ecclesiastes* means "preacher" (hence our word "ecclesiastical"). This is rather strange, because, traditionally, the book has been attributed to King Solomon. The book opens saying, "The words of the Preacher, the son of David, king of Jerusalem." (v. 1)

The content of the book emphatically proclaims all the actions of humans to be inherently "vain," "futile," "empty," "meaningless," "temporary," "transitory" or "fleeting," depending on translation. The author notes that this is because the lives of both the wise and the foolish end in death. While the author clearly endorses wisdom as a means for a well-lived life, no eternal meaning or value is ascribed to it. In light of this ultimate futility, the author's advice is that one should enjoy the simple pleasures such as eating, drinking and enjoying one's spouse and work, which are gifts from the hand of God.

Much of the book of Ecclesiastes is about death, and the author seems pretty cynical as illustrated in the opening words, "Vanity, vanity, all is vanity." Ultimately, I think the point is that unless we live in such a way that we are obedient and our lives bring glory to God, we have really wasted our time. Maybe the strategy is to remind us of our mortality and of the fleeting nature of life. The hope is that, remembering that, we will spend our days for a higher purpose than investing ourselves in that which will not last.

Maybe the preacher in Ecclesiastes was the author of an ancient version of *The Purpose Driven Life*. Perhaps like the preacher Rick Warren, Ecclesiastes is trying to get us to discover, or at least remember, the purpose of a life that endures beyond death. The life lived for self is ultimately lived in vain because it ends in death and is soon forgotten.

While evangelical Christianity tries to get us to focus on where we spend eternity, I'm more concerned with how we spend this life. That seemed to be true for this author as well. Still, the writer knew that, unless we spent this life in such a way that we left behind a good influence and a better place, all the rest was truly vanity.

While I might have said it more positively, I actually agree with the point of the book:
Take pleasure from the simple gifts that are yours. Appreciate them while you have them because you won't have them nearly as long as it seemed when we were kids. And, as you celebrate the gifts of God in this life, trust your tomorrow to God and make as much of a difference as you can. Live your life in such a way that the ultimate judgment is good. Give more than you take and leave behind a better place than you found, because anything else is pure self-absorbed vanity.

SONG OF SOLOMON

Today and tomorrow, we will conclude our whirlwind tour through the wisdom literature of the Bible as we look at the Song of Solomon, or, as it is sometimes called, the Song of Songs.

Some say this is the "dirty book" of the Bible. In chapter 5:1, drunken celebration is encouraged and celebrated. In verses that follow, the woman describes in some detail what her lover does to her body. (vv. 5 and 6) So explicit is the writing in some places that there was an ancient rabbinical tradition that held that Jewish men could not read this book until they were 30 years old. Many claim that the book is merely an allegory of Israel's relationship with God. Those are probably the same people who think you shouldn't learn about sex until you are 30 …

Song of Solomon is one of the shortest in the Bible, and it traces a relationship between two lovers from courtship to consummation. The book is attributed to King Solomon and with 700 wives and 300 concubines, such attribution is not surprising, though one wonders when he had time to write anything. The Solomon tradition is very strong, which poses a problem for those who would hold up the book as scriptural evidence of God blessing monogamous relationships. If this were the case, one is left to wonder which of Solomon's wives with whom he was monogamous and who really was the father of all those other children. Today, the Church of Jesus Christ of Latter-day Saints (Mormons) do not recognize this book as a part of sacred scripture.

The point is that this book has always proved challenging to sex-negative religious leaders, both Jewish and Christian. It is a passionate love poem void of moralism that does not attempt to impose controls. Much of the content is quite explicit and sensual. What is most refreshing is that this is one of the earliest and certainly the most revered record of women being overtly sexual. There were many more modern centuries where the sexuality of half the human race was repressed and denied by academics and moralists.

Yet here we have a biblical witness that the sexuality of woman, and by implication all marginalized people, is a sacred gift from God. Here, at the center of the Bible, we find a book celebrating human sexuality and sensuality. Missing this fact has had terrible consequences for humankind. Religion has taken one of the greatest gifts offered to us by God and made it a source of embarrassment and shame. As you read this love poem, I believe the utter lack of shame by both genders is a sign that this book is inspired by God … that and the fact that fundamentalists haven't torn it out yet.

SONG OF SOLOMON

Next week we begin our journey through the prophets, but, before we do, I want to spend one last moment with the most sexual book in the Bible. The reason to tarry here is not really that the writing is so great or the lessons so important; it is to raise the issue of how the Church has practiced what I call "sexcommunication" without reading the whole Bible.

It seems that every time most of the Church speaks about sex, there is opposition:

- Mainline churches are against adult sexual material, labeling it pornographic.
- They are against sex education, saying it should be left to the home. Yeah, right. As if many parents teach their kids about sex as much as Sunday school teachers.
- Regarding sex, the only option for young people—the population that is at its sexual peak—is to tell them no. Texas spends more on abstinence-only education and has the highest teen pregnancy rate in the country.
- And they are really against homosexuality.
- In fact, they are against any sexual expression between consenting adults outside the bounds of traditional marriage.
- The Roman Catholic Church is against birth control, even in the confines of marriage.
- They are against priests and nuns getting married, which says that if you really want to be holy **you** won't have sex either. It is as if sex somehow corrupts or contaminates our spirituality.

And the truth is, it does. Oh, not sex in and of itself. Sex is nothing more or less than a physical act like eating or sleeping. What gets in the way of our spiritual health is all the guilt and shame we have attached to sex and sexuality. The Church has excommunicated **ALL** sexual expression except that which results in procreation. The consequences of this narrow-minded attitude have been disastrous for humanity.

Since religion is trusted to provide a moral compass for our society, it seems we must either accept the church's distorted view of sexual morality or live as if there are no sexual morals at all. I believe part of what it means for us to be a 21st-century church is that we are to bring sex back to church. We must reclaim it as the wonderful, glorious gift of God that it is. God could have created humans like other species. In the animal kingdom most species only experience strong sexual drives every few months when procreation is a possibility. In humans, that would mean we would feel sexual only once a month.

The truth is, for humans, sexual energy is a part of almost every hour of every day. It is a gift meant for much more than just procreation. According to the Song of

Solomon, sexuality, and sensuality have a sacred place in the Bible and in the lives of the people of God.

Like any gift, it can be misused and abused. However, I can't help but wonder how much of our misuse of our sexuality comes from repression and guilt? For example, in the United States, the rate of alcohol addiction is many times higher than it is in countries like France or Italy where they serve wine with almost every meal. In those countries, even children are served diluted wine with their meals. It is no big deal and does no apparent harm. It might be argued that the number one cause of the high rate of alcoholism is this **prohibition**.

THE PROPHETS

The last section of the First Testament is known as "The Prophets." There are four "major" prophets (Isaiah, Jeremiah, Ezekiel and Daniel) and 12 "minor" prophets. Those designations are purely based on size, and have no relevance to the importance or impact of the prophet. Isaiah and Jeremiah were quite important, but Ezekiel and Daniel are mostly just lengthy books.

The other misunderstanding that we should clear up as we enter these last weeks in this testament is just what is meant by the word "prophet." In modern terms, we may think of the preacher yelling on the street corner who seems like a crazy uncle we don't want to claim. Another idea is that a prophet is someone who predicts the future. While the biblical prophets often did deliver a word from God about what was to come, their words often have been reinterpreted by modern apocalyptic writers to force them to speak about today's events. The only value in that exercise seems to be the millions of dollars that have been put in the pockets of these modern writers/preachers.

The truth is, nearly 2,800 years ago—about the time that Homer was creating the *Iliad* and the *Odyssey*—a movement arose among the Hebrews that lasted about 300 years starting around 750 BCE with the prophet Amos. Prophets arose as a supplement to the voice of the priests, who primarily interpreted and enforced the law and the religious practices that they traced back to Moses. The prophets came to the people bringing a word from God. While that word was sometimes hopeful and comforting, it was also quite often confrontational and rebuking. They were social critics, and were not reluctant to confront those in power, as well as the common person.

As you might imagine, they were not beloved or universally popular people. Unlike those who seek to speak words of critique today, the prophets of Israel didn't gain financial reward, high ratings or a following of fans. They tried to speak what they believed was truth, and no one was safe from their reprimand. We are left to consider what might happen today if a prophet were to walk into the White House or the Kremlin and confront the leaders there in the way that Nathan confronted King David. We also might do well to wonder what might happen if a prophet were to wander into our house …

ISAIAH

Isaiah is considered a major prophet in more ways than one. It is the most important of the written works attributed to prophets. The New Testament alludes to or quotes from it more than 250 times. It is a rich book in terms of its theology, and it strongly shaped the belief systems of Jesus' day and, hence, of ours.

Much of our understanding of the Messiah is derived from the writings of Isaiah. When both Israel and Judah finally fell, it appeared that God's covenant with David had failed. It is hard for people of faith to believe that God had gotten it wrong, but it may have been even harder to believe that they themselves had gotten it wrong. The covenant was that God would establish David's throne forever. Once there was no Hebrew on the throne, the Jews were left to figure out what that promise meant.

The idea of a messiah who was a descendant of David and who would rise up to reunite and reestablish the nation was not universally accepted among the Jews. Of course, Christians interpreted Jesus as the messiah of Isaiah's prophecy. It also should be noted that the word "messiah" is somewhat like the word "angels." While the word "angel" simply means messenger, a rather elaborate mythology has risen up around the messengers. So, while the word "messiah" (or Christ) simply means "anointed," as you know, it came to be understood as much more than simply a leader anointed with oil.

This conversation is important because we must decide if we are going to read Isaiah as if he were writing about Jesus and events that would take place centuries later, or as if he was a prophet for his time whose words also might influence ours. Of course, most objective readers would claim the latter, but I am not sure it is even possible to read some of these passages without seeing Christmas cards and hearing Handel. However, I do think we should try.

Regardless of which verses of the Bible we read, it seems impossible for us to FIRST hear what the author truly meant. It is like listening to the news during a political campaign. What is said is shaped dramatically by the speaker's point of view, values and employer. We know this and choose our channels consistent with our own values. Regardless of what we hear or read, we do this through the lens of our own views, values and experience.

The truth is that those who wrote the New Testament's interpretation of Isaiah did so through the lens of their experience with Jesus and tried to make the prophet's words speak about their own day. Is there ANY hope that we might hear what was said and meant without filters? I believe that, like most of life, just being aware of our filters leads us closer to the truth.

ISAIAH

Isaiah 1-6

The book of Isaiah begins by identifying the author, his father and the period during which the prophet lived. This work claims to span four of the kings of Judah, which would be about a 50-year period. It also should be noted that the work is referred to as a "vision," though the book is not generally understood in that way.

The first chapter is largely a rebuke of Judah and a call to repent. Unlike how I was taught to do it as a preacher, Isaiah wastes no time building rapport. By the time we get to the second chapter, though, we find Isaiah offering a promise of a day when God's reign will be re-established. This passage is quite beautiful and holds one of the favorite promises of the Bible:

God shall judge between the nations,
and shall arbitrate for many peoples;
they shall beat their swords into ploughshares,
and their spears into pruning-hooks;
nation shall not lift up sword against nation,
neither shall they learn war any more.
Isaiah 2:4

This certainly is one of those cases when we hope Isaiah was speaking directly to us. This is a vision of a preferable future that never seemed to come to pass for Judah, and there are no clues that it will come to pass in our day either. Perhaps it refers to the end of the world and the afterlife of peace. I prefer to think that it refers to our common goal and dream. As we work to recreate a world in which all of us are children of the same Creator and not enemies from different nations and peoples, if that common humanity can arbitrate between us, there will be no need for swords and spears, but together we can use our energy and resources for the abundant harvest to feed all.

Many nonprofit groups like *Hope for Peace & Justice* have used this text as the goal of their organization. Many of these peace efforts do not know that this image is one beloved by the prophets. In addition to it appearing here, it can be found in Joel 3:10 and Micah 4:3. Despite the fact that so much conflict and war has been faith-based, it is a long and persistent view that when all is right with the world, war is the first thing to go. Perhaps, though, it is time for people of all faiths to start using all the various instruments of our lives and livelihoods to create peace now rather than waiting for the reign of God to come on earth, as it is in heaven. What are you doing for peace NOW?

ISAIAH

One of the best known passages from Isaiah is the beginning of chapter 6:

> *In the year that King Uzziah died, I saw the Lord sitting on a throne, high and lofty, and the hem of his robe filled the temple. Seraphs were in attendance above him; each had six wings: with two they covered their faces, and with two they covered their feet, and with two they flew. And one called to another and said, "Holy, holy, holy is the Lord of hosts; the whole earth is full of his glory."*

This passage, of course, is the source for that great hymn "Holy, Holy, Holy." It provides a visionary glimpse into the presence of God. I left the references to God as male because that apparently is how Isaiah saw it in his vision. The Hebrew word "seraph" simply means something burning and dazzling, but Isaiah uses this term to refer to some kind of heavenly creature with six wings. This is the only appearance of seraphs in the Hebrew Bible, though similar creatures have a cameo in Revelation.

These days, if someone was to tell us that they had a vision or a dream, we would assume that, while it might have meaning and significance, it shouldn't be taken literally. Isaiah himself called this a vision and attempts to understand God's gender as male, the seraphs as cosmic figures, disrespects the author and what he tried to tell us this was all about. This is why Biblical literalists end up focused on all the wrong things.

What is most significant in this passage is that Isaiah is overwhelmed with the otherness of God. We interpret the word "holy" as a moral state, but that is not how the ancient Hebrews understood it. For them, God, and all that belongs to God, is holy or other. It is like matter coming into contact with antimatter; hence Isaiah's response is to cry out that he is undone. (v. 5) The seraphs take a burning coal from the altar and touch it to his lips to purify him.

Then, having undergone this ritual cleansing, Isaiah is able to hear his classic call from God: *Then I heard the voice of the Lord saying, "Whom shall I send, and who will go for us?" And I said, "Here am I; send me!"* (Isaiah 6:8) God's plea isn't addressed to Isaiah, but it is Isaiah who responds. Every time I read this verse I think of God spending eternity crying into the world for women and men who will answer the call and become emissaries of God's love. The witness of the entire Bible is that, from the moment of creation, God has longed to be in relationship with us. In his vision, Isaiah heard God's call and volunteered to spread that word. Too many religious people, though, have read this passage and seized the hot coals determined to burn up those who didn't agree with them or weren't holy by their standards. God needed more Isaiahs who could see what the world might be, not more seraphs with hot coals.

ISAIAH

Isaiah 7

In this chapter, we find a favorite Christmas image: *Behold a virgin shall bear a son and you shall name him Immanuel.* (Isaiah 7:14)

The word "virgin" used in Isaiah simply means "young woman." Luke has Mary argue with Gabriel about her sexual status, but there is none of that here. The promise is simply that God's sign will come into the world through a child born of a young woman.

Actually, that is how most people are born, but remember that the Bible often holds up the miracle of older women giving birth as a sign of God's blessing. Here, Isaiah simply is saying that the event will be a normal birth. Early Christianity apparently thought that wasn't good enough for Jesus … but I'm getting ahead of the story.

As a kid, I always thought it was strange that we sang "O Come, O Come Immanuel" and read that the "virgin" was to name her child Immanuel, but then Mary named him Jesus. I assumed there must be some logical explanation, but no one ever offered it. As a child, I posed the question to several of my Sunday school teachers, but they had no answer. Well, just in case you were like me and you still wonder that each year, let me explain. The reason no one ever answered my question is that no one knows.

Did Isaiah hear wrong, or was it Mary who messed up? After all, as you can imagine, she was under a lot of stress at the time. Or is it possible that the Messiah named Immanuel that Isaiah talked about really wasn't the Jesus we've come to know and love? I don't know. Isaiah uses the name again in 8:8, and then in chapter 9 records that great birth passage that Handel loved about the *Wonderful Counselor, Mighty God, Prince of Peace ....*

So, are we to ask the question that John the Baptist asked of Jesus: was he the one, or are we waiting for another? I've always believed that all the second-coming theology in the New Testament and in fundamentalist teaching is rooted in this unresolved issue. As great as Jesus was, he didn't seem to fill Immanuel's shoes, at least not the first time around. There is still no peace on earth. The yoke of oppression remains unbroken. God's will is not done on earth as it is in heaven.

So, was Jesus not the messiah of which Isaiah spoke? Are we still waiting on that messiah? Or is God still crying, "Who will I send and who will go for us" waiting on us to bring peace, justice and the reign of God on earth as it is in heaven?

ISAIAH

Isaiah 11

Chapter 10 of Isaiah acknowledges the victory of Assyria over Judah, but promises that a remnant will be saved to rebirth the nation. It ends with a poem or song about how the people of God shouldn't be overly afraid of their enemies because God will cut them down like a forest. (Isaiah 10:33-34)

Then, in chapter 11, Isaiah continues that imagery with the promise, "A shoot shall come out from the stump of Jesse and a branch shall grow out of his roots." (Isaiah 11:1) Jesse, of course, was King David's father and King Solomon's grandfather. This passage is Isaiah's specific attempt to revive the covenant God made with David that David's lineage will perpetually rule the Jews. Here, with the throne vacant and the nation conquered, Isaiah's vision of hope is that, although they may be cut down and though all hope appears to be a dead stump, that stump will sprout again.

This is the origin of the phrase "family tree." Early Christians understood Jesus to be the fulfillment of this prophesy. Both Matthew and Luke seek to establish this with genealogies for Jesus, tracing his lineage back through David. Luke's story of the birth of Jesus taking place in Bethlehem is to establish that Mary and Joseph went there to be registered because Joseph was of the house and lineage of David. What isn't asked is why any of that mattered if Jesus wasn't really Joseph's son.

In verse 2, Isaiah begins to paint a beautiful picture of the reign of this one who is a shoot from the stump. It begins, of course, talking about his being anointed by the Spirit of God. If you recall, the word "messiah" and the Greek work "Christ" simply mean "anointed one." This anticipated future ruler will be anointed with "a spirit of wisdom and understanding, counsel and might." Isaiah makes it a point to say that the anointed will be a defender of the poor. (v. 4) He then goes on to paint the idyllic picture of the wolf living with the lamb, the leopard laying down with the kid, the calf and lion together, and a little child leading them all.

To an age that was perhaps more violent than ours, this must have been a startling vision of peace, of carnivores and their prey together in peaceful repose. This is what life was to be like under the rule of the messiah. This begs the greatest question of all: If Jesus is the messiah, why aren't his people seeking to create this kind of peaceable reign? Early Christians were arrested and executed because they refused to fight in the army, but today you would hardly know from the churches that peace is the ultimate sign of the messiah we claim to follow. Why is that? Was Jesus not the messiah … or just not the messiah we wanted?

<u>ISAIAH</u>

You will say on that day: I will give thanks to you, O Lord, for though you were angry with me, your anger turned away, and you comforted me. Surely God is my salvation; I will trust, and will not be afraid, for the Lord God is my strength and my might; he has become my salvation. With joy you will draw water from the wells of salvation.

Isaiah 12:1-3

After his glorious description of a future where that which appeared to be dead comes to life again and creates a reign of peace and harmony, what is left to say? Isaiah inserts at this point a psalm or hymn of praise to God. It is unclear whether Isaiah is the author of the psalm or he simply inserted one that was used in worship. Either way, the author is calling us to celebrate the Reign of God <u>until</u> it comes on earth.

Worshipping/celebrating our future despite the challenges of our present requires faith. The life of the faithful is a bit like riding a motorcycle as it can be deadly if you only look at the ground beneath you. Instead, you have to keep your eyes/faith focused on where you are going and where you want to end up. Leaders who focus entirely on the challenges of today get overwhelmed and bogged down. However, those who are able hold in their minds the preferable future can almost always find their way through the struggles of the present.

The fact that this section of Isaiah ends with a psalm of praise and celebration says a lot about the rich faith life of the prophet. Remember that he lived in times that were much more desperate than ours—a nation split in two; a long series of inept and destructive leaders; Judah's raid by surrounding nations, taken away resources and kidnapped people; the apparent end of the line—all hope is lost. Then Isaiah has a vision of a future in which hope springs out of a dry, dead stump. This psalm of praise is offered in faith that this future will someday become reality.

One of my favorite verses in all of Broadway is from "The Man of La Mancha" when Don Quixote says, "*True madness is to see the world as it is, not as it should be.*" This was the philosophy of Isaiah and his ministry. He could not fix the present circumstances, but he would prophesy to the people the promise that what they were suffering was not the end of the story. In tough times, we who are people of faith have a responsibility to take up the mantle of Isaiah and become those who bring words of hope. We do not pretend the present isn't tough, but by faith, we offer the promise that these difficult days have "come to pass," but they have not come to stay.

ISAIAH

Isaiah 13-23

The next 10 chapters of Isaiah are not my favorites. They are considered a series of oracles about the fate of the neighboring nations. Most predict coming doom for those who have oppressed the Jews, or were simply just bad neighbors. It is hard to understand the point of these passages since the countries lambasted probably never were aware of this.

At first it seems that Isaiah is like an infuriated driver screaming at the people around him … with the windows rolled up. Perhaps it made him feel better to get it off his chest …. The truth is, though, this kind of venting does little more than fog up the windows. It actually doesn't make us feel better, and it certainly doesn't change the circumstances. In fact, any time we give into rage and direct it at another person or nation, we do not shape *their* behavior, only our own. We feed the beast within and make it stronger every time we exercise it, even privately. Losing patience with other drivers only increases the likelihood that we will lose patience with someone we love.

So, I don't think Isaiah is simply venting his anger and frustration at neighboring nations that didn't come to Judah's aid, and I don't think these passages have been preserved for centuries because they are critiques of other people. We may like to wax eloquently about the faults, failings and foibles of others, but it certainly isn't an activity worth preserving in scripture. So why is this here?

In light of his prophecy of the coming Reign of God led by the messiah, Isaiah apparently wanted to communicate to his readers that this reign included all the nations. This is a passage of inclusion, though they are being included in judgment for how they have conducted themselves which is one of those tough things for liberals to remember. In the name of inclusion, we often turn a blind eye to behavior that is not acceptable.

I had a serious confrontation in a recent meeting because, in order to include an Islamic group, we were being asked to exclude women from leading a service. Eventually, I had to say that, while I didn't believe that Islam was an inferior faith to Christianity, I did believe that prejudices such as sexism in the name of their religion was as wrong as sexism in Christianity. In the name of tolerance and plurality, we cannot fail to raise our voices against the evils of oppression regardless of the religion. Oppression and marginalization in the name of God are especially evil regardless if you do it in Jesus' name or Allah's.

ISAIAH

Isaiah 24-27

In chapter 23, Isaiah finishes his oracles against all the nations and then turns his attention back to Judah and the future. A rough reading of this section is a convincing argument that Isaiah is either on drugs or needs to be on medication. Chapter 24, verses 1-13 is a tirade about how God is about to lay waste to the earth. No one is spared:

> *And it shall be, as with the people, so with the priest; as with the slave, so with his master; as with the maid, so with her mistress; as with the buyer, so with the seller; as with the lender, so with the borrower; as with the creditor, so with the debtor.*
>
> Isaiah 24:2

Chapters 24-27 seem to be a prophecy referring to the end of the world. Yet it is interrupted (as in verses 14 and 15) with verses of worship and praise:

> *They lift up their voices, they sing for joy; they shout from the west over the majesty of the Lord. Therefore in the east give glory to the Lord; in the coastlands of the sea glorify the name of the Lord, the God of Israel.*

Then the woes and warnings resume for the rest of the chapter. Chapter 25 begins with a psalm of praise and worship that includes a reminder that God is on the side of the poor. (v. 4) Verse 8 contains the image of God personally wiping away all our tears. This image is, of course, the climax of the book of Revelation's visions about the end of time, no doubt borrowed from here. Both writers see all this trauma and drama ending in new life and resurrection.

This is one of the earliest introductions of the idea of resurrection in Jewish scripture. In Jesus' day, it was still a highly debated concept among Jewish teachers. The Pharisees largely believed in literal resurrection, as apparently did Jesus. The Sadducees, according to the Gospels, did not believe in a literal resurrection.

This section of Isaiah is so different and seems to flow so erratically that many scholars question whether it was written by Isaiah at all, or if an early editor might have pieced together fragments of writings. Yet there is something compelling about this section that reminds me of my own tendency to swing back and forth between despair and hope. It would be nice to live our whole lives completely and utterly trusting the ultimate victory of the good and of God, but for me at least, that just doesn't seem possible. More often, like Isaiah, I slip into the negative and begin to spiral down, but then catch myself and remember that God is yet alive and so am I. Maybe this section of Isaiah is just proof that the real life of faith is not found in endless trust, but in endless remembering and returning.

ISAIAH

Isaiah 27

This chapter is labeled in my study bible as a "sermon." However, verse one is not included in that sermon. It is as if the drugs that gave rise to Isaiah's apocalyptic vision in the last chapters haven't quite worn off:

> *On that day the Lord with his cruel and great and strong sword will punish Leviathan the fleeing serpent, Leviathan the twisting serpent, and he will kill the dragon that is in the sea.*

Leviathan and dragons are interesting images to find here in Isaiah. You expect them in Revelation, and writers would have made millions of dollars selling books that explained what these creatures represent. However, few Old Testament scholars seem to have a clue, which is probably why their books don't sell well.

Maybe these creatures did exist in Isaiah's time, and he simply is trying to explain how they became extinct. God took a sword and killed them. (Okay smarty, what is your interpretation?) The truth is I don't have a clue what this verse means or what this image represents. I read the analysis of the Hebrew rendering of this verse, and let me say, unless you are having trouble sleeping, don't bother.

The Jews were never seafaring people, so to Isaiah and his readers, these creatures represented the mysterious threats and dangers in life. While I'm not thrilled to see God ever referred to as "cruel," what Isaiah seems to be trying to communicate is that the outcome of life will be the elimination of threats and dangers, both known and unknown, both real and mythical. In fact, the destruction of mythical threats may require more effort from God than ridding us of more tangible threats.

During the popular PBS television series, "The Power of Myth," Joseph Campbell told Bill Moyers, "The images of myth are reflections of the spiritual potentialities of every one of us. Through contemplating these, we evoke their powers in our own lives." Here we have Isaiah offering us an image of the defeat of the fiercest dangers any human could imagine facing. We are not challenged to stoke up our courage, take up our weapons of mass destruction and launch a preemptive strike against the mythical enemies that threaten apocalypse. Rather, Isaiah provides us with a promising image that God, whose people we are, can slay the dragons that threaten us.

I have a small battered plaque on my desk that has been displayed since 1975. You would think that, by now, I would remember exactly what it says. But apparently I don't, because every time I turn around I'm off to slay some dragon. Sometimes, when the dragon threatens others that is what is needed. But most often, my hair is left singed. In those moments, I might do well to read and heed my little desk plaque that simply asks, "Have you prayed about it?"

ISAIAH

Since 1789, Isaiah 40-60 has been referred to, almost universally, as "Deutero-Isaiah" or "Second Isaiah." Some scholars further suggest that another division likely separates chapters 56-60 and credit another author or editor. While there are clear differences in these sections, they are not so extreme that it is impossible that one author or editor was the source of the entire book. If you have been reading ***Liberating Word*** for the past 43 weeks, you know that the writing sounds very different from day to day. The differences may speak to the mental stability of the author, but it could be due to the content about which I'm writing, what is going on in the world on any given day, as well as whether I am writing in my office or on a plane, or any number of other variants.

That is not offered to suggest a single authorship; I frankly have no conclusive opinion or concern about that issue. What I want to do is remind us that whatever we read must be read as a human product, recalling that, from day-to-day, our humanity changes, expands and is diminished.

And so, after a long series of warnings and dire predictions, chapter 40 and this section of Isaiah, open with the words "Comfort, O comfort my people." In churches that follow the assigned lectionary readings, this passage is read every three years on the second Sunday of Advent because it foretells:

> *A voice cries out: "In the wilderness prepare the way of the Lord, make straight in the desert a highway for our God. Every valley shall be lifted up, and every mountain and hill be made low; the uneven ground shall become level, and the rough places a plain. Then the glory of the Lord shall be revealed, and all people shall see it together, for the mouth of the Lord has spoken."*
>
> Isaiah 40: 3-6

Early Christians understood this text to speak of John the Baptist, who prepared the way for the coming of the Messiah. Interestingly, John's work was much more like Isaiah's and the other prophets than it was like Jesus' and his disciples' work. He seemed to know that "one size fits **some**." It is unclear from the text that Isaiah is speaking of two people. That understanding comes from our reading Isaiah through the lens of the Gospels. Still, it does make sense that every movement needs more than one style of communication, and John didn't see himself as the Messiah but apparently as the one to get people ready for the Messiah. That is what we are all called to do.

God may be the one to bring comfort, and our job is to live and love in such a way that people are prepared to believe in a God who actually loves them, even when the circumstances are painful and hard.

ISAIAH

Isaiah 49

This chapter is one of three great poems in this section about the "Servant." The challenge is to try to understand about whom the author is speaking. At the outset, it appears that this is autobiographical: "The Lord called me before I was born, while I was in my mother's womb God named me." (v. 1) In most of the passage, though, the servant is Israel. (v. 3) Of course, the New Testament understood the prophet to be speaking of the Messiah and that Messiah to be Jesus.

I love the middle verses of this chapter (vv. 14-16), which provide one of the most moving images of God, a feminine personification:

> *But Zion said, "The Lord has forsaken me, my Lord has forgotten me." Can a woman forget her nursing child, or show no compassion for the child of her womb? Even these may forget, yet I will not forget you. See, I have inscribed you on the palms of my hands; your walls are continually before me.*

For decades, I have been waging a losing struggle to get people to stop referring to God as "He." I realize it is a hard habit to break, but I don't think it is really a habit. My concern is that we only know the masculine side of God; the result is a religion that is out of balance, too often violent, and too seldom fiercely tender. This is not a matter of pronouns. It isn't a matter of gender either. For me, it is a matter of letting go of the gods of our childhoods and living our lives in the arms of the God who birthed us.

This is more than language, yet the words we use both express the God we truly believe in and shape our beliefs. Theologian Virginia Mollenkott suggests that if we are going to use the word "God" (as opposed to "Goddess") we should pair it with the pronoun "she." That is a bit too much work for me, so I generally try never to use a gender specific pronoun for God. That, too, takes effort, but the effort reminds me to let go of the god of my childhood and embrace my Creator who is happy about my creation. For Christians, we might let Jesus be the masculine expression of God and the Holy Spirit to be the feminine. That is a concept of the trinity that makes sense to me.

What doesn't make sense is how 21st-century people of faith cannot recognize the damage done to our world, our faith and our own souls by our deification of the masculine. If God is male and only male then the feminine is not divine, which means, of course, that women are not really made in the image of God, and effeminate men are clearly inferior, and war gets valued over peace, and strength is defined as power, and exploitation of creation takes precedent over nurturing life. This list could go on and on, but what I'm really advocating is taking this passage in Isaiah seriously, and taking this vision of God into our lives. It is a healing that is long over due.

ISAIAH

Isaiah 52:13-53:12

This section of Isaiah is often referred to as the "Suffering Servant Song." There are several songs in this second section of Isaiah. For the early Church, these songs described the suffering of Jesus, and his suffering, rejection and death thus became signs that he was the Messiah of which Isaiah spoke. Many Jewish scholars, then and now, interpret these passages as a reference to Israel and the redemptive value in all their suffering.

These passages are the original source for several theories of atonement. That is, how Church teachers have understood the significance of Jesus' suffering and death finds its roots in Isaiah more than the teachings of Jesus. Isaiah saw the servant as receiving the punishment due the people. The most ancient understanding was that, as God's chosen people, Israel's suffering had a much greater meaning than simply that they were a small country repeatedly conquered and abused by larger countries.

Isaiah suggests that the servant/Israel's suffering has a healing and forgiving effect:

Surely he has borne our infirmities
and carried our diseases;
yet we accounted him stricken,
struck down by God, and afflicted.
But he was wounded for our transgressions,
crushed for our iniquities;
upon him was the punishment that made us whole,
and by his bruises we are healed.
All of us were like sheep that have gone astray;
we have all turned to our own way,
and the Lord has laid on him the iniquity of us all.

Isaiah 53:4-6

What is interesting to me is that, if Isaiah understands Israel as the suffering servant, it isn't Israel that is redeemed, but humanity—*The Lord has laid on him (Israel) the suffering of us* ***all***. The implication in this is a sort of universalism. Israel bore the iniquities and punishment on behalf of all people.

When the early Church replaced Israel with Jesus in this imagery, they did not understand that his suffering was universally effective for all people, rather only for those who "believe." Does that imply that Jesus' suffering somehow was less effective? Or was believing it a sales tool to expand the church? I've always wondered how salvation can be a gift of grace, yet require our acceptance to be effective. Did Jesus reconcile us to God, or did our own faith? Was Jesus not the suffering servant, or do many Christians think he simply wasn't a very effective one? I'm just asking …

ISAIAH

Isaiah 55-56

Yesterday, we briefly touched on the possibility that Isaiah was a Universalist believing that Israel's suffering made it possible for all people to have their relationship with God healed. That is an important concept when we come to this section, which is one of my favorites.

Chapter 55 begins with the invitation that everyone who is thirsty can come to the water, and those who have no money are welcome to eat and drink. If this seems to be a perversion of capitalism, perhaps it is. As verse 8 explains:

> *"My thoughts are not your thoughts, nor are your ways my ways," says the Lord.*

Then chapter 56 goes on to expound one of the most radically inclusive statements in the entire Bible (and maybe in all of religion):

> *Do not let the foreigner joined to the Lord say, "The Lord will surely separate me from his people;" and do not let the eunuch say, "I am just a dry tree." For thus says the Lord: To the eunuchs who keep my Sabbaths, who choose the things that please me and hold fast my covenant, I will give, in my house and within my walls, a monument and a name better than sons and daughters; I will give them an everlasting name that shall not be cut off.*
>
> Isaiah 56:3-5

This is a specific statement against the kind of nationalism that thinks God practices favoritism and it is a radical inclusion of the sexually disenfranchised. Eunuchs had been excluded from worship and relegated to the outer courtyard of the temple because of their sexuality, yet here is a promise to be given a place and "a name **better** than sons and daughters."

I bet you have never heard a sermon on that text. Just in case we missed the point and think it was only meant for ancient Jews, Jesus quotes the last part of verse 8 in the last days of his life. Seeing that the temple had become a place where people were excluded and abused, Jesus cleared it out and then says, "*Is it not written, "My house shall be called a house of prayer for **all** people?"* Somehow both Jews and Christians largely have missed this message.

Full inclusion is not a peripheral issue of political correctness; it is the very sign of God's rule and reign. Jesus was clear that this was a reign that was to come on earth, and he was willing to start clearing a place for it, even if it would be so violently resisted that he would be killed. What are we willing to sacrifice to ensure that there is a place at God's table for ALL people?

ISAIAH

Isaiah 61:1-3

We come to the end of our study of Isaiah. With just a few weeks left in this year, we will have to hurry through the rest of the First Testament. Still, this book was so important to Jesus and the New Testament writers that it seemed important to spend a few days here.

The 61st chapter begins with words familiar to most Christians. That is because when Jesus was beginning his ministry, he went to his hometown synagogue in Nazareth and they handed him the scroll of the prophet Isaiah. He unrolled it and found this passage in Isaiah 61. That was tougher than it sounded because, of course, it would be many centuries before Isaiah would be divided up into chapters and verses. Jesus found the place because he knew where to look. He had read it many times, studied it, and knew what it said. Our brief study has been a faint imitation of the practice of the one of whom many of us claim to be disciples. This is what Jesus read that day:

> *The spirit of the Lord God is upon me, because the Lord has anointed me; he has sent me to bring good news to the oppressed, to bind up the broken-hearted, to proclaim liberty to the captives, and release to the prisoners; to proclaim the year of the Lord's favor, and the day of vengeance of our God.*
>
> Isaiah 61:1-2

Jesus read this passage and then said that the words were fulfilled in their hearing that day. In other words, he claimed before his hometown synagogue that he had been anointed by God to do this work. This is generally interpreted as Jesus' claim to be the Messiah, the servant about whom Isaiah spoke.

That certainly may be true, or perhaps all Jesus was doing was saying that, like the ancient suffering servant, he, too, had been called to do these things. In the same way, the Church of Jesus Christ can only call itself the "Body of Christ" when we take up the agenda of Christ under the anointing of the Holy Spirit.

When you read the story in Luke 4, you learn that it almost ended badly when Jesus' fellow worshipers tried to throw him off a cliff. Some say that was because he claimed to be the Messiah. I don't think so. I think it was because he left out the last eight words in the scripture we just read. He stopped reading before he got to the phrase, "the day of vengeance of our God." It infuriated them that he left out their favorite part. Then he compounded it by telling two stories in which God sent healing to outsiders.

You see, Isaiah's inclusive vision didn't just get Jesus crucified at the end of his life; it got him in trouble his whole life long. I think making the message of inclusion the cornerstone of our life and ministry might get some of us in trouble today. Maybe that is why we don't.

<u>JEREMIAH</u>

When I was in seminary, I took a semester-long course about the book of Jeremiah. Now I only have a couple of devotions in which to tell you all I know. Think of all that tuition money wasted. Actually, it was a good class, because I learned a lot about how these "books" in the Bible actually were written. Students had to learn this in order to understand why Jeremiah is such a literary mess. This study forced me to finally let go of my fundamentalist view of the Bible and reconsider what I meant when I say that scripture is "inspired." It was in this class on Jeremiah that I finally stopped referring to the Bible as "the word of God" and began listening to the Bible for a word *from* God.

The books of Jeremiah and Lamentations are generally considered to be collections of the writings of the prophet Jeremiah, or of prophecy by Jeremiah recorded by his secretary Baruch. There are certain parts of the Book of Jeremiah that seem inconsistent with either of these sources but seem to be fragments of another work simply included here. The Septuagint, the oldest translation of the First Testament from Hebrew to Greek, was translated about 200 years before the birth of Christ. It is about 2,700 words shorter than the Hebrew texts used for most modern translations, and the arrangement of the book is different.

The text of Jeremiah itself gives some information about why there is so much confusion in the composition of the book:

> *Then Jeremiah took another scroll and gave it to the secretary Baruch son of Neriah, who wrote on it at Jeremiah's dictation all the words of the scroll that King Jehoiakim of Judah had burned in the fire; and many similar words were added to them.*
>
> Jeremiah 36:32

Is the book of Jeremiah simply the memory of an old man about a scroll he wrote years before King Jehoiakim burned it up? Without a word processor or even a notebook, the texts we know as the Bible were written on scrolls of parchment. Sometimes scrolls were damaged or lost, and, when they were translated, they might be put together in the wrong order. This reality is apparent with the book of Jeremiah, but it is also probably true with many works that have no chronological markers to help arrange them.

All of this is simply to provide a bit more information about the book we call the Bible. Its origins are scattered and erratic; its translations inconsistent and often inaccurate. Yet, despite it all, God's voice comes roaring through in undeniable ways, and at other times whispers to us the very words of life. In Jeremiah we find some of the most powerful spiritual truths:

"I know the plans I have for you," says the Lord, "plans for your welfare and not for harm; plans to give you a future with hope."
Jeremiah 29:11

Since Creation was spoken out of chaos, maybe that is the setting in which God works best. If so, that gives me very great hope for my life.

<u>JEREMIAH</u>

Jeremiah 18

Jeremiah often is called the "Weeping Prophet." Who can blame him, given the fact that he is called to preach a message that God says is destined to be ignored? I've identified with Jeremiah many times, like when I speak against capital punishment in Texas. It is enough to make any prophet weep.

Still there are so many great passages in Jeremiah, and even in Lamentations, that I am sorry we don't have more time to explore them together. Let me suggest a couple for you to read on your own. In Jeremiah 18, we are offered this great image of God as a potter. This image is repeated a couple of other times by the prophets, and Paul refers to it in his writings. There are spiritual lessons to be learned here.

Although many of us grew up singing that old hymn, "Have Thine Own Way Lord," nothing could be more contradictory to the lifestyle of those of us who claim to be disciples of Jesus and servants of God. I invite you to spend a bit of time imagining what your life might be like if you really were willing to let your lives be molded by God. What would a Spirit-shaped you look like? How would you act? How would you live?

This all may sound a bit like a sermon excerpt, and maybe it is. However, you need to consider how different the world would be if the Christian Church was shaped a bit more by the values of Jesus. Who would Jesus execute? With whom would Jesus go to war? Who would Jesus disdain or exclude?

With this image of God as a potter trying to shape uncooperative clay, it is no wonder Jeremiah wept. The point of the entire book is that, if the people of God had been shaped by the law and teachings of God, the mess they were in could have been avoided. God tries to shape us into bricks that can be used together to build a new world, and we keep insisting that we are vases to be treated with special care. Thus, the poor potter ends up having to try to build something with bricks that have all decided to put their hands on their hips and stick out their elbows and insist they are vases. We all want to live in Lake Wobegone where "all the children are exceptional."

The next time you use the term "Lord" remember what that means and imagine for just a moment that you were a potter trying to shape your life. Talk about reasons to weep …

JEREMIAH

Jeremiah 29

Before we leave Jeremiah, I want to call your attention to one last passage. In chapter 29, the prophet is trying to give advice to the people of God who are living in exile in Babylon. One might think he would advise them to escape and come back home, or at least practice passive resistance. Nebuchadnezzar had not destroyed Jerusalem, so the city stood ready for them to return. Apparently, many of those prophesying in that day predicted a quick and easy end to this time of exile. Not Jeremiah though; he spoke the cold hard truth, which is probably why he wasn't very popular.

While other prophets advised them to hold on because it wouldn't be long, Jeremiah told them that it was going to be 70 years before they returned. (Jeremiah 29:10) That meant, of course, that few of them would live long enough to see God's promises fulfilled. I would imagine that might have been depressing to the point of defeat. Maybe that is why Jeremiah gives this tangible advice:

> *Thus says the Lord of hosts, the God of Israel, to all the exiles whom I have sent into exile from Jerusalem to Babylon: Build houses and live in them; plant gardens and eat what they produce. Take wives and have sons and daughters; take wives for your sons, and give your daughters in marriage, that they may bear sons and daughters; multiply there, and do not decrease. But seek the welfare of the city where I have sent you into exile, and pray to the Lord on its behalf, for in its welfare you will find your welfare.*
>
> Jeremiah 29:4-7

"Get on with your lives," Jeremiah says "Don't just sit there, don't give up or give in, live fully even when you are in exile."

No one who lives by the values of Jesus or longs for that image of the Divine Realm that Isaiah foretold can help but feel like you are living in exile. We live out our lives in a culture whose true gods are money, power and wealth, and whose true religion is capitalism. We live in a society where militarism and nationalism are unchallenged virtues. And we live in an age where exploitation and consumption destroy the very planet we call home. How could anyone who believes the vision and values of Jesus NOT feel like they are living in exile?

Do you find the news discouraging? Are you frightened by the values of family and co-workers? Do you feel like a "stranger in a strange land?" GOOD! You are living in an age where we are exiled from how life truly should be and Jeremiah says that in such a time we cannot resort to isolation or succumb to despair. We cannot simply dream of the by-and-by and of the "future with hope" God promises later in this same passage. (v. 11) No, we must engage the culture and try to improve it; we must pray for it and work for its welfare. We may not live to see God's reign come on earth in our lifetime, but, even in exile, we must not lose hope. It is not given to us by our circumstances; it is given to us by our God.

LAMENTATIONS

The author of this book historically has been said to be Jeremiah, though many contemporary scholars doubt it. The book's association with Jeremiah is the reason it is placed here in the middle of the four major prophetic books. The book of Chronicles mentions that Jeremiah wrote a lament, and that is likely the reason the book is attributed to him. However, it follows a Hebrew poetic style that is not found in the book of Jeremiah.

Still, it is easy to see the Lament as an expression of the grief that Jeremiah must have felt after his homeland is conquered and the temple destroyed. In times of great grief, sad songs often feel like the only expression that comes close to what we are feeling. Jeremiah no doubt would have written country songs if he lived today.

As it is, the book is pretty amazing ancient literature. Each chapter has 22 verses except for chapter 3, the middle one, which has 66 verses. Part of the book follows a Hebrew acrostic, though chapter five does not. Heard in its original form, it might have been considered an artistic masterpiece. However that gets lost when translated three or four languages later and more than two dozen centuries out of context.

This is a collection of five poems or songs by someone who was an eyewitness to terrible destruction. It wasn't just that he lived in a conquered land, but that the temple, the center of his faith, has been destroyed. Combine that with the fact that, with the fall of the nation, it feels as though God's promises have all been broken, as if the covenant between God and great King David is a lie. There is a confession of sin in the book and a call to all the people to repent, but, unlike the Book of Isaiah, there is no hint of future resurrection. There is no messianic embodiment of the broken covenant.

The lament expresses grief and confesses complicity in the cause for the grief. It requires great faith to do that without moving as quickly as possible to rationalization or to platitudes that "it will all be better." During the worst of the AIDS crisis, the toughest thing was to sit with a young man who was dying and to know there was no hope. There was no cure, and in those days, there was not even a treatment. Often, it would get worse before it would end, and no matter how they begged, I could not tell them that their family was coming when they were not. To be with someone in their absolute grief and have all my nice, Christian platitudes turn to dust in my mouth was the most difficult time of my long ministry. It was also the holiest. Sometimes I could only hold their hands and listen to their lament, but many of them expressed profound gratitude that I did not devalue their grief with clichés. Hopefully, they never knew how I was tempted to leap past their present losses and offer future blessings. To be fully present in the toughest moment is the call of Lamentations to us.

LAMENTATIONS

Lamentations 3:21-30

Right here, in the middle of the Bible's most woeful book, is a beautiful word of comfort. Notice the author doesn't promise that everything will all be alright. The author doesn't speak of a day when God's servant will reign again and life will be restored. There isn't even the promise of a better life in the by-and-by. In fact, there is no hint of heaven or resurrection to be found. Instead, what the author offers is a testimony about God:

But this I call to mind, and therefore I have hope:
The steadfast love of the Lord never ceases,
His mercies never come to an end;
they are new every morning; great is your faithfulness.
"The Lord is my portion," says my soul, "therefore I will hope in God."
Lamentations 3:21-30

The wonderful Christian hymn "Great is Thy Faithfulness" is based on this passage buried in the heart of this book.

It is not my intent to leave you with the impression that life is without hope, that things will get better, that we will heal, or that ultimately God will welcome us. What I do want us to get in touch with is how these people of faith learned to trust God's goodness and love in the midst of tough times, without being bribed by the promise of heaven or resurrection. These promises are such a ubiquitous part of our faith today, but that was not always the case and it is still not the case for many people.

A Buddhist friend once challenged me to imagine how religious people would live if they were not threatened with hell or induced by heaven. He talked about how reincarnation serves that role with Hindus and many Buddhists, and then asked, "What does that say about a faith that isn't adequate simply for today?" I can't help but wonder what that says about the gods we must create in order to get us through the day and compel us to live together in peace and compassion.

The author of Lamentations calls us to trust God's unending steadfast love, even though he didn't believe in heaven or an afterlife. The author calls us to trust God's mercy, even when we are in the middle of a time of grief and pain. For me, the author of Lamentations challenges me to reconsider what I believe and why.

EZEKIEL

Ezekiel

There are four “major” prophets and 12 “minor” prophets at the end of the First Testament. Those labels only refer to the size of the books that bear their names, not to their importance as prophets, nor to the later importance of their writings. Today we come to a case in point. While Isaiah and, to a lesser extent, Jeremiah are key books of the Bible, Ezekiel and Daniel deserve to be considered "major" prophets only because of their book's length.

The book begins with Ezekiel telling us that he is a 34-year-old priest who is living in exile after the fall of Judah. Unlike almost all the rest of the Bible, Ezekiel is fastidious about giving us exact dates. Hence, wc know that this all takes place in the later part of the fifth century BCE.

What is odd about reading this book is how specific it is in places about concrete details, and how completely inexplicable it is about some of the prophecies it offers. Very clearly the prophet is trying to tell those in exile that Jerusalem would be destroyed and that, unless they refrained from worshipping the gods of the people among whom they were currently living, they would be lost themselves.

There is no indication that fire rained down from heaven upon the exiles, but it is true that, as they built houses in Babylon and started businesses, they became increasingly successful and increasingly comfortable. Soon, many of them had no desire whatsoever to return to their homeland to face the tough task of rebuilding. The children who were born to these exiles felt no connection to the land of Moses and David.

For people of faith, comfort is much more dangerous than confrontation. Nothing did more to destroy the religion of Jesus and the movement he gave birth to than the conversion of Emperor Constantine. When Christianity became the religion of the empire, it became invested in its power (military) and its prosperity (capitalism), and we were no longer exiles but new citizens. We who were called to be citizens in the Realm of God became defenders of the status quo and climbers of the material ladders.

True Christianity began to die on the day when Christians were no longer killed for refusing to serve in the army or pledge their allegiance to the empire. The radical faith of Jesus died on the day we started enjoying all the benefits of the exile and forgot about all of those who were left behind.

EZEKIEL

Ezekiel 37

Although it is a strange writing that is not beloved by many, there is one passage in the Book of Ezekiel that many people know. In chapter 37, we find the record of Ezekiel's vision of the valley of dry bones. This vision is a word of promise and hope to Israel, but it also is often used as a parable for the Christian doctrine of resurrection.

Some scholars suggest that the prophet actually may have happened upon the scene of a massacre of exiles whose bodies were left to the animals and elements. It is reminiscent of killing fields of Cambodia or the mass graves in Iraq. It is a sad irony that so much of the land in the Middle East has so often been strewn with the dried bones of human lives.

For Ezekiel, this was a prophecy of hope that Israel might be resurrected from the dead. The bones he had in mind were probably the empty temple and the homes of those who had been taken into exile. As I put myself in the prophet's shoes, I tried to think about the "bones" that litter the landscape of our common lives. Dry and utterly dead, with no hope that a bit of TLC or a mistaken diagnosis would revive them, these were bones … disconnected, utterly lifeless bones.

It is a scene worthy of a Tim Burton film when we find these dry, dusty bones coming together to form first skeletons and then bodies. Still, the bodies are breathless. If the vision had been interrupted, we'd have had a scene right out of "Night of the Living Dead." It doesn't stop, though, and Ezekiel calls upon the winds to breathe life back into the bodies. In Hebrew, the word "ruach" can mean breath, wind or spirit, so the translation of this passage is a bit tricky.

Still, it ultimately is a parable for the Jews whose nation, community, religion and future seem to be as dead as dry bones. Through the prophet, God promises that nothing is ever so dead that the God who breathed life into Creation cannot breathe life back into them. It is a parable of hope in the midst of a scene and situation of utter despair. In verse 3, God asked Ezekiel if the bones could live again. Ezekiel played it safe, shrugged his shoulders and replied, "God knows." After this parable is told to them and to you, though, such answers are no longer possible. Rather, with Jesus, we must affirm in the face of the most utter defeat and death, "With God all things are possible." (Matthew 19:26)

This isn't Pollyanna optimism, but a promise that comes in a valley of dry bones at a time of utter defeat. It is light in the darkness without pretending it isn't dark. It is an acknowledgement that we never really know enough ultimately to despair.

EZEKIEL

Ezekiel 38-39

This chapter in Ezekiel is considered by some to be *apocalyptic* in nature, which simply means "revelatory." It is a type of prophecy, or writing, that arose after the exile, and which is characterized in the New Testament by the book of Revelation. Many conservatives have interpreted it to speak of the end of time, though clearly that wasn't the intent of the author or the understanding of the original reader. Frankly, when I read apocalyptic literature, I am puzzled to know exactly what was either the author or the original reader's understanding.

In Jeremiah's prophecy, the invading armies were victorious and seen as instruments in God's repudiation of the people's unfaithfulness. This corresponds to what historically happened. However, in these chapters of Ezekiel, Gog and Magog are defeated, though no one really seems to know who the heck they were. These apparently mythological nations get a brief cameo in the book of Revelation as well.

When I was growing up, fundamentalist preachers and authors were convinced, and convincing, that Gog represented the Soviet Union, which would someday invade the modern-day nation of Israel only to be defeated by them. This all would be a part of the end of time and the second coming of Christ. I'm not sure what happened to those sermons and all those books after the Soviet Union simply fell apart without ever rising up to attack the faithful as Ronald Reagan's "evil empire."

Frankly, reading this section of Ezekiel makes me wonder what he was smoking. It must have been some really good stuff, because his visions are creative and vivid. He seems to have shared his drugs with Daniel, and wherever they hid their stash, the author of Revelation found them several centuries later.

That is a joke of course, but it is more likely than the fundamentalists' attempts to make these visions descriptive of modern history or predictive of what ultimately will happen in the world. While I could write for paragraphs about apocalyptic literature as an ancient genre, this information isn't likely to enhance anyone's spiritual life.

Perhaps this is the point to simply say, parts of the Bible should just be skipped. While it might have been meaningful to some people at some time, we are not those people and this is not the time … and that is okay. It is narcissistic to assume that everything in the Bible was meant for us, or that everything God ever said was addressed to us. When I get to passages like the 38th and 39th chapters of Ezekiel, I just hear God saying in my mother's voice, "I wasn't talking to you."

EZEKIEL

Ezekiel 40-48

Ezekiel ends with a long section of how the temple, priesthood, and nation are to look and function in some far-off day when the effects of the exile are ended and the nation is restored. There are many parallel passages to be found in the book of Revelation, which, like Ezekiel, describes a far away, fantastical New Jerusalem.

The challenge, of course, is how do we understand this vision? Is it just a fantasy of Ezekiel, or is he describing what he really believes will happen? Remember, all of this apocalyptic vision follows the vision of the valley of dry bones. For this reason, many Christians have interpreted this as a post-resurrection vision. That is, many try to translate this as an end-of-time vision of what life will be like after history as we know it has come to an end.

Again, it is difficult for us, more than two millennia later, to know with any certainty exactly what was meant by this vision. It is like trying to interpret the dreams of someone else from another age and setting. Still, let me give it a stab.

The last verses of Ezekiel describe a city. Revelation calls this the "New Jerusalem," which comes down out of heaven. In both places, the city is HUGE. It would stretch from Dallas to Seattle if it were built in the United States (which makes sense to us, of course, since we think the world revolves around us). The description of its size is the prophet's way of saying that it is as large as it can be, large enough for everyone who had ever lived, at least in that day.

Notice that there are 12 gates. Ezekiel names each gate after one of the 12 tribes. In that day, people immediately would have understood that this was a symbol for access. If you were going to build a city to be defended, to keep people out, then you would only put in one gate. In this city, there are gates on every side. This is a vision of inclusion and welcome. There is room for everyone, and provision is made so that, however you approach the City of God, you find access.

What a powerful image and what a stark contrast to how heaven/eternity has been used by fundamentalists of all religions. This is no exclusive place where only those who believe right and behave right can get in. The ultimate vision of the climax of life is that there is a place of welcome for all.

While Ezekiel's vision is weird and wacky, in the end, he closes the book with a clear statement about where life is headed for us all. His last words describe that place completely in just three words: ***"God is there."*** That is really all we need to understand.

DANIEL

The Book of Daniel is set during the exile after the fall of both Israel and Judah. The central character is an exile who is taken back to Babylon by Nebuchadnezzar. His name is Daniel, known mostly from his episode in the lion's den.

The book has two distinct parts: a series of six narratives (chapters 1-6) and four apocalyptic visions (chapters 7-12). The narratives take the form of court stories that focus on tests of religious fidelity involving Daniel and his friends (chapters 1, 3 and 6), and Daniel's interpretation of royal dreams and visions (chapters 2, 4 and 5).

In the second part of the book, Daniel recounts his reception of dreams, visions and angelic interpretations in the first person. The dating and authorship of Daniel has been a matter of great debate among Jews and Christians. The traditional view holds that the work was written by a prophet named Daniel who lived during the sixth century BC. However, many modern Biblical scholars maintain that the book was written or edited together in the mid-second century BC, and that most of the predictions in the book refer to events that already had occurred. The book was written in both Aramaic and Hebrew, which certainly argues that it is the product of a later author recording legends or parables and apocalyptic visions.

Daniel is arguably the most bizarre book in the First Testament. Having just studied the book of Ezekiel, that is saying a lot! Daniel and his three friends are Babylonian captives who refused to give up their faith or Jewish lifestyle. The book notes that their fastidious eating habits left them healthier, and, despite a couple of major trials, they impressed their foreign captors. Although the God of the Jews was judged as unable or unwilling to protect "his" temple and holy city, the witness of Daniel and company won at least honor for their faith.

That alone is sufficient to call the book to our attention. We serve a God who sides with the losers, the poor, the outcasts. The God of Jesus is not the god of winners, the strong and victorious. There are many who point to their wealth or power as proof that their faith is true. Daniel was the captive of a more powerful military, yet his was the true faith because God was with him … not the God of military might, but the God who goes with us even into dens of death.

DANIEL

Daniel 1

The book of Daniel begins with an account of how King Nebuchadnezzar commands a group of handsome young Jewish men to be rounded up and brought to the palace. There they will be well fed and educated. Daniel (his Hebrew name) and Shadrach, Meshach and Abednego (their Babylonian names) are among the men gathered and were offered this honor.

Daniel, more fastidious than the rest, refuses to eat the food or drink the wine of the Babylonian king. He persuades the Palace Master to let them live on vegetables and water. After three years, Daniel wins over the king by interpreting a dream for him. The reward for Daniel and his friends is to be given royal appointments in the government of the king.

In chapter 4, we find one of the more famous stories of the book of Daniel. Nebuchadnezzar creates a 90-foot golden statue of himself and commands the whole realm to bow down and worship it. Because they refused to bow down, Shadrach, Meshach and Abednego are thrown into a fiery furnace heated to seven times the normal temperature. So hot was the furnace that the men who threw them in were consumed. However, when the king looks in to see how his Hebrew slaves were roasting, he saw them walking around unhurt. In fact, he notices that, instead of three, there are four people in the furnace, and Nebuchadnezzar notes that the appearance of the fourth is god-like.

After they are removed from the fire, the author never identifies the fourth person. Christian preachers are fond of making that fourth person out to be Jesus, but there is nothing in the text to suggest that this is a messianic sighting. Some rabbis have suggested that the fourth was actually Daniel, who is mysteriously missing from this vignette.

No one really knows for certain what the teller of this parable intended beyond the point that God is with those who have the courage of their convictions. The writer may have recalled Isaiah's promise that "when you walk through the fire you shall not be burned." (Isaiah 43:2)

Taking this story literally raises a whole range of issues that we cannot resolve, but, if we treat it like any of the profound stories that Jesus told, we are free to think of all those people of faith who have been through the fires of life, but were not consumed. It is as if God was with them …

DANIEL

Daniel 6

In Daniel chapter 5, we find the story from which we get the phrase "handwriting on the wall," but it is in Daniel chapter 6 that we find the story for which Daniel is forever known. Actually, it is a great deal like the story of the "Fiery Furnace" that we discussed yesterday. This time, though, it was Daniel, not his three friends, whose life was endangered.

Nebuchadnezzar died, and a new king named Darius assumed the throne. Because Daniel had risen to a place of prominence and power without compromising his faith, his rivals decided to get rid of him. They persuaded the new king to issue an edict banning prayer for 30 days. (Daniel 6:7) As they knew he would, Daniel disobeyed the edict and continued to openly practice his faith, regardless of the consequences. The result, of course, was that he was thrown into a den of lions. You remember that Daniel was unharmed by the lions and thus impressed the new king with the power of his God.

To me, the challenge of this story is all of those folks killed by lions in Rome a few centuries later. They, too, refused to renounce their faith. They refused to worship Caesar as a god. Most egregiously, they refused to serve in Caesar's army because they believed being a disciple of Jesus was not congruent with war. Still, God did not intervene and protect them. Was God showing favoritism to Daniel, or were the lions just not hungry at that moment?

Actually, I think that, like so many of these mythical stories, the author wasn't trying to recount history, but trying to offer us a parable containing truth. This story is a summons to faithfulness and courage. Daniel could have gone into his house, closed the door and prayed to his heart's content. It was his practice, though, to kneel in front of the window and pray looking toward the temple in far away Jerusalem. The day after the edict was signed, Daniel prayed in exactly the same manner as he did the day before.

I recently saw a young man dropping his partner off at the airport in Dallas. They embraced and kissed just as they surely do every morning at home. Bill and I have done that for almost 30 years, but then no one can fire me for being gay. I felt a moment of pride that we are coming to a day when people don't have to be ashamed of whom they love. Perhaps this was not what the writer of Daniel had in mind, but I do think it is a parable about having integrity. Who we are, and who our faith calls us to be, ought to be evident, regardless of the circumstances or the threat. Daniel might have gotten off easy, but he had no expectation that would be so. Still, he had the courage to practice his faith and be who he was. That is the only kind of witness that will convince our critics.

HOSEA

We could definitely spend more time in Daniel. However, the visions are mostly inexplicable, and it is arrogance or magical thinking to presume we know their meaning. Hosea, the first of the 12 "minor" prophets, is much more straight-forward.

Again, it is unclear if Hosea's story is a parable or a record of actual facts. In the end, we must always read the Bible, recalling the wisdom of the ancient rabbi who said, "Whether this actually happened or not, I do not know. I do know, however, that it is true." Only westerners are obsessed with the factuality of a story. Other cultures care much more about the truth of the story, and know the difference.

Hosea's book begins with God commanding him to marry a whore (the Bible's word, not mine). He chooses a woman named Gomer who continues to be unfaithful after they are married and even after they have children. Hosea treats her with faithful tenderness, which is offered as a sign to the people of Israel of how they were behaving and of God's continued longsuffering love.

Hosea is divided into three parts. The first three chapters deal with poor Hosea's painful marriage. I sometimes wonder if the fundamentalists who like to talk about "biblical marriage" have ever read about this biblical marriage. Chapters 4-13 deal with Israel's unfaithfulness to the God of covenant love. It offers tender glimpses of God's broken heart, though it is balanced with warnings of judgment and the fact that they "sow the wind and will reap the whirlwind." (Hosea 8:7)

In the end, Hosea is clear that, because of their unfaithfulness, Israel will ultimately be conquered and fall. Still, in chapter 14 in the third section, there is an offer of forgiveness and restoration.

Many years ago, two teenagers came to me confessing that they had "sinned." They were terrified that pregnancy would be the result. They were duly penitent, and I assured them that God loved them and forgave them. The next time I saw them they wouldn't speak to me. She was, in fact, pregnant, and they assumed I had lied about God forgiving them. They thought they were being punished. Now those teenagers are proud grandparents by God's "punishment." Forgiveness doesn't undo the consequences of our actions; however, as Hosea tries to say, God's grace is still ours.

JOEL

On the day of Pentecost, Peter stands up to preach, and he quotes from the prophet Joel, which is the only reason most people have heard of this prophet. It may be the only reason it made it into the Christian canon. No one knows who Joel was and the only information we have is from the book itself. Scholars have no clue when, or even where, he lived.

It is impossible to tell if his writing is addressed to Israel, Judah or, perhaps, the United Kingdom before Solomon's death. He begins with an account of a plague of locusts that provides the context for the book. He describes them as if they were an army of invaders from the north, leaving the land stripped and people starving. Such invasions were apparently common, though they didn't come from the north.

It is possible that locusts are symbolic, or that he simply is using a natural disaster to warn of a coming military invasion. Either way, the prophet sees the disaster as a sign of God's judgment and a call to repentance.

We liberals are not too fond of the theme of judgment. Biblical writers almost always interpret bad things as an expression of God's displeasure. It seems to be a primitive view of God, because today we have scientific explanations for plagues and natural disasters. All of that is well and good, but what is lost in this is that we still have a great need to repent. As much as any people who have ever lived, we need to examine our lives and our lifestyles, vision and values, and turn back toward God. Unfortunately, without the threat of judgment, we are seldom motivated. My partner is fond of reminding me that the church never had financial problems when we had hell with which to threaten people.

In the midst of this disaster, Joel calls on people to "sanctify a fast" (1:14), to put on sackcloth and lament. When we look at the summer sky over most of our cities and hear the wheezing of the elderly and the children, we need the prophet Joel. We need to be called to repent from the natural disasters we are creating because of our lifestyles and the choices we make, or refuse to make. We are destroying the planet and the health of the most vulnerable who suffer an epidemic of asthma, emphysema, sinus infections and respiratory distress. Is this not judgment enough to warrant repentance? Where is Joel to call us to fast and reconsider our selfish ways?

JOEL

Joel 2:28-32

If people know anything at all about the prophet Joel, it is because Simon Peter quotes from this book on the day of Pentecost. A major theme of the Book of Acts, which records that sermon, is inclusion. This passage from Joel is a radical vision of an inclusive age:

> *Then afterwards*
> *I will pour out my spirit on all flesh;*
> *your sons and your daughters shall prophesy,*
> *your old men shall dream dreams,*
> *and your young men shall see visions.*
> *Even on the male and female slaves,*
> *in those days, I will pour out my spirit.*
> Joel 2:28-29

The gift of the spirit is promised to "all flesh," sons and daughters, young and old, male and female, slave and free. The writer of Acts credits Peter for interpreting the coming of the Spirit on the day of Pentecost as the fulfillment of this prophesy. This interpretation has become accepted wisdom for the church, but what is interesting is that Peter was actually "prooftexting" from Joel.

The practice of "prooftexting" is pervasive among preachers, and I must confess my own guilt at times. It means that a preacher or interpreter of the scripture has taken a portion of scripture out of its context. In all fairness to Peter (and me), Jesus did it too. In this case, Peter doesn't bother to quote the whole text, which is probably a good thing because it says:

> *I will show portents in the heavens and on the earth, blood and fire and columns of smoke. The sun shall be turned to darkness, and the moon to blood, before the great and terrible day of the Lord comes.*
> Joel 2:30-31

Joel's vision was clearly apocalyptic, but the moon didn't turn to blood on the day of Pentecost. So was he wrong, or was Peter? Or is it possible that God had a change of heart? Perhaps Pentecost was the beginning of the end. It could be the beginning of the end of excluding religion defined by who is in and who is out. Of course, the way people of faith have behaved the past 2,000 years, it seems more likely that the moon will turn to blood.

AMOS

So, if Joel is one of the more obscure books that made it into the Bible, Amos is the product of one of Israel's greatest prophets. Amos was one of what are called "the Eighth Century Prophets." He is a contemporary of Isaiah, Micah and Hosea. From Tekoa (which is about five miles south of Bethlehem), Amos identifies himself as a herdsman and a "dresser of sycamore trees."

For the most part, Amos addresses his words to the upper and middle classes, as well as a world situation in which the rich were getting richer and the poor were getting poorer. He harshly rebukes an economic system in which wealth is built on the backs of the poor. Amos is clear that, in order for people to do this or tolerate it being done, they have to be worshipping another God.

Amos' prophecy is very strategic. He begins by railing against all the surrounding nations. You can just imagine everyone nodding their heads. It is easy to see the faults and failings of others, and we almost always need a "them" over whom to feel morally superior. Fundamentalism requires the threat of a "them" in order to flourish. In recent years, we have seen conservatives make gay marriage the enemy by which they mobilized their forces. That is a much better fundraising message than addressing the faults and failings of the American nuclear family model. I cannot for the life of me understand how giving same-gender couples civil rights damages anyone else's marriage.

Of course, if you are observant, you already have noted that I was doing what Amos did, and what I accuse fundamentalists of doing. Amos got everyone nodding their heads as he railed against the evils of others. Then, in chapter two, he begins to turn the spotlight closer to home: first Judah (Amos 2:4-5), then Israel (Amos 2:6-3:8), and finally his real target, Samaria (Amos 3:9-4:3).

Despite luring them in, I suspect that Amos had no luck getting those who had to see how they were benefiting at the expense of those who have not. These days almost every leader—religious and political—has abandoned trying to get Americans to see that we are prospering at the impoverishment of others. We complain about the cost of ink for our printers, but in the villages of Mexico where the ink is produced, peasants know what color is being manufactured that day by the shade of their drinking water. And in order to keep products like coffee and bananas cheap for the consumer, American corporations operating in South America pay starvation wages and use child laborers. You didn't know that? I wonder why …

AMOS

Amos 5:21-24

So, if yesterday's lesson on Amos didn't run you off, perhaps I should point out that a prophet feels he has failed if he doesn't make people angry … angry enough to change! Unfortunately, what they usually changed was the prophet. Jesus was just one of a long line of those who gave their lives for telling people the truth.

The Rev. Dr. Martin Luther King, Jr. was part of that long line. He loved the prophet Amos and often used Amos 5:24 as his text:

Let justice roll down like waters,
And righteousness like an ever-flowing stream.

On March 15, 1965, Dr. King wrote in "The Nation":

> *"Let Justice roll down like waters in a mighty stream," said the Prophet Amos. He was seeking not consensus but the cleansing action of revolutionary change. America has made progress toward freedom, but measured against the goal the road ahead is still long and hard. This could be the worst possible moment for slowing down.*

Dr. King saw his role as similar to that of the prophet Amos who confronted the failure of religion in his day to transform how people treated the poor. King addressed his "Letter from a Birmingham Jail" to pastors who were afraid he was an extremist. He wrote:

> *Was not Jesus an extremist for love—"Love your enemies, bless them that curse you, pray for them that despitefully use you." Was not Amos an extremist for justice—"Let justice roll down like waters and righteousness like a mighty stream." Was not Paul an extremist for the gospel of Jesus Christ—"I bear in my body the marks of the Lord Jesus." Was not Martin Luther an extremist—"Here I stand; I can do none other so help me God." Was not John Bunyan an extremist—"I will stay in jail to the end of my days before I make a butchery of my conscience." Was not Abraham Lincoln an extremist—"This nation cannot survive half slave and half free." Was not Thomas Jefferson an extremist—"We hold these truths to be self-evident, that all men are created equal." So the question is not whether we will be extremists but what kind of extremist will we be. Will we be extremists for hate or will we be extremists for love? Will we be extremists for the preservation of injustice—or will we be extremists for the cause of justice? In that dramatic scene on Calvary's hill, three men were crucified. We must*

not forget that all three were crucified for the same crime—the crime of extremism. Two were extremists for immorality, and thusly fell below their environment. The other, Jesus Christ, was an extremist for love, truth and goodness, and thereby rose above his environment.

So what kind of extremist are you?

AMOS

Amos 5:18-24

Although we need to move on if we are going to complete our survey of the First Testament this year, Amos just won't let us go. Perhaps it is because his writings seem so relevant to the state of affairs in the United States and, in particular, how American Christianity is addressing issues such as justice and poverty … or, rather, NOT addressing them.

Churches on the edges of our cities are often packed. We build great facilities and have fabulous music. People call this a "Christian nation." But I keep hearing God speak through Amos:

I can't stand your religious meetings.
I'm fed up with your conferences and conventions.
I want nothing to do with your religion projects,
your pretentious slogans and goals.
I'm sick of your fund-raising schemes,
your public relations and image making.
I've had all I can take of your noisy ego-music.
When was the last time you sang to me?
Do you know what I want?
I want justice—oceans of it.
I want fairness—rivers of it.
That's what I want. That's all I want.

Amos 5:21-24
(The Message translation)

OUCH! You wonder what Amos might say to us today, but with this modern translation of what he said to people of faith 2,800 years ago, I'm not sure I want to know. How has the church so ignored this scripture? Modern prophets rail against gay marriage and activist judges, but whisper about the things about which God seems to shout. Do we really believe that there are no poor? Do people of faith really believe it is God's will that Americans spend more on dog food each year than they give to end starvation?

The panic created by economic downturn is laughable to the 40 percent of the world that isn't sure how they are going to feed their children. We worry about our retirement, and they worry about simply living long enough to see their children raised. Our goal is economic recovery, but, through Amos, God calls us to a different set of values and a different vision for the future. We, who are people of faith, must answer a different call.

OBADIAH

Okay, admit it … you didn't even know there was a book in the bible called Obadiah, right? In 35 years of ministry, I don't think I ever once read from it in church, preached from it, or even quoted it. Still, here it is, right after the very important book of Amos.

Three of the Minor Prophets actually spoke prophecy against other nations: Obadiah spoke about Edom, Nahum about Assyria, and Habakkuk about Chaldea. (You probably hadn't heard of them either). Edom is the name given to Jacob's twin brother Esau, and this supposedly is the nation descended from him. You may recall that Esau was hairy and had red hair. The land southeast of Judah was a desert of reddish sandstone, which may be the real source of its name.

The people were mostly nomadic raiders who were greatly feared in the region. Obadiah was angry that they had not come to the aid of their Jewish cousins when Jerusalem was invaded. Hence, Obadiah believes that they will suffer the same fate. Edom's capital city was Sela, which literally had been carved out of the rocks. The residents thought that it was impregnable. However, as Obadiah prophesied, God brought them down and the nation vanished forever.

The book of Obadiah is only one chapter long; twenty-one verses about a nation that is now extinct. While it is tough to see its scriptural value, I wonder if it is not a parable, like one found in Genesis. Just a few chapters before we find the story of Jacob and Esau, there is another story about two brothers. As you will recall, Cain killed his brother Abel. When he was confronted by God, the murderer's question was "Am I my brother's keeper?"

Obadiah is saying that this is a question only murderers would ask. We are all cousins and have an obligation to help one another if we can. If we ever forget that, the ultimate result will be human extinction. You would think that we would have learned that lesson, but how the world has abandoned places like Darfur and Rwanda offers proof that, even if we don't know about the book of Obadiah, we still need to learn the lesson of the prophet who predicted the fall of Edom because they thought they were secure and prosperous enough not to need to help their neighbors in need.

There are no Edomites on the earth. They are extinct … or are they?

JONAH

Right after Obadiah, the least known book in the Bible, we find the book of Jonah, which is one of the most popular books in the First Testament.

Every child knows a bit of the story of Jonah and the whale, but, like so much of the Bible, we know the story but not the point. I mean think about it, what was the lesson of this story? If you know then I suspect you have a preacher or a Sunday school teacher to thank.

The book is actually about Jonah, not written by Jonah. No one knows who is the true author. The story is a great parable, but, since Jonah doesn't come off looking like the best or even brightest person, it is unlikely that it is meant to be autobiographical. It is also not intended to be historical or factual. Perhaps we have spent so much time wondering how Jonah could survive after being swallowed by a whale because we really don't like the point that the story is trying to make. It wasn't a popular lesson then, and it still isn't today.

Like Obadiah, the book actually addresses a foreign country, but the point was probably aimed at the people of God. Jonah is called by God to go to Nineveh, the capital of the Assyrian empire. The city of Nineveh seems to have been across the Tigris River from the modern city of Mosul. Assyria was a military empire centered in what is modern-day Iraq. They existed for three centuries and were hated by their neighbors who they raided, kidnapped, and abused at will.

God calls Jonah to go and preach to this hated city and call the residents to repent. That isn't Jonah's idea for retirement or a career change, so he flees to the city of Tarshish. No one knows for sure, but it is possible that Tarshish was meant to represent Tartessus, located in southwest Spain. In general, the Hebrews were not seagoing people, so the writer's point in the parable is that Jonah decided to flee from God by going to the very end of the earth.

To what lengths will we sometimes go to avoid being who God calls us to be or doing what God has called us to do? This is especially true when the call of God seems to violate our own prejudices or strong feelings. We will go to "Spain" before we will forgive someone who deserves our anger or even hatred, yet we all know that is what God calls us to do. We will go to the end of the earth to avoid being a servant, though that is the identity Jesus modeled. We flee behind all our rationalizations rather than answer God's call to be generous, compassionate, and merciful people. This is not really the point of Jonah, but if it were, the book would deserve a place in the Bible.

JONAH

So Jonah is a parable about how tough it is for God to get us to offer grace to those we deem unworthy. Jonah was willing to flee to the end of the earth rather than call the people of Nineveh to change their ways and return to God.

In the process of fleeing, the ship Jonah is on is caught in a great Mediterranean storm. The sailors were a suspicious lot and suspected the storm was directed at someone on board. Jonah knew that he was fleeing the call of God, so he came forward and confessed that he was the one causing all the trouble. Although, the sailors were reluctant to throw a paying passenger overboard, it seemed to ultimately be the only option.

From your Sunday school lessons, you know God prepared a "great fish" to swallow Jonah. We call it a whale because that is the only fish big enough to swallow a human whole. The trouble, of course, is that a whale is not a fish, but a mammal, and whales don't swallow people or anything else that size. Still, it makes a good story, and so it is told.

Jonah spends three days and three nights in the belly of this great fish. (Jonah 1:17) The first 10 verses of chapter two contain the prayer that Jonah prayed while in the fish's belly. In verse 2 Jonah calls it the "belly of Sheol," which is, of course, the "place of the dead." It often has been translated as hell, but in Jewish theology, it is the place where we all eventually end up. It is true that we all do sooner or later flee from the best, away from God, and end up in the place of the spiritually dead. In verse 9, Jonah repents and, with a prayer of thanksgiving, promises to keep his vow to God.

Such piety seems more than the fish could stomach, and, after three days, it regurgitates Jonah onto the shore. Jonah immediately sets out to do what God had called him to do. It is little wonder that Jonah terrified people into repentance. He didn't stop to change clothes or even bathe. So, the people of Nineveh heeded Jonah's warning, and everyone, from the King on down, turned from their wicked ways and repented.

In chapter 4, we find a great passage about how angry Jonah is that God has spared the people, which was exactly what Jonah had feared would happen. He didn't want them to change their ways, and he sure didn't want God not to annihilate them. They were enemies, and annihilation was exactly what they deserved. Nothing would have made Jonah happier, and hence nothing could have made Jonah angrier than to see unworthy enemies redeemed. Like all of us, Jonah believed in grace, until he had to offer it to someone he didn't like. Grace is really what most Christians hate most about God.

MICAH

Like other eighth-century prophets, Micah warns that, because of their infidelity, God will punish the people. Most of the book of Micah is unremarkable, except for a couple of passages that seem to have been written specifically for us and for our day.

The first passage is found in Micah 4:3-4. It begins with the promise of a day when God will arbitrate between nations and everyone will beat their swords into plowshares and their spears into pruning hooks. Although it is impossible to tell who originated this phrase, it is clearly the prophet's image of the peaceful reign that God will bring.

What Micah adds is unique (vv. 4 and 5):

They shall all sit under their own vines and under their own fig
trees, and no one shall make them afraid;
for the mouth of the Lord of hosts has spoken.

For all the peoples walk, each in the name of its god, but we will
walk in the name of the Lord our God for ever and ever.

Here we find added to the vision of that Great Day of the Lord the promise that each person will have their own vines and fig trees. The capacity to produce your own food is an assurance to the poor that they will never be hungry again. In fact, that promise is coupled with a phrase, "no one shall make them afraid" that should have great resonance in our day.

Americans living in the wake of the events of September 11, 2001 have only just begun to unpack the horrific impact of a people who have been made afraid. Fear, of course, is the strategy of the terrorist. That fear has had a horrific impact on our culture and corporate psyche. However, it also has been greatly exacerbated by our own government who exploited our fear to stay in office, abandon core principles, and commit a long list of atrocities in the name of security.

Micah knew that those who could be made to feel afraid would have much less tolerance for diversity. That is why we are offered that second verse in this passage. In a land that had great distain for any God but their own, it was a courageous and unheard of thing for a prophet to say that, when creation is restored to its proper order, everyone will have enough, and fear will diminish, and the belief of others tolerated. Wow, how I long for that day!

MICAH

Micah 6:8

You might never have heard of Micah had it not been for this verse in chapter 6. The prophet begins by scoring the religious forms and expressions by which people believed they could win God's favor. Then in verse 8, the prophet is very plainspoken, cutting right through all the visions and symbols:

God has told you, O mortal, what is good;
and what does the Lord require of you
but to do justice, and to love kindness,
and to walk humbly with your God?

"God has told you what is good and what does the Lord require of you?" No ambiguity, no second-guessing, no need for anyone to interpret it for us. What does God expect from us? What does God require?

1. Do justice.
2. Love kindness.
3. Walk in humility with God.

Justice, kindness/mercy, and humility. Could any people less be described by that short phrase than church people?

- Justice: everyone treated equally and fairly, even if you don't approve of their lifestyle or partner choice. Justice: everyone treated equally and fairly, even if they can't afford a high-priced attorney.
- Kindness/mercy: I love the prayer of the little girl who had been around church people all her life: "Dear God, please make the bad people good and the good people nice." I think that is what Micah meant.
- Humility: Notice it is not just humility in how we work or play; it is humility in how we walk with God. It is humility of faith and witness.

That is what God has told us is expected of us: justice, mercy and humility. It is what God values most in the life of disciples.

Several years ago I attended the memorial service for Stanley Marcus, the founder of Neiman Marcus, and a Dallas icon. I knew him a bit, mostly through my friendship with architect Philip Johnson. Both men attended Harvard in the 1920s. Stanley was a deliberately irreligious person, but at his service that day, I found myself wondering if religion was doing most of us much good. At the end of the service, a speaker talked about how Stanley was the one who ordered the restaurants in his stores to be fully integrated, long before Dr. King's witness made that common sense. The speaker concluded about Stanley, "How fortunate we all are that in our time, he came our way." I wonder if that will be said of each of us. Micah thought it should.

NAHUM

My mother used to say, "If you can't say something nice, then say nothing at all." I must confess I'm tempted to take her advice regarding Nahum. I mean just what is this book doing in the Bible?

While the point of Jonah was that God was forgiving and merciful even to people we don't like or think deserve mercy, Nahum is all about how God was going to obliterate the very same people God spares in the book of Jonah. Some scholars suggest that 150 years separate Jonah and Nahum and that, eventually, even God's patience and mercy run out. Maybe. According to Nahum, God is going to utterly destroy Nineveh. In fact, the prophet begins with a description of God as vengeful, wrathful and jealous. (Nahum 1:2) The rest of the book (three chapters) is a description of what this avenging God is going to do to this enemy of Judah.

Ironically, Nahum's name literally means "consolation" or "comfort." That sure doesn't seem congruent with his message … or does it? I mean if you lived in Nineveh, the capital of Assyria, the words aren't very comforting, but it is not likely any Assyrians ever read Nahum's writing or ever heard of him. (Had you?)

Nahum was railing against the Assyrians, but they weren't his audience. His audience, of course, was the people of Judah who had been threatened and harassed by the Assyrians. They were probably **quite** comforted to know their enemies someday would fail. They liked the idea of God bringing vengeance and violence on these hated foreigners. Nahum's theology fit nicely into the image of God that they held dear.

Now, I'd like to say that this primitive image of God was forgotten, much as the book of Nahum has been. Unfortunately, from the way religious people often act, you would think we were disciples of Nahum rather than Jesus. Maybe this book was included in the Bible to remind us that we constantly have to decide if we believe in the God of Nahum or the God of Jonah. We have to choose in each situation which god's values we will live out in our daily lives.

ZEPHANIAH

Like Nahum, Zephaniah is a three-chapter book that talks a lot about the judgment and wrath of God. However, though he talks about how God is going to punish the surrounding nations for their wickedness, Zephaniah's main theme is how the Jews have gone astray and the pain their evil will bring upon them. His major focus is the city of Jerusalem, which was supposed to be the city of God, but had become corrupt.

Zephaniah saw the unifying religion of Judah as diluted with shrines to other gods that served the cravings of the people. His writings are not just a pronouncement of judgment, but they are a warning of the consequences and a call to repentance. In classic prophetic voice, Zephaniah even predicts a day when all will be made right. He ends with a psalm of rejoicing.

This prophetic pattern is probably worthy of our notice, even if the specifics of Zephaniah's prophecy are out of date. While we progressive people of faith are rightly squeamish about the common image of a vengeful God, it is an important reminder. No, I don't believe that God punishes our misdeeds, but the truth is behavior has consequences. We tend to live as if we have no responsibility beyond our own experience. Sometimes we bear 100 percent of the consequences, but far more often, others are punished for our values or choices. For example, the rise in air pollution and respiratory disease because of our vehicle emissions as well as how we consume may not impact us nearly so much as it will for the next generation of children to be born.

In Zephaniah's day, God got the credit or blame for everything. While we understand things differently today, we should not neglect the message of judgment: our choices have consequences and, if we believe we are all connected as a human family, when others bear the consequence, we do too. Zephaniah wants judgment to bring about a change and offers hope that change can bring a new day when we can live together without fear of God or of one another.

When bad things happen in our world or in our lives, I do not believe God is responsible, just as we are not always responsible either. However, the healthiest alternative is for us to pause, look within, and change anything for which we are responsible. That is how we are able to end our lives as Zephaniah ended his book, with a song of joy.

HAGGAI

We come to the last three books of the First Testament: Haggai, Zacchariah, and Malachai. These three books were written after the Jews began to return to Jerusalem and Judah from the exile in Babylon. These prophets correspond to the historic books of Nehemiah and Ezra, which we studied earlier this year.

It is quite possible that Haggai was born in Babylon during the exile and traveled with his family back to Jerusalem around 539 BCE. We know nothing about him except that he returned. Many of the exiles did not. They had become comfortable, even prosperous, in Babylon, and going back to a city that was in bad shape like Jerusalem wasn't appealing to them. Oh, they cared about those who had been left behind, yes; they cared about the temple that was the faith center of their people. Certainly they cared about their heritage and legacy. They just didn't care enough to personally sacrifice or to be inconvenienced. It was similar to how most of us care about things like the environment, poverty, peace or justice. We care, but not enough to be personally inconvenienced or to make any sacrifice.

Haggai came back to a city he probably had never seen, but which he knew had to survive if his faith and people were to endure for another generation. The content of the book that bears his strange name is mostly a call to rebuild the temple and restore the city. The call is accompanied by promises from God about the blessings that will follow, though some might argue that the promises never came to pass since Judah never again became a strong or independent nation. After the Persians came the Greeks under Alexander the Great and after the Greeks came the Romans who, shortly after the lifetime of Jesus, destroyed the nation once and for all.

However, today, despite centuries of oppression and persecution, Jews still bear witness to their faith and to their God. We, who are Christians today, are heirs of Haggai and the exiles who returned and preserved the city and faith until the day that a rabbi named Jesus was born.

Prophecy seldom comes to pass in the obvious way we might expect. Haggai, Zechariah, Malachi, Ezra, Nehemiah and the exiles who made the personal sacrifices to rebuild the temple and city never saw the return to greatness for the land they loved. Still, their faithfulness restored and preserved much of that which we hold sacred today. That is the problem with making sacrifices for the greater good—it doesn't always turn out like we hoped, or we may never know how it all turns out. I guess that is why we call it faith.

ZECHARIAH

Like Haggai, Zechariah was a prophet who lived during the period after the return from exile, and he, too, raised his voice to call for the people to rebuild the temple and the city. I wonder how the residents who had been left behind felt about these returning exiles. I mean, they had been gone a long time! A generation had passed, and those left behind had moved on with their lives. Now, these idealistic strangers come back wanting to "restore" things.

The restoration of the temple met with some resistance and was delayed for about 18 years. Like Haggai, Zechariah is trying to motivate the exiles to get back to work on it. They had gotten distracted with making a living and building a home and forgotten that they had a larger responsibility both to society and to posterity. The prophet's job was to challenge, cajole and harass them into rising up and giving their time and efforts to a larger cause.

Just as the Cathedral of Hope embarked on building an interfaith peace chapel, the economic crisis struck, and, as a result, the project was delayed. As I read Zechariah, I had to pray that this delay would not be for 18 years, but I realized how easy it would be to move on, get distracted, become involved in other activities, or forget we have a responsibility to society and posterity. We, too, must bear witness to a better way. Our goal, of course, is to show that different faiths can work and worship together and that we can be a source of peace rather than conflict. In a world where fundamentalism repeatedly gives rise to terrorism, violence, conflict and war, that message is critical to our future and the future of our children.

Zechariah called the people back to build a temple not just for themselves, but for the future. The last half of his message speaks of a messiah who someday will come to bring peace on earth. The most famous passage of all is found in chapter 9:

> *Rejoice greatly, O daughter Zion! Shout aloud, O daughter Jerusalem! Lo, your king comes to you; triumphant and victorious is he, humble and riding on a donkey, on a colt, the foal of a donkey.*
>
> Zechariah 9:9

My personal favorite, though, is 9:12. It is the appeal of God through the prophet:

> *Return to your stronghold, O prisoners of hope.*

Maybe that is what keeps prophets preaching, calling, harassing and cajoling. They are **prisoners of hope,** which, of course, is a description of all people of faith. We keep on working, praying and believing because we are prisoners of hope who believe the best is yet to be, but that it won't happen by magic.

MALACHI

And so we come to the last book of the First Testament. Next week we will look at some of the inter-testament writings called the Apocrypha. For now, though, you are to be commended for making it all the way through the First Testament!

The prophet Malachi lived some 400 years before the birth of Christ. One would hope this volume would end with a great word of hope; however, the truth is the only reason the Church has ever paid ANY attention to Malachi is that his writing contains the greatest passage in the Bible about the subject of tithing:

> *Will anyone rob God? Yet you are robbing me! But you say, "How are we robbing you?" In your tithes and offerings! You are cursed with a curse, for you are robbing me—the whole nation of you! Bring the full tithe into the storehouse, so that there may be food in my house, and thus put me to the test, says the Lord of hosts; see if I will not open the windows of heaven for you and pour down for you an overflowing blessing.*
>
> Malachi 3:8-10

In the time after the exile, there weren't the resources to restore and sustain the temple or the religion of the people. The people liked the benefits of civil society that religion brought; they even liked the idea that there was a sacred place where they could reconnect with God. They just didn't want to pay for it. Malachi's prophecy was a call to proportional giving, an ancient principle established centuries before.

The rich, middleclass and the poor are all called to give away 10 percent—a tithe—of what they have. In this regard, of course, the poor may not give much, but their gift is honored as being just as generous. This call is coupled with a promise of great blessings poured out from heaven.

I believe Malachi's prophecy is as true today as it was in 425 BCE. I believe it is a core spiritual principle that we who are people of faith ought to give back 10 percent of all we have. I don't mean we have to give it to a church. That is one place where it can help, but there are thousands of other deserving organizations as well. I believe that if we all actually tithed, we could end poverty and much of the disease on our planet … and what a blessing that would be. It is tragic that Malachi has been seen only as a fundraising tool of the church, because the principle of tithing is a God-given solution to much of what ails the world. If we gave it a chance, we might discover that the First Testament actually did end with a great word of hope. Generosity is the cure for much of what ails our world … and us.

APOCRYPHA

This week, we will look at the writings known as the "Apocrypha." These writings may or may not be in your Bible. In fact, they are in the Bible I use at home, but not the one I use at the office. They are in most Bibles authorized by the Catholic Church, but, for most Protestants since 1826, these writings generally are included only in specific study bibles.

The writings generally included in the Apocrypha are:

- 1 Esdras (Vulgate 3 Esdras)
- 2 Esdras (Vulgate 4 Esdras)
- Tobit
- Judith
- The Rest of Esther (Vulgate Esther 10:4-16:24)
- Wisdom
- Ecclesiasticus (also known as Sirach)
- Baruch and the Epistle of Jeremy (all part of Vulgate Baruch)
- The Song of the Three Children (Vulgate Daniel 3:24-90)
- Story of Susanna (Vulgate Daniel 13)
- The Idol Bel and the Dragon (Vulgate Daniel 14)
- Prayer of Manasses
- 1 Maccabees
- 2 Maccabees

All of the above information might help you next time you play Trivial Pursuit, but the real question is do any of these writings contain anything worth reading? Well, frankly there's not much worth taking the time to read, but we will try and dig some nuggets out in the days ahead. For today, what might be worth pondering, though, is why is there an Apocrypha? Why did some writings make the cut and others were left out? Who decided what was in and what was out? For us, it goes to the root of what we mean by "inspired," "scripture" and "Word of God." Are these or aren't these? Who decides? Are you really comfortable with someone else deciding for your what is sacred and what is not? No? Well, then consider what is sacred for you, and why?

1 ESDRAS and 2 ESDRAS

In most Protestant Bibles that include the Apocrypha, the section begins with 1 Esdras and 2 Esdras. The Catholic Bibles based on the first Latin translation called the Vulgate entitled the books of Ezra and Nehemiah as 1 Esdras and 2 Esdras and hence these two Apocryphal books are entitled 3 and 4 Esdras.

The content of 1 Esdras pretty much follows the story recorded in Ezra and Nehemiah. Although mostly disregarded today, it was widely quoted by the first century Jewish historian Josephus and by many early Christian theologians. It is part of the canon of the Eastern Orthodox Church. Most is a repeat of the books found in all bibles, but there is this really strange passage in the third chapter where the courtiers of King Darius debate which is the strongest among the king, wine, women and truth. Zerubbabel wins the debate when the king agrees with him that only truth is stronger than women. As a result, Zerubbabel is allowed to lead a group of exiles home from Babylon to Jerusalem.

While some of my lesbian sisters might argue that this passage is clearly inspired, it doesn't move me. As the only truly unique part of 1 Esdras, you can understand how it got left out of most Bibles.

2 Esdras is a different case entirely. It is believed that this is actually an early Christian writing. The first two chapters of 2 Esdras are included in the Vulgate, but not found in any other translation. Those chapters describe God's rejection of the Jews and God's sending a king to reign over the earth. The rest of the book consists of seven visions attributed to Ezra, who, you will recall, was a priest who led some of the exiles home. It is mostly considered to be Jewish apocalyptic literature. What makes it important is that, like the book of Job, it wrestles with the meaning of suffering. In this case, it wrestles with the sufferings of a nation and a people, whereas Job's suffering was that of an individual.

Job is the oldest book of the Bible. Esdras was written much later, after the nation had been formed and was conquered. Like Job, when bad things happen in our lives, we sometimes ask what we did to deserve it. Quite often the answer is nothing, but, still, it doesn't hurt to ask that question honestly. Far less common, though, is for a nation to examine itself honestly in the wake of tragedy. After the Hurricane Katrina disaster the introspection around our national racism was fleeting. After 9/11 we were too busy getting ready to go to war to ever ask as a nation about responsibility. I don't think anyone in America has ever read 2 Esdras.

TOBIT

The book of Tobit is a part of the Catholic and Orthodox bibles, though not the Protestant bible. The First Testament for Protestants ends about 450 years before the birth of Christ. Tobit is believed to have been written about 200 years before Christ. Some scholars consider it a book of history, but most regard it at as a religious novel. The story is quite fascinating and involves a demon that kills seven husbands on their wedding nights before they have a chance to consummate the marriages. Another main character is Raphael, the angel who helps out in disguise. There is also an attack by a giant fish whose organs are used to defeat the demon and heal Tobit's blindness. The story takes place in Nineveh during the time of exile and is, in part, a love story.

Although most Protestants are unfamiliar with the book, it has shaped Christianity. When the Sadducees challenge Jesus about the resurrection, they refer to the woman who married seven men. This is the primary place where we hear about Raphael who is an angel in Catholicism, Protestantism and Islam. In Islam, Raphael is the one who blows the trumpet and announces the Day of Judgment.

This story shaped much of medieval Christianity's view of angels and the role they play in human life. Raphael was a common figure in art, and he shares a feast day with the other archangels Gabriel and Michael (September 29). Raphael also appears in John Milton's *Paradise Lost* where he is the one who tries to warn Adam against eating from the tree of knowledge.

Tobit is the source of much of the belief of Christians and Jews that angels intercede for us and that we have a "guardian angel" assigned to us. It is interesting that this doctrine has been taken from Tobit, but no one seems to use burning fish liver to drive away demons or fish gall bladder to cure blindness. (Who even knew fish had gall bladders?!?)

It is fascinating what parts of the Bible we choose to believe and integrate into our lives. That is why it is always so dangerous when people try to make the Bible into something it is not or to claim to believe it is "all true." There are truths to be discovered in the book of Tobit, but I personally wonder if angels aren't a bit of a fish story.

JUDITH

The book of Judith is included in Catholic and Orthodox bibles, but generally excluded by Protestants and Jews. As a book of history, the book of Judith has some inaccuracies that are problematic. However, if one reads it as a fictionalized historic novel (perhaps the oldest of all) or as a parable, the story is interesting and has something to say.

The novella begins: "It was the twelfth year of the reign of Nebuchadnezzar, who ruled over the Assyrians in the great city of Nineveh." The story goes on to tell how the mighty Assyrian army is routed by the tiny Israelite town of Bethulia. The hero in the tale is a Jewish widow named Judith. She seduces and then assassinates the head of the Assyrian army and then escapes to tell the tale. Read in its original language, the story is well written, though the author's geographical and historical knowledge was obviously limited.

Judith is the hero, which makes it a unique writing from an age when women were not highly regarded. She decisively takes action when none of the men would do so. She is described as a person of devotion and faith, but the story also makes it clear that she lies, seduces a married man, and murders. Like Moses or David, she is clearly not a caricature of a person of faith. This story is a continuation of the Biblical theme that the people God uses greatly are inevitably flawed and conflicted.

Make no mistake; there are numerous examples of the biblical writers' attempts to glaze over the faults and failings of the heroes of faith, but much less so than one might expect. History often has been selective in its memory. In this country, there often has been a conspiracy of amnesia to remember things as better than they were. Perhaps that is because of how we handle our own personal histories.

Freud warned us about repressing parts of our story, but then he managed to keep many secrets that were discovered only after his death. As the sage points out, ours is the only face we can never see, since even in a mirror all things are reversed. Why do we hide the truth even from ourselves? Writings like the book of Judith try to teach us that God isn't fooled, and that our faults and foibles don't disqualify us from being partners with God and being heroes of faith. Still, we demand perfection of our leaders and discard or discount them when we find their faults. That may be how we treat one another, and even how we treat ourselves, but it isn't the way of God. Great women and men of God have always been deeply flawed. Maybe the only difference is they knew it.

THE REST OF ESTHER

The next book in most collections of the Apocrypha is called The Rest of Esther. About 100 years before Christ, a translator named Lysimachus translated the book of Esther from Hebrew to the increasingly universal language of Greek. There are several relatively minor differences between the Greek translation and the Hebrew manuscripts that have survived. However, there are six extra sections that appear to be additions. Contrary to what was said yesterday, these additions all seemed designed to make the story of Esther more conventional and pious.

You will recall that the name of God never actually occurs in Esther, and that, by and large, Esther risked her life for her people because her cousin Mordecai persuaded her that this was the reason that she was in a position of power. In the supplemental story, it is God who is responsible for rescuing the people.

This is one writing I'm glad was left out. I cannot tell you how weary I am of the artificial piety of religious people like this author. It must make God very tired to watch as the super-pious "protect" the faith, or the Bible, or Christmas, or God. What kind of God needs our protection? It seems to me that the hyper-pious are the ones who give God a bad reputation. In this writing, it was as if the writer couldn't accept that God intervened to save the Jews through a very human woman, Esther.

In our home, our daughters say grace for the family before dinner. Once, when they were young, we were eating out at a restaurant on a school night, which is a very rare occurrence. The girls watched as a family near us said grace aloud in the restaurant. They asked why we prayed at home but not when we ate out. I wasn't sure how to answer—and I don't offer this as a prescription for what others do—but I said, "We pray everywhere we go, but we don't do it in restaurants because it makes the people around us uncomfortable. I hope wherever you are you will say thank you to God in your heart but you don't need to call attention to yourself by using your faith in a way that makes others uncomfortable."

I doubt that meant much back then, but I pray that the girls will grow up to be adults whose faith makes the world better without making them look or feel superior. God works in secret, and Jesus seemed to think that was a good place for us to keep our piety.

WISDOM OF SOLOMON, ECCLESIASTICUS and BARUCH

Wisdom of Solomon, attributed to Solomon, contains wisdom material similar to Proverbs or Ecclesiastes. However, the book really was written in Greek within a few decades before the birth of Christ. It seems primarily designed to encourage Jews who have been scattered (Diaspora) far from the Promised Land. The book ends with a great apocalyptic vision of the end of time. Although this is not held as scripture by the Jews, there are indications that Paul drew some imagery from it.

The next book is called Ecclesiasticus or Sirach. It is included in Catholic and Orthodox bibles, but not Protestant or Jewish ones. The writing is, however, referred to in Jewish teachings and literature. The book begins with a prologue by its first translator, the author's grandson. He says that he worked on translating it from Hebrew to Greek so it would be available to Jews living abroad. There was no Hebrew version of the book available until after 1900. Since then, fragments composing about two-thirds of the original have been recovered in various places. Because of the discoveries, we have a more complete version of the book than what was available for the last 2,000 years. It is a long book of wisdom and proverbs, and a careful reading reveals that Jesus repeats some of its teachings in the Gospels.

The book called Baruch is attributed to Jeremiah's secretary, but was not actually written until the century before Christ. The book is comprised mostly of a prayer of repentance and two poems. It is followed by a short writing that is entitled "The Letter of Jeremiah." It is reputed to be the letter Jeremiah wrote to the exiles in Babylon, and it offers advice on living faithfully while away from Jerusalem. Both books are entitled as they are to give their wisdom credibility, but they actually are addressed to people scattered outside of Palestine.

While artificially attributing work seems deceitful, it is something we all do in other kinds of ways. We omit where we heard or learned something when that information might get in the way of our listeners receiving it. While I think we must avoid deception (despite the biblical writer's poor example) when we are communicating tough truths, we do need to be mindful of Jesus' advice to "be as cunning as a serpent, but as innocent as a dove."

THE ADDITIONS TO THE BOOK OF DANIEL

The next document is called Azariah and the Three Jews. In the Roman Catholic and Eastern Orthodox bibles it is found in the book of Daniel, but it is omitted in the Protestant bible and found only in the Apocrypha.

Azariah is the Hebrew name for Abednego, one of the three young men who were thrown in the fiery furnace for refusing to bow down to a Babylonian idol. The passage begins with a prayer of repentance from Azariah and ends with a hymn of praise when they realize they have been saved. The hymn is found in worship books for the Orthodox, the Anglican *Book of Common Prayer* and the Lutheran Book of Worship.

Because these writings are not found in any of the Hebrew or Aramaic versions of the book of Daniel, they are not referred to in any ancient Jewish writings, Protestant biblical editors removed it. This fact speaks to the editing of the Bible and leaves you wondering just which Bible the fundamentalists believe is infallible and inerrant.

Perhaps more importantly, though, it should leave us all wondering if, since the unanimously authorized version of Daniel was written long after the events were supposed to have taken place, what makes it more inspired than this later passage that is consigned to the Apocrypha? Is the Gospel of Mark more inspired than John since it was written 30 or so years earlier?

The writing entitled Story of Susanna is the next book in the Apocrypha. It, too, is a part of the book of Daniel in Catholic and Orthodox Bibles. The book called Bel and the Dragon is included in Daniel in the original Latin translation *The Vulgate,* but it didn't make the cut even for Catholic scholars.

Both are strange stories, but then the whole book of Daniel is strange. Both appear to have been later additions, but the United Church of Christ insists that *God is still speaking.* If that is so, then who decides what is sacred and inspired by God, and on what basis? If we aren't willing to let others decide for us then we have to be serious about our own study if we are going to be informed enough to decide for ourselves. We must be serious about our own spirituality if we are going to discern the inspirational work of the Spirit. Otherwise you are left with professionals like me to tell you what is and is not "the word of God." And, let me tell you first hand, that is a very foolish thing to do. Make study a new year's resolution!

1 & 2 MACCABEES

You probably never heard of these books, but you should be aware of them. In two volumes, Maccabees tells a very important story of events that created the world into which Jesus was born. Maccabees was written by a Jewish author after the restoration of an independent Jewish kingdom, probably about 100 BC. It is included in the Catholic and Orthodox bibles, while Protestants and Jews regard it as reliable historically but not a part of scripture.

The book opens by talking about Alexander the Great who defeated the Persians and became the de facto ruler of the Jews. Ironically, Alexander is praised in this Jewish document, but the author then describes what happened to the empire after Alexander died. The Greek generals who ruled after the empire was divided were corrupt and evil. Antiochus, Alexander's successor over that region, attempts to secure control over the Jews, desecrates the Temple by setting up an idol, forbids both circumcision and the possession of Jewish scriptures on pain of death, and prohibits observance of the Sabbath and the offering of sacrifices at the Temple. He also requires Jewish leaders to sacrifice to idols. Jewish leaders, adults and children are killed as a warning to others. Antiochus introduced Hellenistic culture, which included the foundation of gymnasiums in Jerusalem. Already forbidden, the practice of circumcision was discouraged further because a man could not conceal himself in a gymnasium, a place where men socialized in the nude. Some Jews even engaged in non-surgical foreskin restoration in order to pass in Hellenic culture.

A priest named Mattathias called for a holy war against the invaders, and his three sons began a military campaign against them. A thousand Jews (men, women and children) were lost when the Jewish defenders refused to fight on the Sabbath. The other Jews then reason that, when attacked, they must fight, even on the Sabbath. In 165 BC, the Temple was freed and re-consecrated. The Jewish festival of Hanukkah is instituted by Judas Maccabeus and his brothers to celebrate this event (1 Maccabees 4:59).

The story of the Maccabean revolt has long been held up as an example of courage by people of faith. I'm more impressed by those faithful Jews who were willing to die rather than violate their value system. Killing for your country and your faith is one type of courage; dying for your convictions is another. Maccabees describes both, but our world only seems to honor those who are killed while killing.

2 MACCABEES

Last week we came to the end of the First Testament for most folks, but with this book we come to the end for everyone. 2 Maccabees is the last book of the Apocrypha in most bibles and was written in Greek, probably in Alexandria. It revises some of the historical account of I Maccabees and introduces the idea of praying for the dead and judgment. It is considered scripture for Catholics and Orthodox Christians, but not Jews and Protestants. Jews, in particular, reject many of the religious teachings of the book, as did Martin Luther.

There is a document called 3 Maccabees, and one called 4 Maccabees. Some compilations of the Apocrypha also include 1 and 2 Esdras, the prayer of Manasseh and Psalm 151. But don't rush out and buy a new Bible that includes the whole Apocrypha. While it is interesting, sometimes enlightening, and even inspirational, there is plenty in the Bible we already have that we don't understand or know well.

Still, there is much about the faith of Jesus' day that we find recorded only in the Apocrypha. Malachi, the last book of the First Testament, was written between 450 and 425 B.C.E. The first book of the New Testament wasn't penned until at least 50 A.D. Are we to assume that God simply was silent for almost 500 years? Were there no prophets? Did God cease acting, stop caring? While some of the books of the Apocrypha are certainly quirky, that also could be said about many of the books that made it into the Bible.

Even if they had been included in the Bible, there still would be a fairly long gap in the narrative. Of course, there are often gaps in the narratives of our lives. That is to say that we all have times when it feels as though God is silent or absent. There are times when we get distracted and don't listen. Were any of us to write our life's story, there would be periods where we would have to strain to recognize the hand of God in our lives. Sometimes those gaps were times of preparation and the work of God in us was underground, hidden even from us.

On this Christmas Day, it is worth wondering if God was allowing silence to settle over the earth so that, when the Word became flesh, human hearing would be more acute. It was into a dark night that the light shined. That may be a good thing to remember, especially when life seems dark and God seems silent. Advent says to us: Look! Listen! It just might happen again.

APOCRYPHA NOW!

Since we have come to the end of the First Testament and the Apocrypha, it is my prayer that you have found this exercise helpful in your daily lives. I am not delusional enough to think that you have read every day's musings and found them inspirational. Heck, some days even I couldn't dig anything out or find anything of interest.

By and large, my mission has been to help progressive folks read ancient texts in a new light. I'm excited about getting to the New Testament. This is, of course, the part of the Bible we all are more familiar with, and the journey may be a little easier.

Blessings,
Michael

Hope for Peace & Justice is a 501(c) 3 non-profit organization that is equipping progressive people of faith to be champions for peace and justice. Founded in 2004 by the Cathedral of Hope, H4PJ is led by the Rev. Michael S. Piazza, a longtime social justice advocate who has been a leading progressive voice in Dallas, Texas for more than 20 years.

Religious dialogue is so dominated by conservative churches, denominations and para-church organizations that the average American is left believing that radical conservative views are the only ones held by spiritual people.

In recent years, it has become apparent that there is a need for an organization that will speak to the values and views that are held by progressive people of faith and give voice to those views in our national dialogue. Seeking justice for the marginalized and advocating for peace have been, and continue to be, values deeply rooted in the tradition of Judaism, the history of Christianity and the authenticity of Islam.

The progressive church has a long and noble history of engaging the political system around issues of peace and justice. From the fight for the abolition of slavery to the modern civil rights struggle, churches, synagogues and mosques have worked for justice. In that tradition, Hope for Peace & Justice was formed to be a vocal force for those of progressive faith and ideology. To accomplish this mission, H4PJ has taken a three-fold approach:

- **The Center for Progressive Renewal** is dedicated to support the birth of new liberal and progressive Christian congregations and strengthen existing progressive churches. In a time when much of the culture in America leans toward progressive values in areas such as civil rights, environmental concerns, peace, and human liberation, churches that espouse these values are in danger of extinction. There is a real danger that the growth of fundamentalism will essentially redefine the Christian faith as a nationalistic, militaristic, and exclusionary system of belief. We find that prospect unacceptable.

- **Art for Peace & Justice** is our principle strategy to create a cultural orientation/bias toward peace and justice using the arts to educate, enlighten and inspire people. Through partnerships with artists and arts organizations, Art4PJ seeks to create a shift in values away from war and violence toward peace with justice.

- **Peace House Dallas** is bringing together North Texas peace and justice organizations to create a world-class coalition for peace and justice programming and advocacy. Resident partners include the Dallas Peace Center, the United Nations Association, Maryknoll Mission Education, Peacemakers Inc., Progressive Renewal, Art for Peace & Justice and Hope for Peace & Justice. Non-resident partners include Resounding Harmony and the Peace Project.

We can't do everything, but we ALL can do something! I encourage you to do something to promote peace and justice in the world. Whether you are a person of faith or someone who has no professed religious or spiritual faith, it is important for you to work to overcome cynicism and complacency and take personal responsibility for making peace and doing justice.

I would love for you to get involved with Hope for Peace & Justice as my partner in this great work. Look for more information about our programs at the following websites:

- **H4PJ.org** – to sign up for your copy of the daily *Liberating Word.*
- **Art4PJ.org** – to learn about the programs and events of Art for Peace & Justice.
- **PeaceHouseDallas.org** – to learn about programs and events of our peace and justice partners.
- **ProgressiveRenewal.org** – for church growth resources and to learn about the work of our leadership consultants.

Hope for Peace & Justice
5910 Cedar Springs Road
Dallas, Texas 75235-6806
(214) 351-1432

Michael S. Piazza is a spiritual visionary, author and social justice advocate who currently serves as Dean of the Cathedral of Hope, a congregation of the United Church of Christ, known as the world's largest liberal Christian church with a predominantly lesbian, gay, bisexual and transgender outreach. In addition to his role as President of Hope for Peace and Justice, a non-profit ministry of Cathedral of Hope whose mission is equipping progressive people of faith to be champions for peace and justice, h is also the co-director and co-founder of the Center for Progressive Renewal, which is renewing Progressive Christianity by training new assertive leaders, supporting the birth of new liberal/progressive congregations, and by renewing and strengthening existing progressive churches.

A native of Georgia, Rev. Piazza has served in ministry for more than three decades, pastoring churches in Texas, Georgia, Oklahoma and Florida. He holds Bachelor degrees in history and psychology from Valdosta State College in Georgia and a Master of Divinity from the Candler School of Theology, Emory University in Atlanta.

The "Advocate" magazine named Rev. Piazza one of the most influential people in the gay and lesbian movement (August 1999). His published books include *Gay by God: How to be Lesbian or Gay and Christian* (formerly *Holy Homosexuals); Queeries: Questions Lesbians and Gays have for God; The Real antiChrist: How America Sold its Soul;* and *Prophetic Renewal: Hope for the Liberal Church,* designed to help restore vitality to liberal congregations. Rev. Piazza and his partner Bill have been together since 1980 and have two daughters.

NOTES

NOTES